The
Corporate
Game

The Corporate Game

A Computer Adventure for Developing Business Decision-Making Skills

David E. Rye

McGraw-Hill, Inc.

New York   San Francisco   Washington, D.C.   Auckland   Bogotá
Caracas   Lisbon   London   Madrid   Mexico City   Milan
Montreal   New Delhi   San Juan   Singapore
Sydney   Tokyo   Toronto

Library of Congress Cataloging-in-Publication Data

Rye, David E.
   The corporate game : a computer adventure for developing business
decision-making skills / David E. Rye.
      p.   cm.
   Includes index.
   ISBN 0-07-054628-2 (acid-free paper)
   1. Business—Decision making—Data processing.   2. Corporate
planning.   3. Strategic planning.   I. Title.
HF5548.2.R94   1994
658.4′03—dc20   93-32447
                                                                              CIP

1 2 3 4 5 6 7 8 9 0 DOC/DOC 9 9 8 7 6 5 4 3

P/N 054628-2
PART OF
ISBN 0-07-911763-5

*The sponsoring editor for this book was Philip Ruppel, the editing supervisor was
Robert C. Walters, and the production supervisor was Pamela A. Pelton. It was set
in Baskerville by Carol Woolverton Studio, Lexington, Mass., in cooperation with
Warren Publishing Services, Biddeford, Maine.*

Printed and bound by R. R. Donnelley & Sons Company.

 This book is printed on recycled, acid-free paper containing a
minimum of 50% recycled de-inked fiber.

Contents

10. The Total Quality Game: In the Race for Quality, There Is No Finish Line   183

11. The Power of Information: Bullets for Corporate Guns   207

12. Changing Corporate America: Learning to Love Change

13. Playing the Corporate Game: Do You Have What It Takes to Win?

Preface

These are tough times for American corporations. Profits are falling at record rates. Foreign competition is eating our lunch. As a result, corporate leaders are aggressively searching for answers and solutions to the dilemma.

To be successful in today's complex business world, you must understand how all the business groups fit together. What does manufacturing have to do with economics, sales, and marketing? Where does accounting and finance fit in? How do you pull all the groups together into a cohesive strategic plan that works? It's all covered in *The Corporate Game*.

This book is written from a leadership perspective. It's a universal management guide that shows, by example, how to apply the business groups to run a winning company. *The Corporate Game* merges the key elements of strategic business planning into a "build your own company" case scenario. The end product is an exciting adventure that instantly catapults you into the position of Chief Executive Officer (CEO).

Your mission is to build a company, from the ground up. The book leads you through a progression of steps and decision points that you must make to achieve brilliant success and avoid catastrophic failure. When you're all done, you'll know how to run any company. Each chapter progressively builds on the strategies and decisions you made in the previous chapters. The book is laced with examples and anecdotes that reinforce its interdisciplinary theme.

As an added challenge, you can play *The Corporate Game* on your personal computer. Each chapter in the book is supplemented with a chapter that you play on your computer. Your strategic business decisions are entered into the computer and subjected to over 300 "real world" economic, political, and business variables that have been built into the game.

You'll be given a million dollars that has one string attached to it! You must use the money to start up a company. You enter into the world of *The Corporate Game* and are suddenly launched into an exciting set of events that progressively move you toward your goal. The scenario follows.

Where do you start? You set up an accounting system and learn how to interpret what the reports are telling you. It's all there in Chapter 1, Accounting for the Facts. What's next? You need a good strategic plan. Without one, your company will die! You're compelled to read Chapter 2, Strategic Planning. The challenge is daunting. Just when you thought you had it made, your master plan goes up in smoke. If you are as good as you think you are, can you adjust your plan and survive in *The Corporate Game*?

Pound for pound, *The Corporate Game* will be one of the best books you'll ever read. It consolidates a whole library of case books into a single master book. This one book gives you the dynamic benefits of the interactive case method approach supplemented with tutorials and the computer game covering all the business disciplines. When you're done, you will have sharpened the skills you need to survive in *The Corporate Game*.

David E. Rye

Introduction

The ground that *The Corporate Game* covers is challenging and exciting. The center of attention is the corporation. What does it take to build and run one? The book takes you through a progressive set of steps that are required to build and run any company.

You'll use all the business disciplines to get the job done. We'll show you how they fit together into one integrated system. When you finish, you will know how to use these disciplines to build and run any company. Along the way, we introduce you to a number of business scenarios relating directly to the building process.

You'll get a workout sizing up a variety of competitive situations. Use the analytical tools provided in the text material. Consider the pros and cons of the various business alternatives. In the final analysis, you decide which strategic plan to implement. Which one will give you the best chance for success?

You will learn how to implement change and how to motivate people to adopt the change, no matter how controversial it may be. You'll become more skilled at what it takes to get ahead in the corporate game by relying heavily on strategic planning as the key interactive process. You'll see how the various pieces of the business puzzle fit together and why the different parts of the corporation must be managed in harmony to survive.

Collection of Cases

We have included a rich diversity of case histories covering interesting companies and situations. Each case study has been selected to complement the topics discussed in the text. Examples are used to explore the issues separating corporate winners from losers. You'll learn about risk taking.

As the CEO, you get to live with the decisions you make and learn what it means to be accountable. You are the one responsible for achieving satisfactory or unsatisfactory results. The whole process is complicated by the enormous number of options you must consider. Trying to unite all the corporation's human resources behind a coherent strategic plan is not an easy task. You have to integrate a lot of material from each of the business disciplines to make it all come together.

Chapter Summaries

Chapter 1, Starting the Corporate Game, covers the actual case history that inspired the creation of *The Corporate Game*. It tells you what happened to a CEO who decided to break the rules of the game.

Chapter 2, Accounting for the Facts, shows you how to build an accounting system that will become the foundation of your company. Reading and interpreting key accounting reports are covered in detail.

Chapter 3, Strategic Planning, covers strategic planning, the lifeblood of your company. You'll learn how to analyze your present strategies and implement new ones. We'll also show you how to determine if your plan is working.

Chapter 4, Managing Economics, weaves all the principles of economics together into a conceptual framework that can be applied to any economic situation. We take the mystique out of economics and show you how to apply it to your strategic plan.

Chapter 5, Getting into the Market, stresses the tool that you can use to size the market for your company's products. We'll show you how to use market research to take advantage of competitive opportunities.

Chapter 6, The Sales Game, analyzes sales strategies from the viewpoint of product life cycles. When should you strive to be the low-cost producer? When does product differentiation pay off? How do you sustain a competitive sales advantage? These are just a few of the issues covered in this chapter.

Chapter 7, Controlling the Production Process, emphasizes the importance of cost controls throughout the organization. Every element of cost is defined and analyzed.

Chapter 8, Manufacturing Just-in-Time, explores the mythical concept of just-in-time manufacturing. Is it the right thing to do? Can you live without it in an increasingly competitive world market?

Chapter 9, Perfection Isn't Good Enough, places emphasis on employee management and on the productivity of people. Without their help, you'll never make it.

Chapter 10, The Total Quality Game, discusses total quality management and why you need it. You'll learn how to integrate TQM into every part of your business.

Chapter 11, The Power of Information, shows why you've got to have good information to make your strategies work. We'll show you how to get and use information to your advantage.

Chapter 12, Changing Corporate America, builds a compelling case for why change is "the name of the game." How you cope with change and make it happen are the key elements covered in this chapter.

Chapter 13, Playing the Corporate Game, takes you through a step-by-step tour showing how to play *The Corporate Game* on your personal computer.

The Computer Game Option

The speed of today's personal computers made it possible to design a "next generation" game. We designed a computer version of *The Corporate Game* to simulate what it takes to run a company in today's tough economic and marketing environments.

It's easy to use and does not require a high-end PC to run the game. All you need is an IBM or 100 percent compatible personal computer with a minimum of 640K of memory and DOS 3.0 or later version. Once the disk is booted up, run instructions appear on your display. Chapter 13 provides a detailed step-by-step explanation for users who may not be familiar with PC operations.

Cars have been chosen as the product of your new company because automobile production is affected by nearly every fluctuation in domestic and international economies. The market is domestic. Your company manufactures and sells cars throughout the United States. Competition is vicious. You match wits against three other car companies that have been built into the game. You can also compete against your colleagues or form teams to compete against each other.

The company that you build and run will have a plant to operate and a work force to compensate. You have inventories to control, accounting and financial data to examine, and capital expenditure decisions to make. You'll analyze marketing and economic data to develop sales forecasts.

You can produce economy, midsize, and luxury cars. Demand conditions, business situations, and cost will vary throughout the game. The competitive spirit of the game hits a new high when you start to produce and sell cars.

It's up to you to determine what corporate strategy to pursue. How many cars do you want to produce? What are your profit objectives? What are your return on investment expectations? You will be challenged to use all your entrepreneurial skills to beat the competition and win the game.

The game covers 12 periods of play. Each period represents a month. You have one year to build and successfully run your company. You can enter any combination of short-run and long-term decisions for a given period.

After indicating that you are done, in a matter of seconds, the PC will subject your company to all of the competitive forces that have been built into the game. When the PC completes its simulation cycle, it closes out the month and produces a set of reports to tell you how well you're doing.

The profit and loss statement report is your scorecard. The scorecard of your company's performance is automatically calculated at the end of each month. If you have a printer, the reports can be printed or they may be viewed on your display.

PC Game Instructions

We conclude each chapter with a section entitled PC Game Instructions. The sections include helpful hints about how to apply what you will have learned from the chapter material when you play *The Corporate Game* on your PC.

We've included a complete tutorial about how to play the game in Chapter 13. If you are not familiar with PC operations, you may want to read Chapter 13 before you proceed. At a minimum, make sure you follow the *copy disk* backup procedures that are covered at the beginning of Chapter 13. Here is how to start the game on your PC. Power up your PC using your normal procedure and follow these instructions:

1. Insert the game disk into a floppy disk drive (e.g., A or B).

2. Assuming that the disk is in drive A, ENTER - A:TCGAME at the DOS prompt.

3. At the start, the Main Menu (Exhibit 1) will appear as follows:

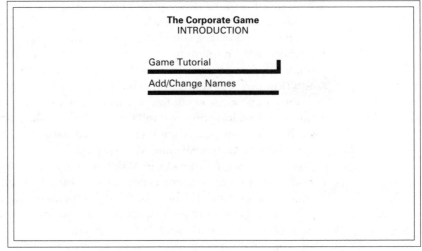

Change Student or Company Name(s)

Exhibit 1

```
┌──────────────────────────────────────────────────────────┐
│                                                          │
│                    The Corporate Game                    │
│                Welcome to the Corporate Game             │
│                                                          │
│                        Introduction                      │
│                                                          │
│    There are twelve months of play (one year) in the Corporate Game's │
│    computer model.  Read the test material, and then apply what you have learned │
│    by playing the corresponding months in the game.  Don't be too concerned if the │
│    early rounds of play seem to be "too simple."  It gets more complicated when │
│    you get into the later months.                        │
│       When you start Month 1 (January), you'll be given one million dollars, │
│    and challenged with building a manufacturing company that makes cars.  The │
│    creators of The Corporate Game realize that in the "real world" it would be │
│    next to impossible to build a car manufacturing company for a million dollars. │
│    It would probably take billions of dollars.  However, we did not want to │
│    clutter up your screen with huge numbers.  Therefore, in the interest of │
│    simplicity, everything is priced relative to a million dollars. │
│       As you proceed through each month of play, enter your business plans and │
│    strategies into the game.  You will have the option to purchase raw materials, │
│    equipment, services, and a labor force along the way as you build your │
│    company.  They may be paid for with cash from the corporate checking account, │
│    charged to your accounts payable account or from money you borrow from a bank. │
│                                                          │
└──────────────────────────────────────────────────────────┘

        F2 Print    F3 Return
```

Exhibit 2

Press the TAB key until the Tutorial option on the Main Menu is highlighted. Then press the ENTER key to select the Tutorial. It's that simple. The tutorial for the introduction to the PC game will now appear on your screen (Exhibit 2). If you have a printer, turn it on and make sure it is in the print ready mode. Press the F2 key if you want to print the Tutorial. Press the F3 key to return to the Main Menu.

When you return to the Main Menu, press the TAB key to highlight the Add/Change Names option. The menu in Exhibit 3 will appear on your display.

```
┌──────────────────────────────────────────────────────────┐
│                                                          │
│                    The Corporate Game                    │
│                       INTRODUCTION                       │
│                                                          │
│                     Add/Change Names                     │
│                                                          │
│         Title 1                     Title 2              │
│         ( ) Dr.                     ( ) President        │
│         ( ) Mr.                     ( ) VP               │
│         ( ) Mrs.                    ( ) CEO              │
│         ( ) Miss                    ( ) CFO              │
│         ( ) Prof                    ( ) PhD             │
│         ( ) NONE                    ( ) NONE             │
│                                                          │
│            Officer's Name                                │
│            John D. Doe                                   │
│                                                          │
│            Company Name                                  │
│            Demon Car Company                             │
│                                                          │
│                  ▄Done ▄        ▄Enter ▄                 │
│                                                          │
└──────────────────────────────────────────────────────────┘
```

Exhibit 3

Press the TAB key to highlight the Title 1 option and use the up/down arrow keys to select your personal title. Press the TAB key to highlight Title 2 and use the arrow keys to select your corporate title. Next, TAB to the Officer's Name field and enter your name followed by the name of your company. When you are done, press the ENTER key.

The personal information that you have just entered is stored on the game disk. Later in the game, your name and the name of your company will appear on special reports that you may print. Highlight the DONE option in the lower left side of the menu. The Main Menu (Exhibit 4) will again appear on your display for Month 1.

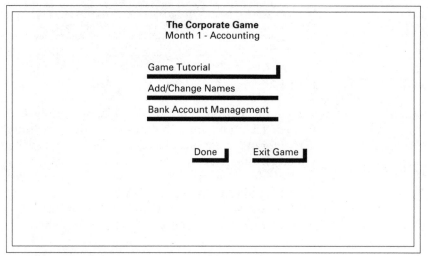

End Work Session - Exit the Program

Exhibit 4

We'll show you how to play Month 1 at the end of the Chapter 1. For now, highlight Exit Game and press the ENTER key. A final exit menu (Exhibit 5) will appear on your display as on the next page.

If you select the Exit–Update option and press the ENTER key, the title and name information that you entered in the first menu is saved on the game disk. If you select the Exit–No Update option, the information that you entered is not saved. You can enter the data again the next time you start the game. Select the Exit–Update option to return to the DOS prompt. Proceed to Chapter 1 in *The Corporate Game*.

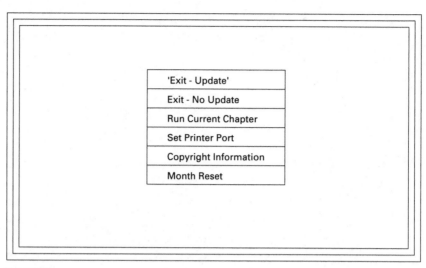

Exhibit 5

The Corporate Game

1

Starting the Corporate Game

Where It All Began

His name was Bill. We called him "Wild Bill." At 33, he was the youngest company president working for a *Fortune* 500 corporation. He had been hired to head up the company's newly acquired subsidiary, Sea Kist Corporation. It was all a part of the parent corporation's master diversification plan. The rich cashflow that the company had been enjoying for decades was being diverted to acquire food product companies like Sea Kist.

Sea Kist was a premier processing facility of frozen lemonade. The company was established in the early thirties in the heart of southern California, the lemon-producing capital of the world.

I first met Bill shortly after he took over as president. He was looking for a vice president of operations and hired me for the job. Bill was everything that you would expect to find in a corporate president. He was a big man with a smile that was as wide as the sunset and a personality to match.

When he spoke, you knew that he had to be right because there was absolutely no doubt in his spoken words. He ran the company with an iron hand. Everybody liked and respected Bill. If he had told us all to jump off a cliff because that was what we needed to do to support the company, we would have done it.

Bill's background was in marketing and sales, and he could sell anything with his uncanny ability to talk. His educational background had been broadened with a Harvard M.B.A. but as far as Bill was concerned, the only business discipline that counted was marketing.

Bill knew just enough about the other business disciplines to make him dangerous. He knew that if you lowered the price of lemonade, consumers would be inclined to buy more lemonade. I think he read Paul Samuelson's *Principles of Economics* and knew what a product demand curve looked like (see Exhibit 1-1).

On the accounting side, he knew that if you increased production even beyond what you could sell, the fixed cost per unit would drop. Since fixed costs are made up of plant and equipment, that makes sense (see Exhibit 1-2). The fixed cost of a can of lemonade drops when the number of cans produced increases.

Armed with these two short-term strategic principles, he proceeded to set up a corporate strategic plan that nearly destroyed the company. To this day, I believe that Bill concocted what he felt was a "sure-fire scheme" to accelerate his fast-track career train.

One afternoon, he called me into his office. I will never forget Bill's immortal words. "Dave, there is something I want you to do for me. I want you to start running our production facility 24 hours a day, 7 days a week."

I stared at him in disbelief. "Bill, we only need to run one shift to meet our current sales plan for lemonade. Besides, that's all the product I have room for in our warehouses." Bill's eyes narrowed and I knew that I had better listen to what he was about to say. "Do it anyway and rent outside warehouse space if you need it. You've got one week to get this game plan started or I will find another team player to get the job done." The coach had spoken!

My carefully selected response followed. "Yes sir, I will get right on it and you can count on me as a team player. It will be done in one week." It actually took me longer than a week to get everything set up for the 24-hour

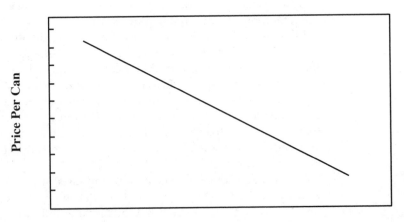

Cans of Lemonade Sold

Exhibit 1-1. Market demand for lemonade.

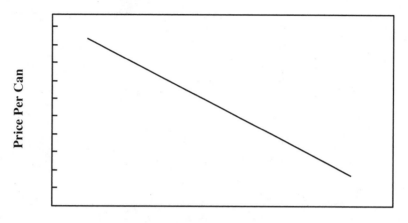

Cans of Lemonade Produced

Exhibit 1-2. Fixed cost per can to produce lemonade.

production cycle. Bill didn't care as long as he could see that progress was being made.

Sea Kist started producing frozen lemonade at record levels. For every three cans of lemonade produced, we were able to sell only one, and we threw the other two cans into a warehouse as surplus.

I had managed to rent every available warehouse in southern California. Our variable cost, mostly attributable to the cost of warehouse space, was going out of sight. Variable costs increase in direct proportion to the quantities of goods produced (see Exhibit 1-3). Bill had totally ignored any impact his decisions had on variable costs.

Nine months later, we had processed and stored enough frozen lemonade to satisfy America's total projected demand for the lemonade for the next three years. The only thing I believed that could stop the incredible production machine we had built up would be a freeze. I wanted a "killer frost" to move into southern California and wipe out the lemon crop. No more lemons, no more lemonade, and no more daily 24-hour production runs.

As it turned out, there was another more powerful force that stopped the lemonade production machine. Thank God for corporate auditors. Every big corporation has them. These are the people that come out of corporate headquarters with a focused mission. They randomly visit the corporation's subsidiaries and review the books to make sure that everything is in order.

They then go back to corporate headquarters and report their findings to the CEO and the executive staff. The auditors paid a visit to Sea Kist. They described what we were doing at Sea Kist as "dressing the profits." That's a polite way of saying "we were manipulating the books."

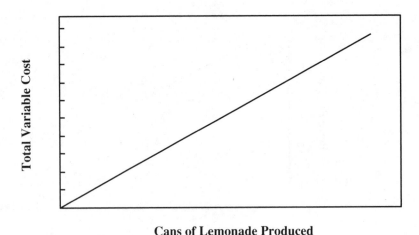

Cans of Lemonade Produced

Exhibit 1-3. Variable cost to produce lemonade.

Bill's fast-track career train came to an abrupt halt. He departed from the company overnight. There were no more buffalo for "Wild Bill" to kill. Shortly after all the smoke had cleared, I can remember thinking, "What a game, what a corporate game. It doesn't have to be played like this."

If Bill had been an executive who understood and truly appreciated all of the business disciplines instead of just marketing he would have known how to use a complement of business disciplines to run the company in a coordinated direction to achieve viable business goals and objectives. By combining Bill's decisions into one graph and adding in variable cost, you can see what happened to Sea Kist in Exhibit 1-4.

Early in the production cycle, Sea Kist was making a profit on each can of lemonade it produced. The fixed cost per can was in fact going down, which contributed to the profit margin. However, look what was happening to variable cost. It was increasing at a faster rate than the decrease in fixed cost to cover increased warehouse expenses.

When the combined fixed and variable cost (total cost line) equaled the total sales, the company was breaking even on each can sold. Add one more warehouse to the variable-cost line and the company went beyond the breakeven point into a loss position. The game was over!

I became obsessed with what had happened at Sea Kist. The story had to be told. It had to be a story that corporate management and aspiring management candidates could relate to and learn from. The idea became a book called . . . you guessed it . . . *The Corporate Game.*

It's about what it takes to run a business from top to bottom. You'll be introduced to each of the key business disciplines you most need to understand to succeed in this game. It starts off with a basic introduction to the

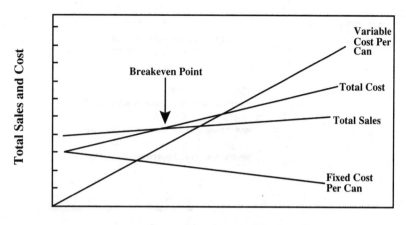

Cans of Lemonade Produced

Exhibit 1-4. Breakeven point to produce lemonade.

principles of accounting and finance followed by economics, marketing, sales, production control, and manufacturing.

To add an element of realism to the game, I begin the whole process by creating a hypothetical company that is in the business of making cars (i.e., not lemons). I carry the same theme throughout all of the chapters to add consistency to the story. It doesn't make any difference what the hypothetical company makes. The principles covered apply to any business.

What is important is that you understand the basic principles and relationships between the business groups. How does accounting support finance? Where do economics, sales, and marketing fit into the game? How does it all roll up into a production plan that subsequently feeds the manufacturing process? How do you "fine tune" your people to compete against your competition?

PC Game Instructions

To start the first month of play, insert the game disk in drive A and at the DOS prompt, ENTER A:TCGAME to start the program. The Main Menu for Month 1 (January) will appear on your screen. (See Exhibit 1-5.)

It looks very similar to the previous Main Menu with one exception. We have added a Bank Account Management option to the Main Menu. Select the option and notice that we have deposited $1 million into your corporate checking account as promised. (See Exhibit 1-6.)

Practice transferring money from your checking account into your savings account. In the Transfer From column, select Checking. In the Trans-

The Corporate Game
Month 1 - Accounting

Game Tutorial

Add/Change Names

Bank Account Management

Done   Exit Game

End Work Session - Exit the Program

Exhibit 1-5. Month 1—Accounting menu.

The Corporate Game
Month 1 - Accounting

Banking Transactions

Transfer from: Transfer to:
( ) Checking   ( ) Savings
( ) Savings   ( ) Checking
( ) Loan Request   ( ) Accounts Payable
                               ( ) Notes Payable

Transaction Amount   0

Account Balances

Checking	$1,000,000.00
Savings	$ 0.00
Accts Payable	$ 0.00
Notes Payable	$ 0.00
Credit Limit	$1,000,000.00

Done   Enter

Exhibit 1-6. Month 1—Accounting, banking transactions menu.

fer To column, select Savings. Next, select the Transaction Amt (transaction amount) option and enter the dollar amount you want to transfer from checking to savings (Exhibit 1-7).

Remember to enter whole numbers. Press the ENTER key and the transfer takes place on the display (Exhibit 1-8). If you change your mind, transfer money in the other direction.

If you had purchased products or services and charged them to your company's notes or accounts payable accounts, you could pay off all or part of the account balances by transferring money from savings or checking into either account.

This exercise completes all that we have to show you about Month 1. To close out the month, select the Exit option at the bottom right corner of the menu and press the ENTER key. The exit submenu will appear on your display (Exhibit 1-9).

Select the Exit–Update option to exit from the game and return to the DOS prompt. Continue on to Chapter 2 in *The Corporate Game.*

```
                        The Corporate Game
                        Month 1 - Accounting
                      Banking Transactions
         Transfer from:            Transfer to:
         ( ) Checking              ( ) Savings
         ( ) Savings               ( ) Checking
         ( ) Loan Request          ( ) Accounts Payable
                                   ( ) Notes Payable

         Transaction Amount   500,000

                        Account Balances
            Checking              $1,000,000.00
            Savings               $         0.00
            Accts Payable         $         0.00
            Notes Payable         $         0.00
            Credit Limit          $1,000,000.00

                     Done  ▄   Enter  ▄
```

Exhibit 1-7. Month 1—Accounting, banking transactions checking menu.

The Corporate Game
Month 1 - Accounting

Banking Transactions

Transfer from: Transfer to:
( ) Checking   ( ) Savings
( ) Savings   ( ) Checking
( ) Loan Request   ( ) Accounts Payable
                                  ( ) Notes Payable

Transaction Amount   0

Account Balances

Checking	$ 500,000.00
Savings	$ 500,000.00
Accts Payable	$ 0.00
Notes Payable	$ 0.00
Credit Limit	$ 1,000,000.00

Done ▗   Enter ▗

Exhibit 1-8. Month 1—Accounting, banking transactions savings menu.

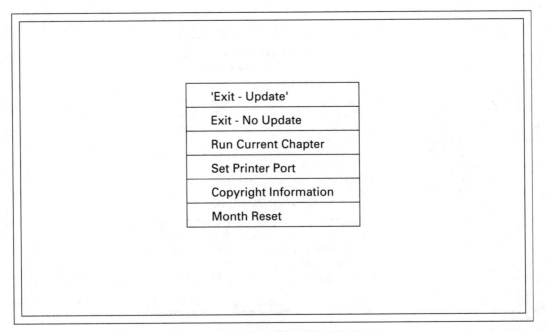

'Exit - Update'

Exit - No Update

Run Current Chapter

Set Printer Port

Copyright Information

Month Reset

Exit - Saving All Changes Since the Last 'DONE' or 'Exit Update'

Exhibit 1-9. Exit menu.

2
Accounting for the Facts

The Bottom Line

Accounting has the distinction of being the oldest of all the business disciplines. The principles of accounting date back to the days of the Roman Empire when ledger cards were used to track army legion payments. Every company uses some kind of an accounting system. It's their scorecard. At some point in time, the business computers stop and the accountants measure two things: profits and return on investment.

Corporate investors and stockholders will be waiting with baited breath for the "official scorecard." If profits and return on investment are high, everybody is happy. The price of stock goes up. The stockholders make money and CEO keeps his or her job. If the numbers go in the other direction, as we saw in the case of Sea Kist Corporation, chaos results.

All businesspeople need to know how to read and interpret accounting reports. More important, they must understand what happens to the balance sheet if something changes on the income statement or visa versa. This chapter introduces you to accounting reports. You'll see how the various reports are interconnected, how to interpret them, and how to make management decisions from accounting information.

Business Environment

The company featured in *The Corporate Game* manufactures cars. Why cars? We could have picked widgets or some other product. We wanted a product that everybody could relate to. It also had to be a product that gets impacted by everything the economy throws out. Cars fit the bill.

9

From this point on, most of the examples and exhibits relate to a car manufacturing company. This format allows us to build an element of consistency into *The Corporate Game*. There is a logical progression of steps that anyone must take to build a company. Each step depends on what you did in the previous step.

As you proceed through the book, your mission will be to determine how to build cars at the lowest cost possible and sell them at the highest possible price. There are three types of cars that you can build; economy, midsize, and luxury cars.

The accounting system you set up for your company is the major source of expense and revenue information. Besides indicating how well you are doing, accounting reports can be used to help develop new game strategies and investigate reasons for the success or the failure of existing strategies.

The Bottom Line

The bottom line of any business is anchored by a set of reports called financial statements. Companies are bought and sold at prices that are based upon a couple of line items in these reports. The price of a corporation's stock can swing north or south, depending upon what is reported by the accountants.

In the final analysis, management careers are made and lost on bottom-line numbers. If you're going to make it in this game, you had better know how to read and interpret financial reports. Your career depends on it. It's the first step you must take to build a strong company and career.

All accounting systems produce financial statements that consist of two primary reports: a balance sheet and an income statement. They show a company's performance and financial picture at a given moment in time.

This chapter starts by discussing the purpose and function of the balance sheet. An example of a simple balance sheet is shown. The discussion leads you into the subtle complexities of the balance sheet. There are several examples along the way to help ease the transition.

Next comes the income statement. The same approach that is used to explain the balance sheet is used here. When you complete the chapter, you will know how to read and interpret financial statements. More important, you will know how to apply information derived from these reports to improve the performance of any business.

The Balance Sheet

The balance sheet is a record of the dollar value of three accounting categories; assets, liabilities, and owner's equity. A simplified example of the report format is shown in Exhibit 2-1. Assets are items that have value and are

Balance Sheet

End of Month 1

Dollars in Thousands

Assets

Cash	$41
Inventory	$30
Plant & Equipment	$120
LESS: Depreciation	($10)
Total Assets	$181
Liabilities	$165
Owner's Equity	$16
Liabilities & Owner's Equity	$181

Exhibit 2-1. Balance sheet.

owned by the corporation. The amounts of money you have on deposit in checking and savings accounts are examples of asset accounts. In a manufacturing company, the value of raw materials and finished goods inventory generally represent the largest assets in terms of dollars.

An expanded version of our original balance sheet is shown in Exhibit 2-2. The headings of the report include the name of the company and the period of time that the report covers (Month 1 or January in the example). It is a "snapshot" report showing what the corporate assets, liabilities, and retained earnings were at a specified moment in time. In our example, this moment in time is January 31.

Assets

An asset is anything that has a monetary value to the corporation. In some cases, the asset values are easy to quantify. If you have cash in a corporate checking account, then the account balance of the checking account on January 31 will be the value of the cash asset. Assets that depreciate over a period of time, such as capital equipment, are more difficult to estimate in terms of cash value.

To determine depreciation, we first estimate the useful life of the asset.

Demon Car Company

Balance Sheet

End of Month 1

Dollars in Thousands

Assets		Liabilities	
Cash in Checking Account	$35	Accounts Payable	$140
Cash in Savings Account	$6	Notes Payable	$25
Materials Inventory	$5	Total Liabilities	$165
Car Inventory	$25	**Owner's Equity**	
Plant & Equipment	$120	Retained Earnings	$16
Less: Accumulated Depreciation	$10		
Total Assets	$181	Liabilities & Owner's Equity	$181

Exhibit 2-2. Demon Car Company balance sheet.

Next, we reduce the asset value accordingly by a term accountants call *accumulated depreciation*. If your accountants have done a good job in establishing depreciation rates, the net value of your assets after deducting accumulated depreciation should be what the asset is worth on the open "used" market.

If you start from the left side of the report in Exhibit 2-2, the Demon Car Company accumulated $181,000 in total assets (or $181 thousand dollars with the zeros omitted to simplify the report format). The company has $35 in a checking account and $6 in an interest-bearing savings account.

The balance of the assets is made up of inventories, plant, and equipment. The materials inventory is probably located in the company's warehouse where it will soon be used to manufacture cars. Car inventories represent the value of the cars at their manufactured cost since they have not yet been sold.

There are several methods companies use to track the cost of their inventories. The method that we use throughout the book is called the *inventory averaging method*. It's one of the most common methods used today. In its simplest form, the value of a unit of inventory is set at its average value.

Let's say that you purchased a ton of steel for $1000 in January. Because you didn't use the steel you "carried over" January's steel inventory (1 ton) into February's inventory. During the month of February, you bought an additional two tons of steel at $1500 per ton ($3000 total). What is the average unit value of your steel inventory?

$$\text{Value of steel} = (\$1000 \text{ for 1 ton}) + (\$3000 \text{ for 2 tons})$$

$$= \$4000$$

$$\text{Average price per ton} = \$4000/3 \text{ tons}$$

$$= \$1333/\text{ton}$$

There are two other methods commonly used to record the cost of inventory: LIFO and FIFO. LIFO stands for last-in, first-out and FIFO stands for first-in, first-out. LIFO is a popular inventory costing method to use in inflationary periods. Let's go back to our example to see how LIFO works.

As we saw, the price of steel jumped from $1000 a ton in January to $1500 a ton in February. If we had used a ton of steel in the production process in February, we would have charged $1500 to the cost of steel used instead of $1333 under the average cost of inventory method, because $1500 was the last- in price we paid per ton of steel.

It was, therefore, the last-out inventory that we used. The use of this method is popular with corporations that want to run up monthly expenses as a means of deferring corporate income tax payments.

The reverse situation happens under the FIFO method. If we had used a ton of steel in the production process in February, we would have charged $1000 to the cost of steel used instead of $1333 under the average cost of inventory method or $1500 under LIFO since $1000 was the first-in price we paid per ton of steel.

It was, therefore, the first-out inventory that we used. The use of this method is popular with corporations that want to reduce monthly expenses and show temporary windfall profits.

Switching back and forth between inventory methodologies is an act that is frowned upon by the Internal Revenue Service. In fact, it's illegal. Corporations must declare the methodology they will use to account for the cost of inventory. They must be consistent in the method used for corporate tax-reporting purposes.

Plant and equipment are real property that is owned by the corporation. For this reason, they are sometimes referred to as *real assets*. Real assets include the land where the plant is located, buildings, and fixtures. Equipment includes manufacturing machines, tools, and any other assets used in the manufacturing process.

Depreciation.   Notice that in Exhibit 2-2, accumulated depreciation is deducted from the asset account. *Depreciation* is an accounting term used to record a decrease in the value of an asset through wear, deterioration, and obsolescence. For example, suppose you bought a machine (asset) for $120. This particular machine is expected to last for 12 months before it wears out. The depreciation period for this asset would therefore be 12 months at a depreciation cost of $10 per month ($120/12 months = $10).

The value of the machine at the end of the first month would be $110 (Asset Value − Depreciation or $120 − $10). This is an example of *straight line depreciation*. It is the simplest and most common method used by corporations for determining depreciation.

Accumulated depreciation is the sum of year-to-date depreciation expenses for applicable assets. In our example, it was $10 at the end of Month 1. If we were reporting depreciation in Month 2, it would have been twice that amount ($20) if we assume that no additional depreciable assets were acquired.

In the "real world," there are several other ways to calculate depreciation. Sum-of-the-years' digits and double-declining balance are two examples of depreciation methodologies used by corporations to achieve tax advantages.

The federal government's corporate tax structure plays an important role in establishing depreciation rates and methodologies. For example, the number of years that you are allowed to assign a useful life to an asset is partly controlled by tax laws.

Liabilities

Liabilities are the next account category on the balance sheet. Liabilities are a corporation's commitments to pay off assets or services received from suppliers. They are used to help fund the capital side of the business. Liability claims are generally held by banks, vendors, and mortgage companies. Accounts payable and notes payable are two examples of liability accounts.

If you own your company, you have a claim to the assets after all liability obligations have been met. This is what is referred to as *owner's equity*. It is the difference between total assets and total liabilities.

Two types of liability accounts are shown. The company owes a bank $25 (notes payable) for money that was perhaps borrowed to buy equipment (notes payable). Notes payable are considered long-term loan obligations (six months or longer). Accounts payable generally covers short-term obligations to vendors (less than two months). The company owes $140 in accounts payable to various vendors and suppliers.

Owner's Equity

The difference between total assets and liabilities is owner's equity ($16) in the company. It represents what the corporation would be worth if it were to go out of business, sell off all its assets, and pay off all its liabilities.

Owner's equity will increase as long as there is a positive flow of revenues. Sales income brings assets in the form of cash and accounts receivable into the business. Expenses cause the outflow of assets (i.e., cash reduction) to occur to help generate more sales revenues.

If revenues are greater than expenses, the increase in assets simultaneously increases the owner's equity. If revenues are less than expenses, the owner's equity decreases. Increases in owner's equity caused by a profitable operation are called *retained earnings*. These earnings are retained to fund the growth of the company.

The Income Statement

The income statement identifies the profits or losses of the company at a given moment in time (e.g., end of the month). The purpose of this report is to measure the overall effort of the company in terms of what it cost to run its operations during the month. Total costs are matched against the company's accomplishments, which are measured in terms of income earned during the month. If income exceeds costs, the company made a profit. A loss occurs when costs exceed income.

Three primary accounting categories make up an income statement: sales, cost, and profit. A simplified example of the report format is shown in Exhibit 2-3. Sales are the revenues that a company derives from the sale of goods and services it produces.

Income statements are often confused with cashflow statements. One could assume that if the corporation made a $5 profit at the end of the month, the company has $5 more than what it needed to cover expenses. This may not be the case.

The sale of an item could qualify for two different types of asset accounts. In a cash sale, the company deposits the money from the sale into a cash asset account (i.e., checking account). The money is instantly available to pay off expenses or liabilities.

In a credit sale, the sale gets "booked" against the accounts receivable asset account. The customer owes the company money at some future point in time. The money from the sale is not immediately available to pay off current expenses.

The company may not have a sufficient reserve of cash on hand to cover all expenses. A cashflow report would have brought this point out. It matches cash inflows against required cash outflows. We will cover cashflow reports in more detail in the next chapter.

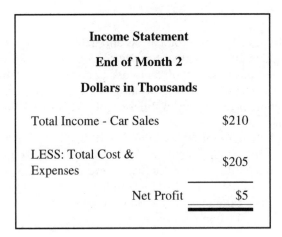

Income Statement

End of Month 2

Dollars in Thousands

Total Income - Car Sales	$210
LESS: Total Cost & Expenses	$205
Net Profit	$5

Exhibit 2-3. Simple income statement.

The costs of manufacturing products are deducted from sales to determine the amount of profit made. If costs had exceeded sales, the profit exhibit would have been a negative number reflecting the dollar amount of loss to the company.

Our simplified version of the income statement has been expanded to show more detailed information about the company's overall performance. Exhibit 2-4 breaks down the company's sales by the types of cars sold. Both sales units and dollars are shown. There is also a breakdown of what it cost to produce cars. Our expanded income statement includes a year-to-date column that is an accumulation of the previous months' totals for sales and expenses. In the real world, most companies officially record and report income over 12 monthly periods.

Like the balance sheet, income statement report headings include the name of the company and the period of time that the report covers (Month 2 or February in Exhibit 2-4). It too is a "snapshot" report showing what the company's profits or losses were at a specified moment in time. In our example, this moment in time is February 28.

Cost of Goods Sold

Cost of goods sold is an accumulation of all the expenses the company incurred to produce automobiles. The company's total cost of cars sold was determined by calculating the difference in cost between beginning car inventory, plus the cost of cars manufactured in February, less the cost of the ending car inventory.

It shows that the company had 10 cars in stock at the beginning of February. It manufactured an additional 10 cars during the month and, there-

Demon Car Company

Income Statement

End of Month 2

Dollars in Thousands

Car Sales	Curr $	Units	YTD$	Units
Economy Sedans	$50	5	$195	13
Midsize Sedans	$90	7	$201	15
Luxury Sedans	$70	3	$104	4
Total Car Sales	$210	15	$500	32
Cost of Cars Sold				
Cost of Beginning Car Inventory	$122	10	$245	15
Cost of Cars Manufactured	$104	10	$205	20
Cost of Cars Available for Sale	$226	20	$450	35
LESS: Cost of Ending Inventory	$108	5	$225	3
Total Cost of Cars Sold	$118	15	$225	32
Profit				
Gross Profit on Sales	$92		$275	
Less: Sales & Overhead Expense	$87		$200	
Net Profit	$5		$75	

Exhibit 2-4. Demon Car Company income statement.

fore, had a total of 20 cars available for sale during the month. The total cost of cars available for sale was $226,000.

Demon sold 15 of the 20 cars that were available for sale. The inventory at the end of the period was therefore 5 cars valued at $108. The company started off with 20 cars valued at $226 and ended up with 5 cars worth $108. The $118 ($226 − $108) difference is "booked" as the total cost of cars sold. The 5 cars that were left over at the end of the month will show up in next month's income statement as the beginning car inventory valued at $108.

Cost of Cars Available for Sale

The cost of cars available for sale is the sum of two separate but related cost components. It includes the cost to produce the cars that are in inventory plus the total manufacturing cost in the current period. The cost components are the same in both categories and include labor, materials, and factory overhead.

Here is how manufacturing and inventory cost gets "rolled up" into a cost of cars available for sale on the income statement. First, we'll talk about how we arrived at the cost of cars manufactured. The cost information in Exhibit 2-5 shows what it cost to make each car model.

We know from the income statement that we produced a total of 10 cars in February. The report doesn't tell us what models were produced or how many cars were in the month's beginning car inventory. That is because the income statement in Exhibit 2-4 is a summary report. The month's beginning car inventory is shown in an expanded income report (Exhibit 2-6).

Exhibit 2-6 shows the number of car units that were in inventory and were produced in February. Our total cost for all cars is also shown. If we apply the cost information in Exhibit 2-5 to the calculation that follows, we can quickly see how the accountants determined what it cost to manufacture economy cars in February.

$$\text{Economy car cost} = (\text{Material \$} + \text{Labor \$} + \text{Factory overhead \$} + \text{Selling expense \$})$$

$$= (1.5 \text{ tons steel} \times \$1200/\text{ton}) + (100 \text{ parts} + \$10/\text{part}) + (100 \text{ hrs. labor} \times \$25/\text{hr.}) + (\$500 \text{ selling expense}) + (\$2585 \text{ overhead})$$

$$= \$9100$$

Description	Unit Cost	Economy Car	Midsize Car	Luxury Car
Steel (tons per car)	$1,200/ton	1.5	2.0	3.0
Parts per Car	$10 each	100	210	350
Direct Labor Hours	$25/hr.	100	150	300

Exhibit 2-5. Material and labor required to build each car model.

Demon Car Company

Income Statement

End of Month 2

Dollars in Thousands

Car Sales	Mon $	Units	YTD$	Units
Economy Sedans	$50	5	$195	13
Midsize Sedans	$90	7	$201	15
Luxury Sedans	$70	3	$104	4
Total Car Sales	$210	15	$500	32

Cost of Cars Sold

Beginning Car Inventory

	Mon $	Units	YTD$	Units
Economy	$36	3	$100	5
Midsize	$42	3	$101	6
Luxury	$44	4	$44	4
Cost of Beginning Car Inventory	$122	10	$245	15

Cars Manufactured

	Mon $	Units	YTD$	Units
Economy	$40	4	$55	5
Midsize	$42	4	$98	5
Luxury	$22	2	$52	5
Cost of Cars Manufactured	$104	10	$205	15
Cost of Cars Available for Sale	$226	20	$450	35
LESS: Cost of Ending Inventory	$108	5	$225	3
Total Cost of Cars Sold	$118	15	$225	32

Profit

	Mon $		YTD$	
Gross Profit on Sales	$92		$275	
Less: Sales & Overhead Expense	$87		$200	
Net Profit	$5		$75	

Exhibit 2-6. Demon Car Company income statement.

That's how we arrived at the total cost of cars manufactured. What about the inventory side of the cost formula? In the previous period (January), the cost of cars manufactured was determined using the exact same methodology that we used in February. What we didn't sell in January, we carried over into February's beginning car inventory. In our example, we had 10 cars valued at $122.

Profits

The balance of the income statement is relatively easy to explain. Gross profits are determined by subtracting the cost of cars sold from car sales. *Gross profits* are defined as profits that are realized after all directly related manufacturing costs have been deducted from sales. When you subtract the indirect costs associated with car sales, you end up with net profits or what is sometimes called the bottom line.

As the example in Exhibit 2-6 shows, selling expenses are treated as an indirect expense and include commissions paid to salespersons for cars sold. Factory overhead represents all the costs that are associated with running the manufacturing facility and includes expenses such as rent for factory space.

If total sales are greater than total costs, profits will be a positive dollar amount ($5 in Exhibit 2-6). In this example, profits represent a cash surplus (asset) that will appear in one of the balance sheet asset accounts (i.e., checking, accounts receivable, and so on).

Your understanding of the corporate cost concepts will become a critical factor in assuring the success or failure of your company. As a general rule, a company that cannot control costs will go out of business.

An important piece of information in our profit analysis is missing. All we know at this point is that the company made money in February. We don't know what the profit contribution was for each of the car models sold. The numbers are easy to get if we consolidate the data from Exhibits 2-5 and 2-6. Profit margins by model are shown in Exhibit 2-7.

Car Model	Sales Price	Unit Cost	Profit Margin	Profit %
Economy	$10,000	$9,100	$800	8%
Midsize	$14,000	$11,800	$2,200	16%
Luxury	$19,000	$15,500	$3,500	18%

Exhibit 2-7. Profit margin by model.

The contribution that each product line makes to the corporation's total profit is critical to the ongoing success and survival of the company. Abrupt up and down shifts in a product's profit contribution must be recognized in a timely manner so that appropriate adjustments can be made to the company's operating plan.

Balance Sheet versus Income Statement

Up to this point, we have discussed the components of the balance sheet and the income statement as though they were separate, unrelated reports. On the contrary, a direct relationship exists between these two financial statements that should not be ignored.

There are decisions you can make as a result of your interpretation of the income statement that can have a positive or negative impact on the balance sheet. Changes that you make to the balance sheet can also have a positive or negative effect on the income statement. One of your primary strategies should be to improve your company's equity position. Let's review the procedures for determining owner's equity.

Owners equity = Total assets − Total liabilities

THEREFORE:

If assets increase and liabilities decrease

THEN equity will increase

OR the reverse is true

What happens to owner's equity if the company makes or loses money? The Demon Car Company recorded a $5 net profit on their income statement in Exhibit 2-6. This represents a surplus of money the company earned after it met its current period expense responsibilities. As the CEO, it's your responsibility to determine how to invest the profits earned by the company.

If we assume that all profits are deposited in a corporate checking account, then cash on hand in February would have been $40 ($35 + $5). The balance sheet for February with the increase in the checking account balance is shown in Exhibit 2-8.

Suppose Demon lost $5 in February. The company pays for its losses using cash from the checking account. If the cash on hand in the previous period was $35, then the current period cash in Demon's checking account would have been $30 ($35 − $5).

The effect of a $5000 loss on the balance sheet is shown in Exhibit 2-9. As you can readily determine, a relatively small profit or loss can significantly impact the balance sheet. The profit assumption resulted in a favorable eq-

Demon Car Company

Balance Sheet

End of Month 2

Dollars in Thousands

Assets		Liabilities	
Cash in Checking Account	$40	Accounts Payable	$137
Cash in Savings Account	$6	Notes Payable	$18
Materials Inventory	$5	Total Liabilities	$155
Car Inventory	$25	**Owner's Equity**	
Plant & Equipment	$120	Retained Earnings	$21
Less: Accumulated Depreciation	$20		
Total Assets	$176	Liabilities & Owner's Equity	$176

Exhibit 2-8. Demon Car Company balance sheet showing profit.

uity position of $21 (Exhibit 2-8), whereas the loss assumption resulted in a negative equity position of $11 (Exhibit 2-9).

Making Financial Decisions

Now that you understand financial statements, it's time to put your accounting knowledge to work making financial decisions. Financial statements provide an essential ingredient to this process. They can be used by management to monitor the company's performance or serve as a decision-making tool used by external groups as well.

Banks may or may not grant you a loan based upon financial statement information. Rating agencies like Standard & Poor's and Dun and Bradstreet will set bond and credit ratings for your company based upon the performance shown in these reports.

What are these agencies looking for? What should you be looking for to assure the financial health of your company? Corporate financial health can be monitored by using financial ratios that measure short-term and long-term liquidity.

Short-term Liquidity

Webster defines *liquidity* as "having the capability to quickly convert over to cash." In corporate terms, that means having sufficient cash reserves to pay bills and stay in business. Liquidity means survival and the lack of liquidity can lead to bankruptcy.

Liquidity is measured by dividing current liabilities into current assets to calculate what is called a *current ratio.* Accountants tend to think of the current period of time as less than one year. Therefore, current assets and liabilities could be either sold or paid off within one year. The balance sheet in Exhibit 2-10 shows current and long-term assets and liabilities.

Demon Car Company

Balance Sheet

End of Month 2

Dollars in Thousands

Assets		Liabilities	
Cash in Checking Account	$30	Accounts Payable	$137
Cash in Savings Account	$6	Notes Payable	$18
Materials Inventory	$5	Total Liabilities	$155
Car Inventory	$25	**Owner's Equity**	
Plant & Equipment	$120	Retained Earnings	$11
Less: Accumulated Depreciation	$20		
Total Assets	$166	Liabilities & Owner's Equity	$166

Exhibit 2-9. Demon Car Company balance sheet showing loss.

Demon Car Company

Balance Sheet

As of Month 2

Dollars in Thousands

Assets		Liabilities	
Current Assets		**Current Liabilities**	
Cash in Checking Account	$10	Accounts Payable	$137
Cash in Savings	6	Notes Payable	5
Accounts Receivable	$20	Total Current Liabilities	$142
Credit Sales	$60	**Long-term Liabilities**	
Material Inventory	5	10-year Mortgage	$73
Car Inventory	$25	Total Long-term Liability	$73
Total Current Assets	$126	Total Liabilities	$215
Long-term Assets		**Owner's Equity**	
Plant & Equipment	$120	Retained Earnings	$11
Less: Accumulated Dep.	(20)		
Total Long-term Assets	$100		
Total Assets	$226	Total Liab. & Equity	$226

Exhibit 2-10. Demon Car Company balance sheet.

Current Ratio. The current ratio derived from Exhibit 2-10 is .89 (Current Assets/Current Liabilities or $126/$142). Current ratios are typically expressed as "1.5 to 1" or ".89 to 1" in our example. It shows what would happen if a company was liquidated (sold) at a given moment in time.

In the example, we had enough current assets to cover $.89 on every dollar that we owed in current liabilities. Most banks and financial institutions consider current ratios greater than 1 as a good indicator of liquidity.

Turnover Ratio. Turnover ratios can be used to help isolate problems that may be present in the current ratio. Turnover is a measure of how quickly corporate assets are used to return cash (liquidity) to the company. There are three turnover ratios used for this purpose:

Accounts receivable turnover

Accounts payable turnover

Inventory turnover

The credit sales in Exhibit 2-10 are $60. Accounts receivable turnover is determined by dividing credit sales by accounts receivable. In this example, the accounts receivable turnover is 3 (Credit Sales/Accounts Receivable, or $60/$20). Receivables are "turning over" three times a year.

Turnover can also be expressed in days. If we divide 365 days in a year by 3, we get the number of days (365 days/3, or 122 days) it takes on average to collect each dollar billed. Receivables that are in excess of 45 days signal problems with liquidity and a company's ability to collect money for the goods and services it sells.

Accounts payable turnover shows how current a company is in paying suppliers. Cost of goods sold is divided by accounts payable to determine this ratio. If we divide the cost of goods sold from Exhibit 2-6 ($118) by accounts payable ($137) in Exhibit 2-10, we end up with .86 times per year. It takes us almost a year or 86 percent of a year to pay off a supplier. While that may be good for us and bad for our suppliers, it is an indicator that our company may be on "thin ice" in the field of supplier relations.

Inventory turnover is derived by dividing cost of goods sold by the cost of inventories. It indicates how fast we are able to sell each product produced. That's important for a couple of reasons. Although finished good inventories are recognized as assets on the balance sheet, their value is shown at cost.

The asset value increases significantly if we sell the asset at a profit. We not only recover our cost but also add the profit margin to our cash account. If we divide the cost of cars sold ($118 in Exhibit 2-6) by car inventories ($25 in Exhibit 2-10), we can determine the inventory turnover rate:

$$\text{Inventory turnover rate} = \text{Cost of cars sold/Car inventories}$$

$$= \$118/\$25$$

$$= 4.7$$

$$\text{Inventory turnover days} = 365 \text{ Days per year/Turnover}$$

$$= 365/4.7$$

$$= 77 \text{ days}$$

The inventory turnover ratio tells us is how long it takes to sell a product. In our example, it took an average of 77 days to sell one car or unit of inventory. The higher the ratio, the faster the company is able to realize a profit from its capital investment.

Long-term Liquidity

The test of long-term liquidity focuses on the corporation's ability to meet its long-term debt obligations. The ratio of long-term debt to equity is one measure of long-term liquidity. If we use the numbers from Exhibit 2-10 and divide our long-term debt by total long-term capital and equity, we end up with an equity position of 51:25. Our calculations are summarized as follows:

Long-term debt		$ 73
Owner's equity:		
Capital	$100	
Retained earnings	($ 11)	$111
Total long-term capital structure		$184

$$\text{Long-term liquidity} = \text{Long-term debt}/\text{Long-term capital}$$

$$= \$73/\$184$$

$$= .40$$

In this example, we have almost twice as much capital as would be required to pay off our long-term debt. Better than a 2-to-1 ratio is considered "good" by most industry standards.

Return on Investment

As the CEO of the company, you are responsible for earning a competitive rate of return for the funds invested in your company. Investors may include your partners, stockholders, or lending institutions. Therefore, you want to earn at least as high a rate of return on the money that has been invested in the company as could be earned from alternative investment opportunities with similar risks.

Let's assume that you are an outside investor and you've invested $10 million into the Demon Car Company. The company is currently returning 5 percent on your investment. Suppose that the banks are currently offering a 10 percent return from a safe money-market account.

As an investor, you would probably be less than satisfied with your investment in Demon when you could be making twice the return in a money-market account. If you were given the opportunity, you would fire Demon's

CEO. Therefore, in the interest of job security, you need to know how to measure the earning powers of your company. The basic measure of earnings power is called return on investment (ROI).

The ROI is used as a financial tool to help identify problems and evaluate alternative uses of money for making investments. Many consider ROI to be the ultimate qualifier in making financial planning decisions.

ROI calculations are derived from income and balance sheet data as a series of ratios used by management to help make logical decisions based upon past and anticipated company earnings. The two financial components used to calculate ROI are profitability rate and turnover rate.

Profitability Rate

The profitability rate is computed by dividing net profits by net sales. Net profits are the actual profits earned by the corporations after all applicable expenses have been deducted. An example of how net profit is calculated as follows:

Net profit = Gross profit – Sales and overhead expenses

Net sales are the actual sales retained by the corporations after all sales related deductions have been allocated. An example would be sales discounts.

Net sales = Gross sales – Sales discounts

The profitability ratio highlights the profits earned from sales and measures the company's success at controlling cost. When net sales decline, most companies will experience lower profits. To offset lower sales dollars, expenses are generally reduced in order to maintain profit levels. The profit rate from Exhibit 2-6 is calculated as follows:

Profitability rate = (Net profit)/(Net sales)

= ($5)/($210)

= 2 percent or 2 cents profit for every sales dollar

Turnover Rate

The other ROI measurement is the turnover rate. It is computed by dividing the corporation's investments into net sales. This rate reflects the efficiency with which capital assets committed to the company are being used. The turnover rate formula calculated from Exhibits 2-6 and 2-10 is shown in the calculation that follows:

$$\text{Turnover rate} = (\text{Net sales})/(\text{Total assets} - \text{Current liabilities})$$

$$= (\$210)/(\$226 - \$142)$$

$$= (\$210)/(\$84)$$

$$= \$2.50$$

In our example, $5.40 of net sales are generated for every $1 the company has invested in total assets. In other words, we are turning our assets over five times (2.5-to-1 ratio) to produce sales. If we divide 365 days by 2.5, we end up with 146 days. That is how long it takes the company to generate enough cash from car sales to cover its assets.

This same ratio can be used to calculate the turnover rate of new capital equipment. The turnover rate for capital equipment reflects the efficiency with which capital assets will contribute to the overall profitability of the company. In the final analysis, ROI can be increased by increasing the use of existing capital, reducing expenses, or a combination of both.

Accounting for the Facts

You are sitting in your office thinking to yourself, "Now that I'm a CEO, I don't have to concern myself with all that accounting stuff." You hated accounting when you took it in college and your lack of love for the subject hasn't changed. Besides, if you're the CEO, you can hire "bean counters" to take care of all your number-crunching needs.

Suddenly, you remember your good old friend Bill at Sea Kist. He didn't like accounting any more than you do. He ignored it when he put together one of his strategic plans and drove the company into a severe loss position. He also lost his job because of that situation.

You decide to take a renewed interest in accounting. You contact Jane, your controller, and tell her, "Jane, I want you to help me put together the key accounting information required to support our strategic plan. I want the report to come out monthly. It's got to show high-level accounting information that will indicate to me if we have potential problems in any one segment of our business."

Jane digests your request for a moment and comes back with a response that you like. "If you can give me a day, I can create a mock-up of the report you're looking for." The next morning, Jane comes back to your office eager to show you her proposed report. Using your overhead projector, she displays the proposed report on the screen (see Exhibit 2-11).

She proceeds to explain her report. "You will notice that there are only seven lines of data shown on the report. It has been designed to give you a quick snapshot of how our company is doing at any one moment in time.

Accounting Information	Current Month Actuals	Current Month Plan	Current Month Variance	Year-to-Date Actuals	Year-to-Date Plan	Year-to-Date Variance
1. Net Sales	$210	$200	$10	$500	$495	$5
2. Cost of Cars Sold	$118	$125	$7	$245	$255	$10
3. Net Profit	$5	$20	$15	$75	$80	$5
Turnover Ratios						
4. Accounts Receivable	77 days	70 days	7 days	70 days	75 days	5 days
5. Accounts Payable	.86	.90	.04	.90	.80	.10
6. Inventory	4.7	5.0	.3	4.2	4.0	.2
7. Assets (ROI)	12%	11%	1%	13%	15%	2%

Exhibit 2-11. The accounting part of the corporate strategic plan ($ in thousands).

Actual dollars from our balance sheet and income statement will be summarized and recapped on the report."

"Month and year-to-date actuals for each category will be compared against our strategic plan numbers for the same category. Actual-to-plan variances will be easy to identify. Negative variances can trigger a more in depth analysis of what went wrong so that corrective action can be taken to resolve any problems."

You tell Jane that you like what you see and want the report to be implemented immediately. For the time being, you are satisfied with Jane's report as the first step in your strategic plan. You plan to refine your strategic plan in the next chapter.

Summary and Conclusions

This chapter began by stating that your company's accounting system can provide you with critical information about how your company is doing. Several examples were used to demonstrate how a company's financial performance is tied to loan rates, bond prices, and stock prices.

The first report discussed was the balance sheet. A simple example of a balance sheet was shown. Next, we built an expanded version of our balance sheet and showed how to read and interpret each line item on the report.

The income statement followed. We started off again by showing an example of a simple income statement and followed up with a more complex example. Each line entry in the report was carefully explained.

We talked about the interrelationship that exists between the balance sheet and the income statement. We emphasized the importance of this issue by showing you several "what-if" examples. The importance of the exercise was to show you what would happen to the income statement if something changed on the balance sheet.

We then talked about how you make financial decisions based upon the information contained in the income and balance sheet reports. To help you with the decision-making process, we explained how to calculate various ratios to show how your company is performing at any one moment in time.

You worked with your controller to put in place an accounting report that could be used to quickly identify potential problems. You also want to use this accounting information to supplement the company's strategic plan. But, as yet, you don't have a strategic plan.

You've bought a book called *The Corporate Game*. You know that the title of Chapter 3 is Strategic Planning. You decide to read the chapter to see if you can get some ideas about how to set up a strategic plan for your company.

PC Game Instructions

Turn your PC on, insert the game disk into a disk drive (i.e., drive A) and ENTER A:TCGAME. The game's Main Menu will appear on your screen (Exhibit 2-12). If you have not closed out Month 1, you will need to do this before you can start Month 2.

The Main Menu for Month 2 includes two new options: View Last Month's Report and Financial Planning. The View Last Month's Report option allows you to do just that (Exhibit 2-13). Select the option. The first page of your company's balance sheet will appear on the display. As you page down (i.e., PgDn key) through the report, the income statement will follow.

If you have a printer, we recommend that you print both reports by pressing the PF2 key. Make sure your printer is powered on and in the ready mode. Review the reports. They are a statement of how well your company performed financially in Month 1. Return to the Main Menu by pressing the PF3 key.

Select the Financial Planning option. The submenu that appears on your display is an entry panel (Exhibit 2-14). Whole numeric numbers are entered into the data fields just like we showed you in the Bank Account Management submenu. The data fields are self explanatory and represent forecast fields for different account categories.

Account forecasts that you enter into the Financial Planning menu will

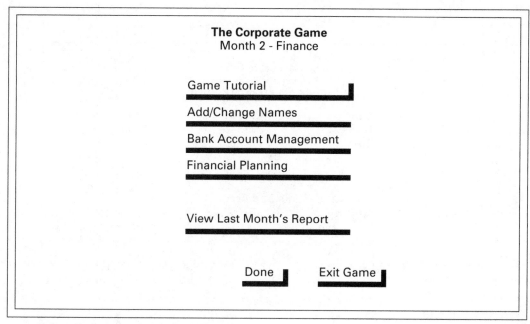

The Corporate Game
Month 2 - Finance

Game Tutorial

Add/Change Names

Bank Account Management

Financial Planning

View Last Month's Report

Done   Exit Game

End Work Session - Exit the Program

Exhibit 2-12. Month 2—Finance menu.

The Corporate Game
BALANCE SHEET FOR MONTH - 1
Demon Car Company

Mr. John D. Doe, President

	ACTUAL	FORECAST
Checking Acct. Bal.	$ 500,000.00	$ 0.00
Savings Acct. Bal.	$ 525,000.00	$ 0.00
Car Inventory Value	$ 0.00	$ 0.00
Raw Materials Value	$ 0.00	$ 0.00
Factory Space Owned	$ 0.00	$ 0.00
Equipment Owned	$ 0.00	$ 0.00
Total Assets:	$ 1,025,000.00	$ 0.00
Notes Payable to Bank	$ 0.00	$ 0.00

F2 Print   F3 Return

Exhibit 2-13. Screen showing balance sheet for month 1.

The Corporate Game
Month 2 - Finance
FINANCIAL PLAN & MASTER BUDGET

Type of Car	# Cars to Make	Cost to Produce	# Cars to Sell	Minimum Sell. Price
Economy	10	$120,000	5	$ 13,000
Midsize	0	$ 0	0	$ 0
Luxury	0	$ 0	0	$ 0

Estimates of Month End Account Balances

CHECKING	SAVINGS	ACCTs PAYABLE	NOTEs PAYABLE
$ 0	$ 0	$ 0	$ 0

Estimate the value of your:

FLOOR SPACE	PLANT EQUIPMENT	RAW MATERIALs	INTEREST INCOME
$ 0	$ 0	$ 0	$ 0

NEW--------INVENTORY

'OTHER' INCOME	COST	SIZE	DONE ■	ENTER ■
$ 0	$ 0	0		

Exhibit 2-14. Menu for financial plan and master budget.

appear on the income statement next to the equivalent actual account category. This will allow you to easily compare your company's actual performance against its forecasted performance. Forecast numbers play another important role that we will tell you about when you start Month 5. For now, practice entering numbers into the menu so that you will become familiar with this menu. You may also want to check your bank account balances. When you are all done, close out the month.

3

Strategic Planning

The Lifeblood of the Corporation

Why is strategic planning referred to as the lifeblood of the corporation? The Answer: If you don't have a strategic plan, and we mean a good one, your company will die. It will simply go out of business. A good strategic plan that is both dynamic and flexible is key to the success of any business.

If you don't believe us, walk into any reputable bank and tell the loan officer that you want to take out a commercial loan on behalf of your company. The loan officer will ask you for a copy of your strategic plan. If you tell the loan officer that you don't have one, your loan request will be denied.

The savings and loan story dramatically illustrates what happened when bank officers did not require a strategic plan as a prerequisite for a loan. Unscrupulous corporate executives would walk into an equally unscrupulous bank and ask for a commercial loan. The loan officer, knowing that the loan would be federally insured, would say, "Not a problem as long as you pay the loan points up front." The loan officer pocketed the loan point money and the borrower pocketed the loan money. The loan balance was never paid off. And, as Paul Harvey would say, "You know the rest of the story."

A strategic plan was not required as a prerequisite for the loan. Over a relatively short period of time, both the banks (lenders) and the corporations (borrowers) went out of business. The federal government got stuck with the bad debts. We will be paying for that fiasco for the next several decades.

The balance of this chapter shows you how to develop and implement a good strategic plan. We'll build on the plan as we proceed through the remaining chapters to help assure the financial integrity and survival of your company.

What Is a Strategic Plan?

Some companies call it a financial plan, a five-year plan, or an operational plan. It doesn't make any difference what you call it. The bottom line is that corporate planning functions are all the same. For consistency, we'll call it a strategic plan. It's the road map a company uses to pilot its way toward specific goals.

A strategic plan is a comprehensive view of the company's goals and objectives. They are typically expressed in the form of forecasts encompassing the expected impact of all corporate financial and strategic planning decisions. A good plan covers all of the functional areas of the business, exploits the company's strengths, and minimizes its weaknesses. Weaknesses are openly identified and are supported with corrective action plans.

Who Needs Strategic Planning?

Over the past several years, there has been a growing dissatisfaction with the way things have not been working in this country. The burgeoning national debt has caught everybody by surprise. Major name-brand corporations are, for the first time in their history, having a tough time making it.

The complexities of the economy and world markets demand new and better ways of doing things. The speed of technological change is already making new products obsolete a year after they are introduced into the market. To complicate matters, some corporate decisions require long-term commitments that won't pay off for a decade or more. In an era when capital is costly and economic uncertainty is high, the use of strategic planning to reduce risk becomes essential.

In a poorly run company, strategic planning is nothing more than a management ritual. Management is assembled into some kind of "pecking order" at an annual meeting and presents a budget to their respective bosses. If they answer all of the questions right, they pass the forecast exam and are left alone for another year.

Occasionally, you'll hear about a progressive company that does "grassroots" planning. Such a company is run by a CEO who understands planning concepts and is strongly committed to the disciplines that are required to make planning work. Corporate planning starts from the top and rolls down to every employee (see Exhibit 3-1). Detailed plans are prepared at

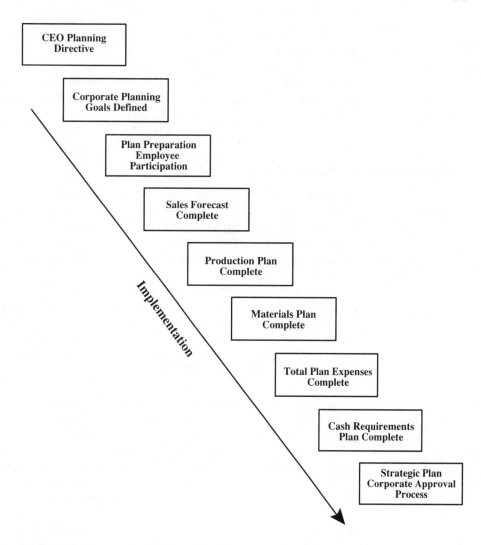

Exhibit 3-1. The strategic planning and implementation process.

the lowest level and rolled back up through the various organizations. They are then consolidated into a single strategic corporate plan.

When it's all done, employees know exactly what is expected of them. The plan is blessed by top management and the marching orders are given. It's subjected to a performance review at least once a month. If something isn't working, the plan is either fixed or changed so that it will work. Again, there is a common focus and everybody in the company understands what their respective roles are within the framework of the plan.

Employee-integrated strategic planning makes a lot of sense. Nobody wants to be left out of the plan. If someone is left out, it carries the connotation that "I must not be very important." That attitude fuels anger and distrust for the plan. As a result, those that have been excluded from the plan will do everything they can to sabotage it. Nobody wins in this kind of a scenario.

Organizational Requirements

Let's talk about some of the organizational components that must be in place to make planning work. For starters, if the CEO does not want an employee-integrated strategic plan, it will not happen. If that is the case in your particular situation, you can skip this chapter and go on to the next. Planning without serious management direction and commitment is a waste of time.

Assuming that you have management backing for the kind of planning that we are talking about, the next step is to remove fear of the consequences of planning from the employees who will be involved in the planning process. A good plan must address worst-case scenarios. For example, if you don't make your profit objectives, what short-term actions can you take to get back on track? The recovery issues here could involve cutting expenses and layoffs.

Can the people involved in the planning process stand up to these kinds of probing questions? They can if they are backed by good management. In poorly run companies, management keeps the hidden agenda of the strategic plan to themselves. Everybody knows they have one. Nobody knows what it is. And yet, everybody is expected to meet the objectives of the plan.

People must know what the plan is before they can participate in it. That statement is so basic that we are almost embarrassed to put it in the book. The fact remains that few corporations do it, for whatever reason. Some managers will offer up the excuse that they can't trust their employees to not divulge the secrets of the plan. If you can't trust your employees, then you've got problems that go well beyond the contents of the plan. How can you run a successful company with people you can't trust?

Forecasting

One of the basic challenges of strategic planning is knowing how to anticipate what is likely to happen to the company over periods of time. A manager who fails to anticipate events can improperly allocate company resources. This could result in unsold inventory, decreased profits, and sometimes in the financial failure of the company.

Forecasting plays a critical role in assuring that all company resources are effectively used. First, it provides a basis for long-range planning. Areas affected by long-range planning include production, capital allocation, and the acquisition of plant and capital equipment. Forecasts are also used to establish short-range schedules. Examples of short-range schedules include production scheduling, determining manpower, and material requirements.

In the overall scheme, forecasts are used to predict the future demand for the company's goods and services. Forecasts summarize the objectives of all the departments in a corporation. It's "your best guess" of what will happen to the company over some future period of time. The use of sound strategic planning techniques will help you make good forecasting decisions.

Forecasts can also be used as a tool to develop management plans and monitor performance expectations. In the real world, the constantly changing economic environment will generate all kinds of unanticipated events that will raise chaos with even the best of plans. Your forecasts should be formulated to reach the expected performance level of your strategic plan.

Types of Forecast

Three primary techniques are used to develop forecasts: (1) qualitative methods, (2) time series projections, and (3) mathematical methods. In this section, we briefly describe each of the forecast techniques.

Qualitative Forecasts.   The qualitative method relies on input from experts to establish the forecast. The experts could come from within or outside the corporation. Using this technique, a company may poll, at periodic intervals, a number of experts who have insight on a key forecast area considered vital to the company's interest. For example, an oil company might poll, on a quarterly basis, a select group of 25 national resource experts to assess future energy needs.

The experts may be asked to complete a questionnaire where they respond to questions designed to determine the likelihood of technological or market changes occurring over a specific period of time. A summary of the survey results is prepared and reduced to points where the experts agree. For example, 80 percent of the experts may have agreed there will be a major shortage of gasoline this coming summer. Based upon this input, the oil company may revise its forecast for consumer gas prices.

A revised corporate forecast is subsequently prepared and sent out to the experts for comments and analysis. If a majority of the experts agrees with the company's forecasted position, a final forecast is prepared and submitted to top management for approval.

Time Series Forecasts.   Time series forecasts rely on the maintenance of historical indicators to derive future projections. The method analyzes past activities and extrapolates from historical events to forecast future events. For example, economic indicators may be used to establish a group of historical forecast indicators.

The ups and downs of the indicators are carefully tracked to gauge which way the forecast numbers may be going. *Business Week* publishes an index that can be used to predict the status of the entire economy at any one moment in time. The time series method is popular for predicting product sales over a relatively short period of time (i.e., two years or less).

Mathematical Forecasts.   The mathematical forecasting technique is popular with manufacturing companies that are heavily dependent upon inventory control. Moving averages are a popular method used to establish inventory forecasts. In its simplest form, here is how it works. Suppose your unit sales for economy cars were 100, 150, and 300 units over the last three months. Your average monthly car sales would therefore be 183 units (550 units/3 months). One could conclude, based upon car sales over the last three months, that you will be able to sell at least 183 cars in Month 4.

However, we are missing an important ingredient to our mathematical forecast. An important related technique called trend projecting needs to be added. If we apply trending to our original calculation, we know from history that our car sales jumped 50 percent in Month 2 (150 units/100 units = 150 percent) and a whopping 200 percent in the third month (300 units/150 units = 200 percent). If we are aggressive, we may want to revise our moving average forecast of 183 units up 200 percent to 367 units (183 units × 2 = 367 units) for Month 4.

Analyzing the Integrity of Forecasts

Forecasts versus actual comparisons are used by all companies to determine "how well they did" over a given period of time. They'll also compare current month's results against last month's results, which may or may not portray an accurate picture of what is happening. For example, suppose that your current month's car sales are better than the previous month, or that current costs are lower than expected. This may be encouraging, but it is by no means a conclusive measurement of the company's success.

The fact that you may have sold 100 cars compared to 90 cars in the previous month could be dampened by the fact that you could have sold 120 cars, if you had maintained adequate levels of inventories. The major weakness of using historical data to judge current performance is that the two periods may have been affected by completely different events. Hence, the comparisons are not always meaningful.

Forecast Planning

Forecast planning integrates all the functions of the business so that corporate financial goals and objectives are satisfied. For example, the sales plan must be integrated into the production plan. Production must then plan to have the appropriate levels of materials and manpower available to produce the number of cars needed to satisfy the sales plan. The final step in the planning process is to integrate the forecast units and dollars into the company's financial statements. Financial forecasts have been integrated into the income statement in Exhibit 3-2.

Note that no actual figures appear in the income statement in Exhibit 3-2. Remember, forecasts represent your best projections of what you expect will be the performance of your company at the end of a period of time. The computer game will prompt you to enter forecast figures into your financial statements. You have the option to ignore the forecast process, or enter forecasts into a strategic planning menu. If you elect to enter forecast figures, the model will produce financial statements at the end of each month which will include your forecast entries.

Preparing a Strategic Plan

There are six interdependent steps that you take to develop the financial part of the strategic plan. For example, do you have enough inventory on hand to cover projected sales? Does your company have adequate cash reserves to cover current expenses?

If you choose to omit any one of the steps, you'll end up with a partial strategic plan. A partial plan is nearly worthless. Go back to Chapter 1 and read the Sea Kist story again. The CEO attempted to implement a partial strategic plan. It almost destroyed the company. The six steps are summarized as follows:

1. Establish financial goals and objectives
2. Estimate sales units and dollars
3. Prepare a production plan
4. Develop a material requirements plan
5. Estimate expenses
6. Project cash requirements

Let's develop a sales and cost forecast for your company. Before you can start the process, you will need basic cost, inventory, and production information about what it takes to manufacture a car. Study the data that we have provided for this purpose in Exhibit 3-3.

Demon Car Company				
Income Statement				
End of Month 2				
Dollars in Thousands				

	Actual $		Forecast $	
Car Sales	Mon $	Units	YTD$	Units
Economy Sedans			$195	13
Midsize Sedans			$201	15
Luxury Sedans			$104	4
Total Car Sales			$500	32
Cost of Cars Sold				
Beginning Car Inventory				
Economy			$100	5
Midsize			$101	6
Luxury			$44	4
Cost of Beginning Car Inventory			$245	15
Cars Manufactured				
Economy			$55	5
Midsize			$98	5
Luxury			$52	5
Cost of Cars Manufactured			$205	15
Cost of Cars Available for Sale			$450	35
LESS: Cost of Ending Inventory			$225	3
Total Cost of Cars Sold			$225	32
Profit				
Gross Profit on Sales			$275	
Less: Sales & Overhead Expense			$200	
Net Profit			$75	

Exhibit 3-2. Demon Car Company income statement.

Description	Unit Cost	Economy Car	Midsize Car	Luxury Car
Steel (tons per car)	$1,200/ton	1.5	2.0	3.0
Parts per Car	$10 each	100	210	350
Direct Labor Hours	$25/hr.	100	150	300
Factory Overhead	Each	$715	$950	$1,430
Selling Expense	Each	$500	$900	$1,500
Total Cost per Car		$6,515	$10,100	$17,530

Exhibit 3-3. Material, labor, and overhead required to build each car.

Here is how to interpret Exhibit 3-3. A car can be produced from two basic materials—steel and parts. Parts include everything from spark plugs to tires. The average price of steel is $1200 per ton. The average part costs $10 each. Direct labor used to manufacture a car costs $25 per hour. Factory overhead covers the total cost of running the factory and will vary depending upon the type of cars you manufacture. Selling expense covers the sales commission paid for each car sold. From this data, we can project what it will cost to produce each car model.

Establishing Financial Goals and Objectives. The corporate act of selecting financial goals and objectives establishes the financial targets management has deemed important to achieve. Goals and objectives are compared against actual financial results to monitor the success of the company. Key results may include achieving a certain size and rank in the industry, annual growth in earnings, return on investment, and increasing market share. Examples of strategic financial goals and objectives of some well-known corporations follow:

Federal Express: To become the largest and best transportation company in the world.

General Electric: To become the most competitive enterprise in the world by being number one or number two in market share in every business the company is in.

Quaker Oats: To achieve a return on equity of 20 percent or more. Be a leading marketer of strong consumer brands and improve profitability of low-return businesses.

Both long- and short-range objectives are needed. Long-range objectives are used to establish the actions to take now in order to reach a targeted long-range performance goal. Long-range planning forces management to consider the impact of short-range decisions on long-range goals.

Short-range objectives are used to identify the immediate and near-term goals that must be achieved. They tend to be very specific regarding expected results and the time frame in which the results will be achieved. Generally, short-range objectives are in line with and support long-range objectives. For example, if a company has a long-range profit objective of 15 percent that is consistent with its short-range profit objective, then the short- and long- range objectives coincide.

Schedule 1: Financial Goals.   Your first step in building a strategic plan will be to establish financial goals and objectives for your company. In the example that follows (Schedule 1), management set a 20 percent profit objective for the company. They choose to maintain a surplus of raw material inventories to avoid running out. They want to build more cars than they can sell "just in case" their sales forecast is low.

Schedule 1
Corporate Financial Goals

1. The selling price of each car will cover total cost and yield a 20 percent net profit.

2. The ending inventory levels of raw materials must be sufficient to cover 25 percent of next month's expected material needs.

3. Car inventory levels at the end of the month will be 10 percent of the expected sales for the month.

At the same time, the plan must be flexible enough so that it can be quickly changed to accommodate changes in economic or competitive events. The forecast is the target. Without something to shoot for, your company will lack direction, problems will not be foreseen, and growth will be virtually impossible.

We will refer to Schedule 1 as we work to complete the five remaining planning steps and schedules. Our intent is to make sure that the financial plan supports the corporate's strategic plan, goals, and objectives. Upon the completion of each step, a financial schedule is prepared. You will end up with five schedules that when consolidated will become the financial part of the strategic plan.

Schedule 2: Sales Forecast.   The sales forecast in Exhibit 3-4 is the starting point for the planning process. Inventory levels and production costs are geared to the rate of sales activity. Let's review the process to see how the sales forecast was developed.

Car Model	Desired Car Sales	Cost per Unit	Price per Unit	Profit per Unit	Total Sales
Economy Sedan	300	$6,515	$8,144	$1,629	$2,443,200
Midsize Sedan	150	$10,100	$12,625	$2,525	$1,893,750
Luxury Sedan	100	$17,530	$21,912	$4,382	$2,191,200

Exhibit 3-4. Schedule 2—sales forecast ($ in thousands).

You have asked your vice president of sales, Jim, to prepare a sales forecast and meet with you later in the day. Jim enters your office at the scheduled meeting time to start his presentation. He assures you that all of his numbers have been reviewed by the accounting, finance, sales, marketing, and production control departments.

"What we sold last month is what we can probably sell next month. Unit car costs were calculated from the data in Exhibit 3-3." He shows you how he derived the cost to produce an economy car in Exhibit 3-5.

Jim proceeds to show you how he arrived at a sales price for each car. "One of our financial goals was to achieve a 20 percent net profit on each car sold. Our car prices include a 20 percent profit margin. For example, I used the following calculation to determine the sales price of an economy car:"

$$\text{Desired price for 20 percent profit} = (\text{Cost per unit})/(80 \text{ percent})$$
$$= \$8144$$

$$\text{Profit per unit} = (\text{Desired price}) - (\text{Cost per unit})$$
$$= \$1629$$

$$\text{Unit profit as percent of sales} = (\text{Profit per unit})/(\text{Sell price per unit})$$
$$= (\$1629)/(\$8144)$$
$$= 20 \text{ percent}$$

Jim concludes his presentation with a carefully guarded remark. "Our sales price and profit margin are heavily dependent upon the cost numbers that we have been given by production. If they change unit cost, we'll have to go back to the drawing board and assess the impact of any change." You thank Jim for his presentation.

Total Cost = Material Cost + Labor Cost + Factory Overhead + Selling Expense

= (1.5 tons steel)($1,200/ton) + (100 parts)($10/part) + (100 hrs.)($25/hr.) + ($715 overhead) + ($500 selling expense)

= $6,515

Exhibit 3-5. Material, labor, and overhead cost to build one economy car.

Schedule 3: Preparing a Production Plan. The need to coordinate the complex activities of workers and machines to produce products falls under the domain of production control. Production control uses the sales forecast (Schedule 2) to develop a production plan (Schedule 3).

A production plan is therefore prepared after the sales forecast has been completed. The total production needed will be the sum of the desired ending inventory (financial goals) plus the number of cars needed to satisfy the sales forecast. Total production requirements will be reduced by the number of cars that are in the beginning inventory. Your production control department used Jim's sales forecast to determine their production requirements (see Exhibit 3-6).

Staying with the economy-car example, here is what Exhibit 3-6 tells us. We already know from Schedule 2 that we plan to sell 300 economy cars. When we established our original financial goals, we wanted to maintain a surplus of cars (ending inventory) at the end of each month that would be equal to 10 percent of the units sold. In this example, we would need 30 economy cars (300 units sold × 10 percent = 30 cars) in ending inventory.

Production Requirements	Economy Sedan	Midsize Sedan	Luxury Sedan
Desired Ending Inventory	30	15	10
Plus: Sales Forecast	300	150	100
Less: Beginning Inventory	-50	-25	-10
Units to be Produced	280	140	100

Exhibit 3-6. Schedule 3 production plan.

We already have 50 economy cars in the beginning car inventory. How many cars do we need to produce to meet our sales and inventory objectives for economy cars? We need a total of 280 economy cars (30 ending inventory + 300 for sales – 50 in beginning inventory).

Schedule 4: Develop a Material Requirements Plan. Material Requirements Planning (MRP) is a widely used manufacturing allocation tool to determine the amounts of raw materials needed to support the production plan. Most MRP systems are computer based and merge information about the structure of a manufactured product, the availability of its parts, and the required order lead times with the needs of the sales forecast. In its simplest form, MRP systems look at the materials needed to support the production plan (Schedule 3). An example of an MRP flow is shown in Exhibit 3-7.

Each of the steps represents management decisions that evolve as the

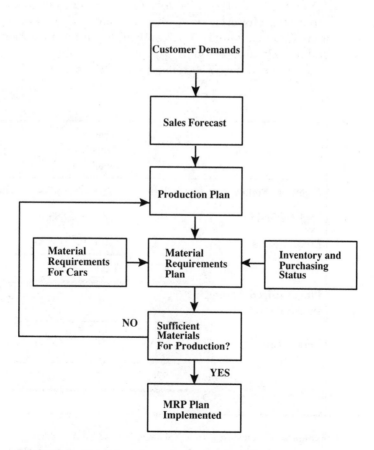

Exhibit 3-7. Material requirements plan functional flow.

MRP system cycles through the process of obtaining all the materials manufacturing needs to satisfy the sales forecast. The inventory system will first attempt to pull the materials it needs from current inventory. If it can't find the materials in inventory, purchase orders are created to procure the materials needed.

The materials plan is prepared after the production and sales plans have been completed. Material requirements are influenced by the expected materials usage for the production of cars taken from Schedule 2. The desired ending inventory levels for materials and the beginning car inventory balances are included in the materials plan. A materials plan is prepared by your purchasing department and comes together in Exhibit 3-8.

Here is how they determined how much steel and how many parts are needed to produce 280 economy cars. You know from Exhibit 3-3 that it takes 1.5 tons of steel and 100 parts to produce one economy car. We also know steel costs $1200 per ton and parts are $10 each. The simple formulas to calculate total steel and parts cost are summarized in Exhibit 3-9.

You need a total of 1230 tons of steel to produce the desired mix of all three cars. However, recall that we stated in our financial goals that we wanted to maintain a 25 percent surplus in raw materials inventory at the end of each sales period.

You want to have 250 tons of steel (25 percent × 1000 tons = 250 tons)

Car Model	Cars to Make	Steel Tons Need	Steel Cost	Parts Need	Parts Cost
Economy Sedan	280	420	$504	28,000	$280
Midsize Sedan	140	280	$336	29,400	$294
Luxury Sedan	100	300	$360	35,000	$350
Total Units and $	520	1,000	$1,200	92,400	$924
Plus: Desired Ending Inventory	N/A	250	$30	23,100	$231
Less: Begin Inventory	N/A	(20)	($24)	(20,000)	($200)
Totals	520	1,230	$1,206	95,500	$955

Exhibit 3-8. Schedule 4—material requirements plan ($ in thousands).

$$\text{Total Steel} = \text{(280 Cars) (1.5 Tons/Car)} = 420 \text{ Tons}$$

$$\text{Steel Cost} = \text{(420 Tons)(\$1,200/Ton)} = \$504,000$$

$$\text{Total Parts} = \text{(280 Cars)(100 Parts/Car)} = 28,000$$

$$\text{Parts Cost} = \text{(28,000 Parts)(\$10/Part)} = \$280,000$$

Exhibit 3-9. Material units and cost to build 280 economy cars.

left over at the end of the month. You now need a total of 1480 tons of steel (1230 tons + 250 tons = 1480 tons) less the 20 tons that you already have in inventory, or 1460 tons. The same logic would be carried through to determine the total number of parts you need.

Schedule 5: Expense Forecasts. Your accounting department has rolled all of the data from Schedules 1 through 4 into Schedule 5. Forecasts for labor, factory overhead, and selling expenses are shown in Exhibit 3-10. Labor expenses cover the direct labor required to build cars. Factory overhead covers the cost of plant and capital equipment used in the car manufacturing process. Selling expense covers sales commissions and administration costs that are associated with the sale of a car.

Unit volumes were derived directly from the production plan (Exhibit 3-8) and the cost information (Exhibit 3-3). You know from Exhibit 3-3 that

Production Component	Economy Sedan	Midsize Sedan	Luxury Sedan
Production Units	280	140	100
Direct Labor Hours	28,000	29,400	30,000
Direct Labor Cost	$700	$735	$750
Factory Overhead	$715	$950	$1,430
Selling Expense	$500	$900	$1,500
Total Cost	$1,915	$2,585	$3,680

Exhibit 3-10. Schedule 5—labor, overhead, and selling expense estimates ($ in thousands).

it takes 100 labor hours at a cost of $25 per hour to build one economy car. Factory overhead and selling expense are derived from the same exhibit and amount to $715 per car.

It now becomes a relatively simple task of extending the total cost to produce 280 economy cars (see Exhibit 3-11). Once this same process is completed for the midsize and luxury cars, you will know what your total costs are for labor, factory overhead, and selling expense.

Schedule 6: Cash Requirements Schedule. The final schedule to consider is the cash requirements plan. It is used to forecast the amount of cash required to fund the operation of the company. Cash plans cover monthly periods of time and help to avoid having unnecessary idle cash or cash deficiencies. As an astute CEO, it's your responsibility to develop and monitor a program that keeps your cash requirements balanced to the needs of your company. Your finance department has prepared Schedule 6, the cash requirements plan (see Exhibit 3-12).

Schedule 6 is relatively easy to interpret. Let's walk through it anyway to make sure we cover all the points. The top of the schedule starts off with a category called Cash Available. It represents the total amount of cash we expect to have available to pay for the financial part of our plan over the time period covered by the plan (e.g., one month).

The beginning cash balance represents the balance of cash in the corporate checking account. The $6568 is the money we expect to make from the sale of cars. We are also expecting to earn interest ($8) from money the company has invested in the corporate savings account. The bottom line is that we believe that the company will have a total of $6566 available to fund the plan. Is that enough cash?

Review the Cash Required side of the schedule. From the exercises that we conducted when we prepared Exhibits 3-10 and 3-11, we know how much raw materials to purchase to support our production plan. Based upon current prices, we expect to order $2124 in raw materials. Labor, selling, and overhead expenses were calculated in Exhibit 3-12. The company

---

Labor Hours =	(280 Cars)(100 Hrs./Car) = 28,000 Hrs.
Labor Cost =	(28,000 Hrs.)($25/Hr.)= $700,000
Overhead =	(280 Cars)($715/Car) = $200,533
Sales Cost =	(280 Cars)($500/Car) = $140,000

Exhibit 3-11. Labor, overhead, and sales cost required to build 280 economy cars.

	Budget	**Data Source**
Cash Available:		
Beginning Cash Balance	$30	Balance Sheet
Expected Cash - Sales	$6,528	Schedule 1 & 2
Cash from Interest	$8	Balance Sheet
Total Available Cash	$6,566	
Cash Required:		
Payments for Materials	$2,124	Schedule 3 & 4
Direct Labor Payroll	$2,185	Schedule 5
Selling Expense	$416	Schedule 5
Notes Payable to Bank	$150	Balance Sheet
Payment - Factory Overhead	$476	Income Statement
Total Cash Required	$5,351	
Cash Surplus	$1,215	

Exhibit 3-12. Schedule 6—cash requirements plan ($ in thousands).

had borrowed money from the bank (e.g., notes payable) and planned to pay $150 to the bank. Based upon our analysis, we need $5351 to cover all operating expenses.

The concluding line on the cash requirements schedule is the Cash Surplus line. It's considered surplus because, according to our schedule, the company anticipates that it will take in more money than it plans to spend. The planned surplus of $1215 was derived by subtracting total cash required from total cash available ($6566 − $5351 = $1215).

Had the numbers been reversed, and the cash available was less than cash required, the company would have been in a cash-deficit position. If this situation had occurred, the financial plan would have to be modified to bring expenses in line with sales, or sales would have to be increased to cover expenses. As a third alternative, the company could borrow the money that it needed to cover the deficit portion of their cash requirements plan.

Financing Your Plan

No major corporation develops a strategic plan without first having a financing plan in place. The financing plan may be as simple as securing a line of credit that can be used at the discretion of the company just in case the company needs some ready cash. Longer-term financing may be needed to build a plant, purchase capital equipment, and to build up inventory levels for strategic reasons.

If you are playing the computer side of *The Corporate Game,* you will be pleased to know that a bank called The Great American Bank lives out there on your game diskette. It's a typical commercial bank that is in the business of making loans to companies just like yours.

And, like all good banks, The Great American Bank likes to loan money as long as it knows, beyond a reasonable doubt, that you will pay it back. Banks loan money to companies in much the same way that they loan money to individuals. For example, companies or persons can obtain unsecured loans (i.e., no collateral required) with only their signatures. If you are signing on behalf of a company, you generally must be an officer of the company with a signature authorization preapproved by the company and on file with the bank.

In either case, the size of the loan granted will be determined in part by the reputation of the individual or company, respective credit and payment histories, and annual incomes. On large loans, banks will require some form of collateral. The bank wants assurance that if you, as an individual or corporation, were to go bankrupt, the bank could sell off the secured assets to recover the original loan.

Interest Rates

We all know that interest rates are the cost of borrowing money (see Exhibit 3-13). The interest rates charged to corporations tend to vary significantly over what is charged to individuals. This is where the comparison ends. Banks apply a more complex credit rating system to corporations than to individuals. There are a couple of good reasons for this. Corporations borrow money in far larger amounts than what we mortal individuals typically borrow. Hence, the exposure to the bank goes up proportionately with the size of the loan.

The second reason for the disparity is that a corporation is an "innate being." By legal definition, a corporation is "a being that exists only in the eyes of the law." It can be sued just like a person. It must obey the laws just like a person. But, it has no human or living personality. This one missing human attribute tends to make bank managers nervous about corporations.

For example, let's say a bank has been loaning money to your family who

Interest Rate	Three Months	Six Months	Nine Months	Twelve Months
10%	$338.90	$171.56	$115.79	$87.91
11%	$339.46	$172.05	$116.26	$88.38
12%	$340.02	$172.54	$116.17	$88.84
13%	$340.58	$173.04	$117.21	$89.31
14%	$341.14	$173.54	$117.69	$89.78
15%	$341.70	$174.03	$118.17	$90.25
16%	$342.26	$174.50	$118.64	$90.73
17%	$342.86	$175.02	$119.13	$91.20
18%	$343.38	$175.52	$119.16	$91.68

Exhibit 3-13. Monthly interest and principal payments necessary to amortize a $1000 loan over various time periods.

runs a farm. The farm was originally owned by your grandfather, then your father, and now you. It's been in the family for over 60 years. The bank knows how productive your farm has been over all those years just like it would know how productive a corporation had been over that same period of time.

The big difference is in what banks call *the continuity of management*. In the country farm example, individual and personal ownership counts for a great deal. The farm has only passed through three owners and they were all related. Furthermore, the bank knows that the owners have "family skin" in the game and they're the bosses.

In a corporation, the owner is often another corporation. Hence, the corporation the bank is about to loan money to is a subsidiary. The CEO and senior executive staff may be the greatest people in the world but chances are, none of them have been with the company for more than five years. Other than their paychecks, they have "no skin in the game." The bank knows that if things get really tough, the entire strategic executive team could just "uproot and leave the company for another job."

The banks created the concept of *prime* to bring stability and continuity into corporate loan criteria. *Prime* is the shortend term for *prime interest rate*. It is the interest rate that bankers apply to loans made to their best corporate customers. If your company is something "less than best," and you ask for a loan, you're quoted an interest rate that is "prime plus some add-on interest points."

By now, the begging question that should be jumping into your mind is "How do I qualify my company for prime?" Unfortunately, corporate prime status is established just like it was with the family farm, i.e., over time. The one major difference was that the bank used subjective judgment—like family and tradition—to establish a prime for the farm. Not so with corporations.

They want to see hard historical numbers for corporations. Where do these numbers come from? Your financial plan, of course. That makes sense when you consider the fact that every time you ask the bank for a loan, you are asking the bank to bet on your financial future. The bank, therefore, has every right to ask how successful you have been in the past. If you've done a perfect job and can show good consistent performance, you may qualify for prime.

Contingency Planning

Now that you have got all your managers and employees firmly behind your strategic plan, what's next? All of the projected scenarios have been included in the plan. The sales forecast for the year has been carefully laid out. Corporate expense items have been meticulously evaluated.

The final plan is brought before your management team for its final review and approval. Somebody in the back of the room raises a hand. You politely ask, "Do you have a question that I can answer?" The person in the back of the room speaks up. "What is the contingency plan . . . you know, what do we do if the plan fails? How are we going to implement it?" The meeting room grows deadly silent. Everybody is thinking to themselves, "What does this person mean by saying if the plan fails . . . I've got my name on that plan. If it fails, I'm dead."

As the presiding CEO, you are an avid believer in employee-integrated strategic planning. You decide to break the silence. "You are absolutely right. We do not have contingencies to cover the plan in case parts of it fail." You tell your planning team to "go back to the drawing board" and prepare the missing contingency planning sections.

Even the most sophisticated of plans will fail if equal attention has not been directed at how the plan will be executed and what contingency plans will be activated if the plan deviates from its target objectives. Execution and the effective implementation of contingency plans is a planning requisite. Exhibit 3-14 summarizes the development and execution steps required to implement a strategic plan.

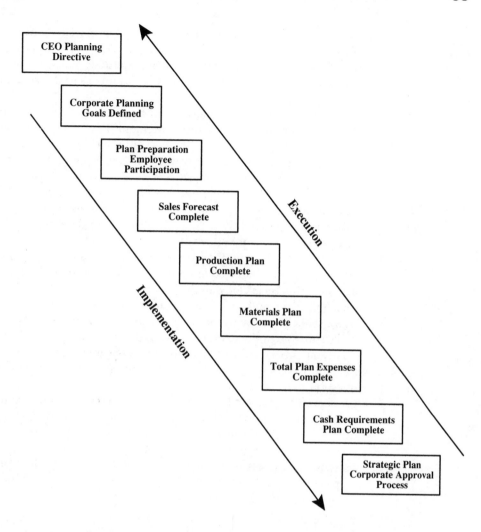

Exhibit 3-14. The strategic planning and execution process.

Tracking Your Plan

How do you monitor your financial plan over a period of time to determine if your original estimates were accurate? What steps can you take to learn from your mistakes and improve the planning process? To reiterate what we said earlier, the most valuable part of strategic planning is the learning process. It is based upon the premise that mistakes will be made and that those who have been involved in preparing the plan are not afraid of making mistakes.

Most mistakes can be corrected. Therefore, the strategic planning process assumes that you are constantly correcting mistakes and improving the planning processes to run a better company. Over time, your company continues to improve. One of the principal methods of determining if you are "on or off" plan is to compare your plan estimates to the actual results that you experienced.

We have taken the numbers from the planning schedules and inserted them into the corporate income statement. Let's move the clock ahead to the end of Month 2. Your controller, Jane, has just updated the financial statements for February and you are anxiously awaiting the result to see how accurate your financial projections were when compared to February actual. Jane enters your office to present this month's financial results. She starts off the presentation with an impetuous grab at glory by flashing up February's financial results (Exhibit 3-15), using the report format that she had prepared for you last month.

"Look at our bottom line. We exceeded our 20 percent profit objectives by 4 percent and managed to reduce our expenses by a whopping 2 percent overall." This is certainly all good and you couldn't ask for anything more than that. You pull out your scientific calculator and start performing a "sanity check" on the numbers. You trust your accountants but you want to make sure you understand everything they are telling you.

As you proceed through your number-crunching exercise, you realize that you have more than just a few questions to ask of Jane. The nagging question that stares you in the face is whether or not this was really such a great month after all, based upon the limited analysis that you're coming up with. In the interest of full disclosure and team spirit, you write all your questions on an overhead foil and display them on the screen.

1. Why did we sell more more economy cars than we had planned at a price that was less than our budgeted sales price? In fact, our net profit on economy-car sales was not 20 percent but rather 15 percent.

2. Why did our luxury cars sell at a higher price than we expected, which resulted in a 25 percent profit per unit? Luxury-car sales made up for the loss in profits from economy-car sales.

3. Our cost of cars manufactured dropped 2 percent. Why?

4. Why did our sales and overhead expense increase by 5 percent over forecast?

Jane breaks the tension by making a neutral statement. "I don't know what to say or how to answer your questions. I thought that we had a great month but you are obviously disappointed." You decide to pull the knife out just a little. "Yes, we had a great month. I believe that it could have been a lot better if we had been a little smarter at implementing our strategies. Here is an example of what I'm talking about."

Demon Car Company

Income Statement

End of Month 2

Dollars in Thousands

Car Sales	Curr $	Units	Est. $	Est. Units
Economy Sedans	$264	33	$244	30
Midsize Sedans	$180	14	$189	15
Luxury Sedans	$230	10	$219	10
Total Car Sales	$674	57	$652	55
Cost of Cars Sold				
Cost of Beginning Car Inventory	$10	1	$81	8
Cost of Cars Manufactured	$509	66	$499	52
Cost of Cars Available for Sale	$519	67	$580	60
LESS: Cost of Ending Inventory	$100	10	$152	5
Total Cost of Cars Sold	$419	57	$225	55
Profit				
Gross Profit on Sales	$255		$224	
Less: Sales & Overhead Expense	$116		$89	
Net Profit	$139		$135	

Exhibit 3-15. Demon Car Company income statement.

1. If we had held firm on our higher economy-car price, we would have sold fewer units, but our total sales would have been about the same. We would have met our 20 percent profit objective.

2. Overall, luxury-car sales profits made up for the reduced profits from economy-car sales. Our focus was on economy-car sales. Maybe we should have placed more emphasis on luxury-car sales.

3. Our cost of cars manufactured dropped. If I look at our inventory turnover ratio, we may have used cheaper raw materials to achieve a one-time drop in manufacturing cost.

You continue the conversation by telling Jane that "in spite of this, we're making progress. Before we had Jane's report, which now includes forecast data, none of us knew where our business was going. We clearly need to add more information to our report to help us predict where the market is going (i.e., luxury cars). Let's get Harold who's got a good mind for economics to take a look at what we've got and what we may want to add to our strategic plan." You proceed on to Chapter 4 to find Harold.

Summary and Conclusions

Strategic planning is an important part of any successful corporation. Poor strategies or plans can lead to serious problems, no matter how efficient the company may be. We introduced you to the basics of the strategic planning process. The basic process was based upon accurate forecast. Several alternative forecast techniques were explored.

We then started the process of actually preparing a strategic plan. Six basic steps (schedules) were covered. Each step was dependent upon the accuracy of data from the previous step. Numerous examples where shown to help explain the process.

In the end, you presented your strategic plan to your management staff for a final review. One of your team members asked you if you had thought about a contingency plan. It was the one major point that you had not considered. The omission was corrected. Actual results were compared against the plan's projections.

The results were favorable but you could have done better. You realize that you needed to build upon your strategic plan. You need economic data to improve the integrity of your forecast projections. You have an economist on your staff, and you decide to seek out his advice in the next chapter.

PC Game Assignment and Instructions

On a separate piece of paper, prepare a strategic plan for your company. Start the process by developing the six schedules that we have covered and carefully record your assumptions, plans, and strategies. When you have completed the process, enter your forecast and planning figures into the game. The purpose of this exercise is to familiarize you with the steps that you should follow to prepare a forecast. The game will allow you to make changes to your original forecast as you complete the later chapters. Now, load the game into your PC. The Main Menu for Month 3 should appear on your display (Exhibit 3-16).

Select the View Last Month's Report option. The first report (Balance Sheet) will appear on your screen. As you page down (PgDn key) through the report, you will find that the Income Statement will follow. If you have a printer and it is on, press the PF2 key to print the report. Review the results of both reports to become familiar with the report formats. Press the PF3 key to return to the Main Menu.

Select the Financial Planning option. The submenu that appears is an entry panel (Exhibit 3-17). Practice entering your forecast numbers into the entry fields. Remember to enter whole numbers (i.e., enter 1000 instead of $1000). Whatever number you enter into the Financial Planning menu will be printed under the forecast column in end-of-month financial statements. When you have completed the exercises, update and exit the month.

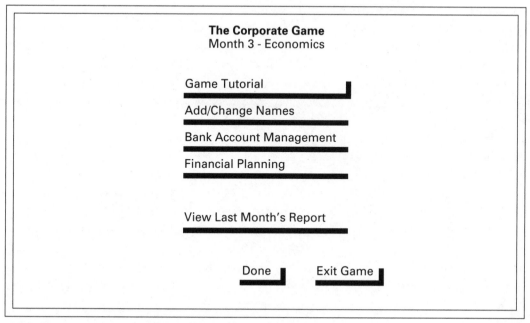

Exhibit 3-16. Month 3—Economics menu.

```
┌─────────────────────────────────────────────────────────────────────────┐
│                                                                           │
│                          The Corporate Game                               │
│                           Month 2 - Finance                               │
│                   FINANCIAL PLAN & MASTER BUDGET                          │
│                                                                           │
│   Type of Car        # Cars          Cost to        # Cars      Minimum    │
│                      to Make         Produce        to Sell    Sell. Price │
│                                                                           │
│   Economy              10          $120,000            5        $ 13,000   │
│   Midsize               0          $      0            0        $      0   │
│   Luxury                0          $      0            0        $      0   │
│                                                                           │
│              Estimates of Month End Account Balances                      │
│                                                                           │
│    CHECKING         SAVINGS         ACCTs PAYABLE      NOTEs PAYABLE       │
│    $        0       $       0       $        0         $        0         │
│                                                                           │
│                    Estimate the value of your:                            │
│                                                                           │
│   FLOOR SPACE   PLANT EQUIPMENT    RAW MATERIALs     INTEREST INCOME       │
│   $        0    $        0         $        0        $        0           │
│                                                                           │
│                    NEW--------INVENTORY                                    │
│   'OTHER' INCOME      COST              SIZE      DONE ▮   ENTER ▮         │
│   $        0      $        0              0      ▃▃▃▃▃▃▃  ▃▃▃▃▃▃▃         │
│                                                                           │
└─────────────────────────────────────────────────────────────────────────┘
```

Exhibit 3-17. Menu for financial plan and master budget.

4
Managing Economics

The Laws of Supply and Demand

In today's world economy, corporate managers are constantly faced with many economic choices. If the economy takes a downturn or an upturn, how will consumers react? When should companies increase or decrease production and sales forecasts? Should they buy or lease plant and equipment? Economics is used to provide answers to these and other important questions. It helps us to understand the nature of consumers who buy products and the nature of the companies that produce products. Economics can also be used to guide the way in which way corporate resources are allocated to satisfy consumer needs.

As the CEO, you have to balance your company's economic interest when thousands of other companies are independently doing the same thing. You don't know what they are all doing that could adversely affect your economic plan. The problem gets more complicated. At the same time, millions of consumers are independently choosing how much and what mix of products they will buy at any one moment in time. Can a happy balance be reached?

Let's review some economic theory to help us understand how prices are determined in a competitive market. We also want to know how prices influence what companies produce. How do changes in external forces such as technological change and market conditions independently affect the entire economic process?

Two schools of economic theory provide answers to these questions; microeconomics and macroeconomics. Microeconomic principles are used to analyze specific product and service levels. Macroeconomics focuses on the

59

behavior of the economy as a whole, and how events affect the national and international economies. Examples of macroeconomic events are the government's monetary policy, unemployment rates, and inflation.

Although microeconomics and macroeconomics are taught as separate college courses, they have important connections. Both are used to analyze, from a different perspective, how prices and quantities of goods and services are determined. Both look at what has happened in the past to predict what will happen in the future. If interest rates were down last quarter, will they stay down next quarter? If unemployment drops, will it continue to fall? Out of this economic analysis process, rational business decisions are made.

Microeconomics

Microeconomics is concerned with how quantities and prices of individual commodities are determined. Here's a quick outline of how microeconomics works. Let's create a hypothetical market for economy cars to find out about how prices and production quantities are set. Assume that there are four car companies making economy cars. All cars are exactly alike. Consumers have no preference over which company's car they buy. All four companies have identical manufacturing facilities with the same labor cost, materials cost, and technological capabilities.

Hence, the costs to produce a car are the same for each of the four companies. We know that total cost increases in direct proportion to output.

Units Produced	Total Cost	Marginal Cost
1	$10,000	$10,000
2	$16,000	$6,000
3	$21,000	$5,000
4	$31,500	$10,500
5	$42,500	$11,000
6	$54,000	$11,500
7	$66,500	$12,500

Exhibit 4-1. Marginal cost to produce one additional car.

This is what economists call *marginal cost,* which is the added cost of producing one additional unit or car (see Exhibit 4-1).

The data points in the exhibit are plotted in Exhibit 4-2. The cost per unit of output decreases to Point *A* on the graph before unit cost begins to increase. This phenomena is what economists refer to as *economies of scale.* Unit cost may decrease as factory output is increased up to Point *A.* The closer a plant's production moves toward full capacity, the more cost effective it becomes to produce each additional unit of output. Once full capacity is reached, any attempt to increase output beyond full capacity results in an increase in unit cost.

Let's assume that the objective of the four car companies is to maximize their profits (Profits = Price − Cost). Each can sell as many cars as they like at the going market price. Maximum profits are then reached when price equals marginal cost. This makes sense when you consider that every car sold above the cost line generates a profit. We can show this concept by adding two columns to our original exhibit (see Exhibit 4-3).

Given our original assumption that all four companies want to maximize profits, they will be inclined to sell all the cars they can make at a price that is equal to or greater than their marginal cost. For obvious reasons, they will not be willing to sell any car at a price that is less than their marginal cost, because this would result in a loss on each unit sold. This concept reveals the product supply side of economics. Companies will continue to supply products as long as they can recover their cost.

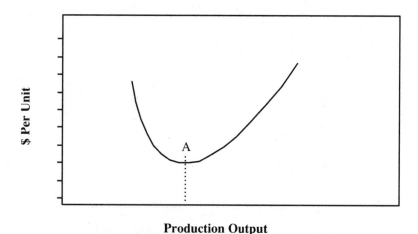

Production Output

Exhibit 4-2. Marginal cost when production output increases.

Units Produced	Total Cost	Marginal Cost	Price per Car	Profit per Car
1	$10,000	$10,000	$9,500	$500
2	$16,000	$8,000	$9,500	$1,500
3	$21,000	$7,000	$9,500	$2,500
4	$32,000	$8,000	$9,500	$1,500
5	$42,500	$8,500	$9,500	$1,000
6	$54,000	$9,000	$9,500	$500
7	66,500	$9,500	$9,500	$0

Exhibit 4-3. Marginal cost to produce one additional car.

Market Demand

The quantity of a product people will buy in part depends on price. The higher the price charged for a product, the less people will buy. Conversely, if you lower the price, people will generally buy more. We can conclude that there is an inverse relationship between price and quantities demanded. This relationship is called a *demand curve*. If we plot the price and quantity figures from Exhibit 4-1, we can create a demand curve (see Exhibit 4-4).

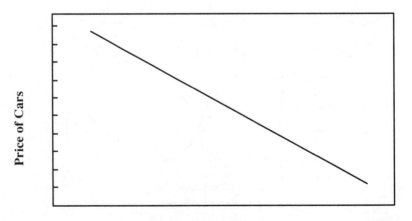

Quantity of Cars Demanded

Exhibit 4-4. Market demand for cars.

The higher the price of a car, the lower the quantity demanded. The vertical scale in the graph represents the various alternative prices of cars. The horizontal scale shows the quantity of cars that could be sold at different prices. Demand curves slope down and to the right. The quantity of cars demanded increases as price falls. All demand curves cover specific periods of time. In our example, the curve covers the current month. As a result, they are directly influenced by the economic events occurring in that time period.

If you had set your price at $14,000, you would have sold 25 cars. However, if you lowered the price dramatically to $12,000 per car, you would have sold five more cars than you would have at the $14,000 price. At some point, consumers may only be willing to acquire so much of a given product, regardless of how low the price might be. For example, if everybody already owns two cars, their desire to own a third new car may be substantially reduced.

How do economic events affect demand curves? Suppose we knew that the unemployment rate will double next month. We would see a different car demand curve next month (Exhibit 4-5). Some potential consumers will be out of work and will delay purchasing cars. The demand curve shifted down and to the left. Consumer demands have adjusted for the increase in unemployment.

To illustrate what happens when the demand curve shifts down, let's assume that the price of economy cars remained the same during the two months ($14,000). In the first month, you would have sold 50 cars at that

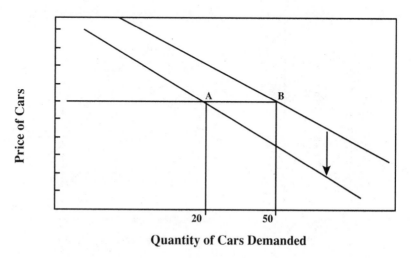

Quantity of Cars Demanded

Exhibit 4-5. Downward shift in demand for cars.

price (Point *B*). However, in the second month, quantities would have fallen to 20 cars (Point *A*) as a result of higher unemployment.

Another example of an economic event that can influence the demand curve is taxes. If consumer income increases across the board as a result of reductions in federal income taxes, they could afford to buy more than they did previously. In this scenario, the position of the demand curve for cars shifts up and to the right (Exhibit 4-6). If economy-car prices remain the same ($14,000), they will buy ten additional cars (Point *B*) than they did before the curve shifted.

The price of competitive products can also influence the position and shape of a demand curve. For example, rapid transit can be used as a substitute for commuter cars. If the price of rapid transit is high, more people may choose to purchase cars to commute to work. If the price of rapid transit drops, people may be motivated to substitute rapid transit for commuter cars. Thus, the price of rapid transit could shift the demand curve for commuter cars up or down.

Other economic events can influence product preferences. If the price of gas goes up dramatically like it did during the oil crisis of the mid-1970s, consumers will switch from large gas-guzzling cars to small economy cars. Suppose we encounter an across-the-board decrease in consumer income. The inflation rate jumps from 5 to 15 percent. All these kinds of economic activities serve to influence consumer demands. The demand curve reacts by shifting up and down the scale when the events occur.

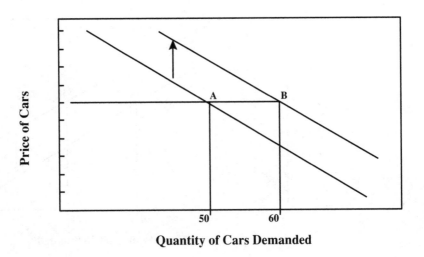

Exhibit 4-6. Upward shift in demand for cars.

Allocation of Demand

All companies are faced with the problem of choosing alternative ways to manufacture products. We live in an economy with only so many people, factories, and natural resources. The economy must decide how these resources are to be allocated to produce the proper mix of goods and services consumers want.

One of the principal objectives of economics is to address the allocation question. What determines the way that consumers allocate their income among various commodities? The answer to this question varies among people. Some may desire luxury cars while others may prefer to spend their money on home improvements.

To illustrate this point, let's see how consumers allocate their income between only two commodities, food and cars. Assume that all the resources of the country are directed to produce food. There will only be a maximum amount of food that farmers can produce and that people can consume. Assume that the maximum amount is 10 million pounds of food. At the other extreme, if all resources are directed to manufacture cars, assume the maximum output that can be produced is 10,000 cars.

Given these two extreme possibilities, we can then assume that people must eat to stay alive, and they can only consume so much food. If their maximum consumption level is something less than 10 million pounds of food, then resources can be taken out of farming and directed back into the manufacturing of cars. Exhibit 4-7 illustrates this point.

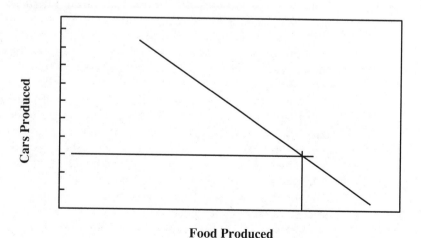

Exhibit 4-7. Alternate production possibilities.

If you go to any point on the graph, you can determine the number of cars you could manufacture and the amount of food you could produce at the same time. How do you determine the maximum number of cars consumers will buy before they must allocate the rest of their earnings to buy other goods and services?

When you complete this chapter, you will develop an understanding for the economic allocation principles that influence consumers to buy more or fewer commodities. Allocation factors have been built into the computer game. They will challenge your ability to second guess what's going on in the economy so that you can maximize your company's car sales.

Price Elasticity of Demand

We have discussed some of the factors that influence the position of demand curves. The shape of a product's demand curve varies from one product to another and from one market to another. As was stated earlier, product demanded is highly sensitive to price and economic events.

For some products, a small change in price can result in a large change in the quantity demanded. For other products, a large change in price may not significantly change the quantity demanded. To measure the effect of a change in price on quantity demanded, economists have developed a measurement technique called *price elasticity of demand*. It is the percentage change in quantity demanded resulting from a 1 percent change in price.

Suppose that a 1 percent reduction in the selling price of a car results in a 3 percent increase in the quantity demanded. In this instance, the price elasticity is 3 ($.03/.01 = 3$). As you would suspect, price elasticity will vary from one type of product to another and from one period of time to the next. The example in Exhibit 4-8 illustrates the price elasticity concept.

If you know that the price elasticity is 3, what would happen if you lowered the price of economy cars to $9900? As the example in Exhibit 4-8 shows, you would have sold an additional 30 cars at the lower price and increased sales by $197,000.

It would make sense to lower the selling price if your objective is to increase total sales. Let's consider a second example where the reverse scenario may be true. Suppose that a 4 percent price reduction results in a 1 percent increase in cars sold. The price elasticity would be .25 ($.01/.04 = .25$). The economics of this scenario can be shown in Exhibit 4-9.

In this example, the increase in sales units from the 1 percent increase in demand did not compensate for the loss in sales dollars resulting from the price reduction. Sales decreased by $304,000. How do you estimate the price elasticity of the market demand? Suppose that you have access to a market demand schedule showing the number of cars sold at various prices in previous months. Exhibit 4-10 shows incremental changes in prices and quantities sold last month.

Given: A 1% reduction in price results in
a 3% increase in the quantity
demanded

Assumptions: Price and quantity demanded
before the reduction were
$10,000 and 1,000 cars

Then: The net increase in the demand
for cars resulting from a 1% price
reduction can be calculated

Sales before Reduction = Price (Quantity)

= $10,000 (1,000 Cars)

= $10,000,000

Sales after Reduction = Adjusted Price (Adjusted
Quantity Demanded)

= (($10,000)(.99)) ((1,000)(1.03))

= ($9,900)(1,030 Cars)

= $10,197,000

Net Increase in Sales = (Sales after Reduction) - (Sales
before Reduction)

= $10,197,000 - $10,000,000

= $197,000

Exhibit 4-8. Calculating the price elasticity of demand.

Using the market demand data in Exhibit 4-10, we can compute a price elasticity of 1.5 percent. It tells us that the quantity demanded will increase by 1.5 percent every time we reduce our sales price by 1 percent. In this example, if we reduced our sales price by 1 percent or $200 ($20,000 – $19,800), we would increase demand by 3 percent or 30 cars (1000 cars × 3 percent = 30 cars).

Given: A 4% reduction in price results in
          a 1% increase in the quantity
          demanded

Assumptions: Price and quantity demanded
              before the reduction were
              $10,000 and 1,000 cars

Then: The net increase in the demand
         for cars resulting from a 4% price
         reduction can be calculated

Sales before Reduction = Price (Quantity)

                       = $10,000 (1,000 Cars)

                       = $10,000,000

Sales after Reduction = Adjusted Price (Adjusted
                         Quantity Demanded)

                      = (($10,000)(.96)) ((1,000)(1.01))

                      = ($9,900)(1,010 Cars)

                      = $9,696,000

Net Decrease in Sales = (Sales before Reduction) - (Sales
                         after Reduction)

                      = $10,000,000 - $9,696,000

                      = $304,000

Exhibit 4-9. Calculating the price elasticity of demand.

If we wanted to sell 60 additional cars next month, how far would we have to lower our price given a price elasticity of 1.5 percent? We know that a $100 price reduction increases our market demand by 15 cars. It then follows that a $400 reduction in price will result in an increase in demand of 60 (4 × 15 cars) cars for a total estimated demand of 1060 cars.

Price per Car	Quantity Sold
$19,800	1,015
$20,000	1,000
Price Elasticity Calculation	

Price Elasticity =	((Qty. Change)/(Previous Qty. Demanded))/((Price Change)/(Previous Price))
=	((1,015 - 1,000)/(1,000))/(($20,000 - $19,800)/($20,000))
=	1.5%

Exhibit 4-10. Luxury cars sold at various prices last month.

Market Supply Curves

Up to this point, we have covered the market demand side of economics. The market has a supply side that can be represented by a supply curve. It shows the total quantity of goods and services that companies will supply at various prices. Companies have a different price motivation than do consumers. The higher the price that they can get for their cars, the more they are willing to supply. If our four car manufactures are still faced with the marginal cost in Exhibit 4-2, then we can show what the market-supply curve looks like in Exhibit 4-11.

Like demand curves, there is a direct relationship between the quantity of cars companies will supply at different prices. If the price of cars increases, companies will be motivated to supply more cars to improve their profit position.

The vertical axis of the graph shows alternative car prices. The horizontal axis measures the quantity of cars that will be supplied at the various prices. Like the demand curve, the supply curve covers a specific period in time and can change from one period to the next. Notice that the supply curve slopes upward and to the right. Quantities supplied will increase as unit prices increase. Most goods and services share this characteristic.

Like demand curves, economic events can influence the position and shape of supply curves. An example would be a technological change. Suppose it costs $12,000 to produce a car that sells for $14,000 returning a $2000 profit. An important technological change has just occurred making

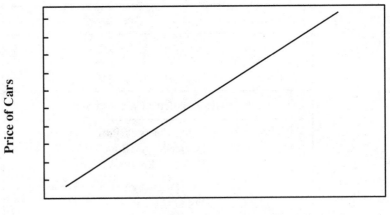

Exhibit 4-11. Market-supply curve for cars.

a new type of machine available. Manufacturing cost can be reduced by $1000 per car by using this machine.

If there are no changes in the selling price and you purchase this machine, your company's profit margin would increase from $2000 to $3000 per car. As a sharp business executive, you would be motivated to supply more of your now cheaper cars to maximize your profits. In this example, the supply curve shifts down and to the right (Exhibit 4-12).

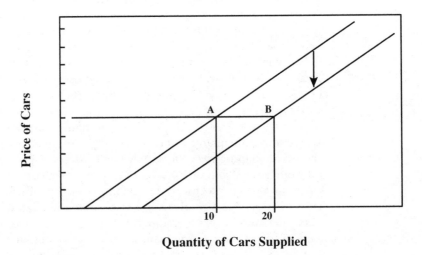

Exhibit 4-12. Shift in market-supply curve for cars.

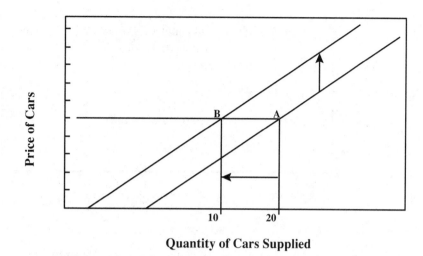

Exhibit 4-13. Shift in market-supply curve for cars.

Prior to the purchase of this machine, you were willing to supply 10 cars at the $14,000 price (i.e., Point *A* on Exhibit 4-12). With the cost savings realized when you acquired the machine, you are now willing to supply 20 cars (Point *B*) at the same price.

Other factors influencing supply curves are changes in the prices of manufacturing resources such as labor and materials. A decrease in the price of resources makes it cheaper to produce cars. The supply curve will shift down and to the right as we showed in the previous example. However, increases in manufacturing costs would reduce profit margins and reduce the number of cars companies would supply. In this example, the supply curve shifts up and to the left (see Exhibit 4-13).

Price Elasticity of Supply

As we have seen, supply curves are sensitive to changes in price and cost. We can use a concept called *price elasticity of supply* to measure the degree of change. The elasticity of supply can be defined as the percentage change in the quantity supplied that results from a 1 percent change in the unit price. If a 1 percent increase in the price of car results in a 3 percent increase in the quantity supplied, then the price elasticity is 3.

We can determine the price elasticity of supply in the same manner that we used to calculate the price elasticity of demand. The example shown in Exhibit 4-14 estimates price elasticity of supply when prices increase from $20,000 to $20,200.

Price Elasticity =   ((Quantity Change)/(Previous Quantity
                      Supplied))/((Price Change)/(Previous Price))

              =   ((1,030 - 1,000)/(1,000))/(($20,200 -
                  $20,000)/($20,000))

              =   3.0%

Exhibit 4-14. Price elasticity calculation for market supply.

Let's review the significance of a 3 percent supply elasticity factor. It tells us companies were willing to supply 3 percent or 30 additional cars if prices increase by 1 percent ($20,200 each). This example assumes that manufacturing costs remain constant, and the higher selling price contributed to the profits of the corporation. In the real world, prior period prices and the quantities that were produced at those prices are available to corporations who are willing to do some investigative research.

Market Equilibrium

This concludes our analysis of the events that can influence market demand and supply curves. If we combine our analysis of demand and supply, we can see how market price is determined. Up to this point, we have assumed that all prices are possible. We have said that consumers will demand just so many cars and that companies will supply just so many cars at various prices.

Three questions remain to be answered. What will be the final market price? How many cars will be produced or supplied? How many cars will be sold or demanded over a given period of time? If you evaluate just the demand or supply curves alone, you cannot answer these questions. What happens if we combine both the demand and supply schedules onto one graph as we have done in Exhibit 4-15?

The demand and supply curves intersect at a point economists call the *market equilibrium point*. Exhibit 4-9 shows the only price for cars that manufacturers are willing to supply at a quantity that consumers are willing to purchase.

At any price below the equilibrium price, the manufacturers would incur a loss on each car sold. They would probably store unsold cars in warehouses rather than sell at a loss. If one producer tries to price above the

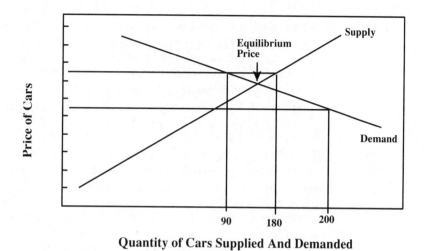

Quantity of Cars Supplied And Demanded

Exhibit 4-15. Market equilibrium price for cars.

equilibrium price, the other three producers would find it profitable to continue charging at the lower price to draw customers away from the "price hiker."

Let's consider the option in Exhibit 4-15 where cars are selling for $17,500. Is this a viable price? The answer is an obvious "no." At $17,500, car companies will be willing to supply 180 cars to the market at this high price. Consumers, on the other hand, will only demand 90 cars at this price.

What happens? Car companies will end up with a surplus of 90 cars (180 − 90 = 90) at the end of the month. Their normal reaction will be to reduce their prices as they gear up for the second sales month. They will be motivated to sell their surplus inventory of 90 cars.

Now, let's go to the other extreme where the price is reduced to $15,500. Can this price persist? The answer is "no." Even though consumers are willing to buy 200 cars at this lower price, no company will be willing to produce cars when the price falls below their cost.

Consumers will become frustrated because they cannot buy what they want. They will go back to the marketplace prepared to pay more for a car. Consumers begin to exert upward pressure on prices as they move "up the demand curve."

The equilibrium price is reached when the demand and supply curves cross or intersect. This is the only price that can last. It represents the number of cars companies will supply and consumers will demand at a balanced price. The fact that the market may have experienced some shifting up and down on the two curves is a normal occurrence. The price will finally stabilize at the equilibrium price.

What happens if one of the four manufacturers decides to lower its price below the equilibrium point? You might ask why a manufacturer would want to do this and incur a loss on each car sold. The manufacturer's strategy may be to lure consumers away from the other three manufacturers. Will the competition stand for this? The answer is "no." They'll react by dropping their price to protect their respective market shares. In the real world, this kind of scenario can erupt into a price war.

Price wars ultimately come to an end because none of the manufacturers can survive by selling cars at a loss. Sanity will, in time, return to the industry and they will all move their price back to the equilibrium point. Competition ensures that the market price will prevail at the equilibrium point.

Because all four manufacturers receive the same price for the same product, distribution across the industry is efficient. They will all hold their prices in line with each other and resort to the use of other tactics, such as advertising, to establish product differentiation. If their tactics are successful, they'll increase their market share at the expense of their competitors. You've seen the ads. My product is better than their product for reasons that are listed in the ad.

Suppose that one of the car companies develops a cost advantage over its three competitors. It has discovered a new method to reduce its production cost. The marginal cost for this company now drops below the marginal cost of the other three companies, giving it a decisive competitive advantage.

The company can now afford to supply more cars at a lower price and still make a profit. It doesn't take the competition long to find out what's going on. They will immediately implement their own cost-cutting analysis programs in an all-out effort to become competitive with the new price leader. They know that if they cannot meet the lower price and make a profit, they'll be forced out of business.

The Monopoly Game

If all cars are manufactured by a single company, this company would be called a monopolist. Webster defines a *monopolist* as a company that controls a market by commanding exclusive rights to a supply of products consumers want. Assume that the objective of the monopolist is to maximize profits. Because there is no competition, the monopolist is free to choose a point (price) on the demand curve that maximizes profits. A concept economists refer to as *marginal revenue* is used by the monopolist to achieve this goal. Marginal revenue is the increase in revenue that is generated from each additional unit produced.

The profit-maximizing monopolist will produce and sell cars up to the point were marginal revenue equals marginal price. The monopolist will restrict output (supply) below the equilibrium point (Exhibit 4-16) to maximize profits at the expense of consumers.

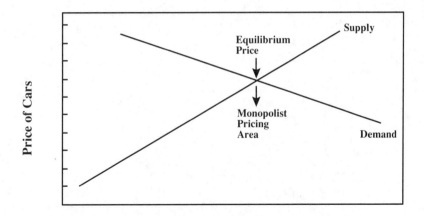

Quantity of Cars Supplied And Demanded

Exhibit 4-16. Monopolist position to maximize profits.

Macroeconomics

We saw how microeconomics is concerned with how product quantities and prices are established by companies and consumers. Macroeconomics addresses how the economy affects aggregate industrial output. Aggregate output in the United States is measured by an economic term called *Gross National Product* (GNP).

GNP is a measure of the market value of the goods and services produced by all industries over a specified period of time. The GNP is adjusted after inflation to determine the "real" GNP value. Leading economic indicators are a set of indexes used to project changes in the GNP. The challenge of macroeconomics is to predict what effect fluctuations in major economic events will have on the overall rate of economic activity.

It's the mission of macroeconomics to predict the up and down sides of the economy as a whole. To accomplish this, it relies on the analysis of aggregate demand and supply curves. An example of how this happens is shown in Exhibit 4-17.

Let's review the aggregate supply (AS) curve first. Aggregate supply curves do not slope up and to the right like microeconomic supply curves. In contrast, the curve is vertical at some level of output. This macroeconomic orientation implies that the amount of output all producers are willing to supply does not depend on price.

The supply remains constant because the price level is an average of all prices, including prices paid by producers for all manufacturing resources (i.e., labor and raw materials). If prices for resources increase by 10 percent, macroeconomics assumes that consumer prices will increase by 10

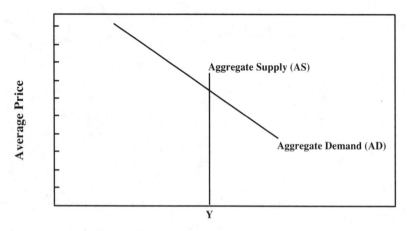

Exhibit 4-17. GNP market demand and supply.

percent. Relative prices remain unchanged. Profit-maximizing output levels of the producers remain unchanged.

Now, let's look at the aggregate demand curve in Exhibit 4-17. It shows the total amount of goods and services consumers are willing to purchase from the economy at different average prices. Like its microeconomic counterpart, the demand curve slopes down and to the right but for different reasons. The descent is due to the effect price changes have on the money supply. Money supply represents the total stock of available money in circulation at any one moment in time. Hence, aggregate demand is closely linked to changes in interest rates and investments.

Investments include business purchases of building and capital equipment. The amount of investment that business consumers wish to take on is sensitive to interest rates. When interest rates go up, the cost of borrowing for investments goes up and the number of investments goes down. Interest rates are, in part, dependent upon the quantity of money in circulation. If the supply of money is down, money is scarce and interest rates are high.

Suppose the aggregate demand curve was initially at the *AD1* position in Exhibit 4-18. At this position, an average price level of $15 for the output demanded and the quantity supplied is established. The economy is at full employment at the *AD1/AS* intersection point of the aggregate demand and supply curves (Point *B*). Suppose there is a sudden economic event which causes the aggregate demand curve to shift down and to the left (*AD2* position). A sudden increase in interest rates has reduced the output of quantity demanded. What's the impact of the demand shift on GNP?

If the average price level falls to *P2,* the quantity of output demanded

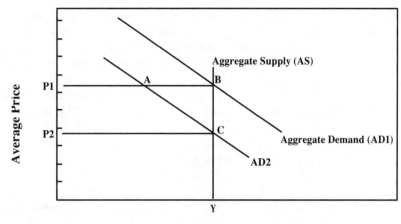

Real Gross National Product (Y)

Exhibit 4-18. Effect on GNP when demand declines.

would equal the supply level of *Y* units, and the economy would remain at full employment. If prices are flexible, the economy is always assured of sustaining its full-employment position. In the face of a general decline in demand, producers would lower their prices to the new equilibrium point.

Putting It All Together

You finally made it through Chapter 4 and have a better understanding for what economics is all about. How can you apply what you have learned about economics to your business? What about Harold, your company's economist? In the previous chapter, you concluded a meeting with Jane where you had expressed concerns about the accounting data she had presented to you. All the accounting information dealt with the past. You want to get your hands on information that can be used to predict what will happen in the future. Maybe Harold can help.

You are particularly interested in coming up with a better way of pricing your cars. For example, if you can predict that the market is bullish for luxury cars, then you can price your luxury cars accordingly. You call your secretary and ask her to find Harold. As soon as you hang up the phone, here comes Harold. You wonder how he could get to your office so fast. At your meeting with Harold, you say "Harold, I have got a problem that I would like you to work on for me. I want access to economic data that will tell me what the economy is doing to the car market at any one point in time. I want to use this information to help determine the best price that we can get for our cars. Can you help me?"

Harold reaches into his shirt pocket and pulls out a 3×5 card. "I think this is what you are looking for." He shows you the card (Exhibit 4-19). You're impressed with the fact that Harold can seemingly pull instant answers out of his shirt pocket. But you are puzzled. You are not sure how to interpret the card that Harold gave you.

Harold senses the problem and without an introduction proceeds to explain the information that's on the card. "The data on the card show the average selling prices of cars and the number of units that were sold over the last two months for the industry. From that data, I can calculate the projected car price and units that will be sold next month. We economists call this the price elasticity of demand."

You remember seeing something about price elasticity of demand in Exhibits 4-8 and 4-9. Harold has got your undivided attention. You ask him to continue with his explanation. "Here is the calculation I used (see Exhibit 4-20) to come up with next month's average luxury-car price and the total units that will probably be sold.

"What all of this seems to indicate is that the demand for luxury cars has been exceptionally strong over the past two months. It's showing up in the premium prices that dealers are getting for the luxury models. I've reviewed the accounting information that Jane put together. I would like to add economic demand data to the same report. Here is what the revised report would look like." Harold shows you Exhibit 4-21.

You can't get the words out fast enough. "Do it. It is exactly what I need to put together a decent pricing strategy for this company." Harold cuts back in. "You're missing one thing. You need to add market research data to ver-

	Economy	Midsize	Luxury
Last Month's Price	$8,000	$12,000	$20,000
Units Sold Last Month	1,000	800	1,000
Price Two Months Ago	$8,500	$13,000	$20,000
Units Sold Two Months Ago	700	850	1,030

Exhibit 4-19. Harold's 3×5 economic card.

Price Elasticity = ((Qty. Change) - (Previous Qty. Demanded))/((Price
Chg.)/(Previous Price))

= ((1,030 - 1,000)/1,000))/(($20,200 - $20,000)/$20,000))

= 3% or a 1% reduction in price results in a 3% increase in
quantity demanded

Sales before Reduction = (Price) (Quantity)

= $20,000 (1,000 Luxury Cars)

= $20,000,000

Sales after Reduction = (Adjusted Price)(Adjusted Quantity Demanded)

= (($20,000)(.99)) ((1,000)(1.03))

= ($19,800)(1,030 Cars)

= $20,394,000

Net Increase in Sales = (Sales after Reduction) - (Sales before Reduction)

= $20,394,000 - $20,000,000

= $394,000

Exhibit 4-20. Harold's projection for next month's luxury-car sales.

ify what the economic numbers are telling you. I know your marketing people have been experimenting in this area. You might want to talk to them."

You thank Harold for his help. As soon as he leaves your office, you call
your secretary and ask her to send Harold a $1000 bonus check. You then
take off to find your marketing team. You'll find them somewhere in the
next chapter.

Summary and Conclusions

Economics deals with the way in which resources are allocated among alternative uses to satisfy human wants. Human wants are partially determined
by the prices consumers are willing to pay on a demand schedule. What
companies are willing to produce is also partially influenced by prices re-
flected on a supply schedule.

Historical Sales Analysis				
Description of Plan Element	Mon. 1	Mon. 2	Mon. 3	Mon. 4
Forecast Car Unit Sales	52	48	45	49
Actual Car Units Sold	38	36	36	34
Forecast Less Actual Sales	14	12	9	15
Forecast vs. Actual % Delta	37%	33%	25%	44%
Forecast Car Unit Sell Price	$14,800	$14,100	$14,200	$15,100
Actual Car Unit Sell Price	$13,500	$12,900	$12,700	$13,100
Forecast vs. Actual $ Delta	$1,300	$1,200	$1,599	$2,000
Forecast vs. Actual Price %Delta	10%	9%	12%	15%
Economic Analysis				
Consumer Demand Unit Reduction per $100 Increase in Sell Price	.10	.09	.08	.07

Exhibit 4-21. Sales plan for economy cars.

The economic system that has been built into the game will challenge you with three tasks. You must first allocate resources within your company to produce cars to meet consumer demands. Second, you must determine what types of cars to produce to satisfy the different demands of consumer groups.

Finally, you must establish the prices that you are willing to accept for your cars to maximize your profits. We would encourage you to selectively use different prices for your cars as a technique to measure the level of demand from one period to the next.

Game Assignments and Instructions

When you load the game into your PC, you should see the Main Menu for Month 3 if you exited the game without updating. That was our recommendation in the last chapter. There are no new options to tell you about. However, we recommend that, at a minimum, you review last month's financial statements and update your financial plan. When you're all done, exit and update Month 3.

5

Getting into the Market

Does Anybody Want It?

Marketing is based on the principle that consumers have needs and wants which are satisfied through the acquisition of goods and services. Most societies function under the market principle of exchange where commodities are produced and sold to satisfy market demands. In Chapter 4, we discussed economic principles that can influence market demands. Marketing relies heavily on economic principles to quantify and qualify markets.

The market qualification process calls for a considerable amount of subjective planning that extends beyond the scope of economics. For example, suppose that an artist spends a year creating a beautiful painting and now wants to sell it for $100,000. The question the artist faces is whether there is anyone who will exchange $100,000 for the painting.

If the artist can find at least one buyer, then there is a qualified market for the painting. The size of the market may vary with price. If the artist reduces the price, the market size may increase because more people can afford to buy the painting. Market size depends upon the number of persons who both have an interest in a product and are willing to pay for it.

Market Plans

The qualification of a market comes under the general heading of market planning. How do you prepare a market plan? You first need to analyze the potential market size for your cars. Next, establish a price consumers will pay for your product and that meets your corporate sales objectives. There are three marketing concepts to consider when developing marketing plans:

1. Product concept
2. Selling concept
3. Marketing concept

The Product Concept

The product concept assumes consumers will always buy quality products. The concept also assumes that the company producing the product is not required to initiate any marketing or sales effort to achieve its desired sales levels. By itself, the product concept may overlook important buyer needs since it does not rely on market analysis.

The following story of a filing cabinet company illustrates the limits of the product concept. The company manufactured the world's strongest and most expensive filing cabinets. However, the company's sales were on a steady decline. One day, the frustrated director of manufacturing was found complaining to a coworker. "We should be selling more filing cabinets. They are the best in the world. You can drop one from a four-story building and it will not be damaged." The coworker agreed. "But maybe our customers don't need filing cabinets that can be dropped off four-story buildings."

The Selling Concept

The selling concept assumes that consumers will not buy products unless they are subjected to intense selling and promotional efforts. The main task of the selling-concept company is to sell its products at some desired sales level using various sales techniques. Companies strictly practicing the selling concept assume that their goods are sold and not bought.

There are inherent risks in the selling concept. Consider what would happen if you decided to cut car manufacturing cost by using a cheap paint and increase your advertising budget with the money saved. Initial sales may increase until the consumer becomes dissatisfied with your inferior product.

The Marketing Concept

The marketing concept integrates consumer needs and wants. It incorporates the proper mix from the product and sales concepts to achieve the most effective marketing strategy for the company. There are two underlying premises of the marketing concept.

First, the corporation plans its production levels to meet the wants of identified consumer groups. Second, the corporation uses an active market-research program to identify consumer needs and wants. The marketing concept is used to drive the production process to produce products that best meet consumer needs. It relies on the sales programs to assure that consumers can get what they want.

Market Demands. The market-concept approach can be used to develop practical methods for estimating market demand. It can be used to determine the total market potential for a product. Total market potential is of interest to a company whenever it is facing a decision to introduce a new product, drop, or expand the sales of existing products.

One method of estimating market potential is known as the *market-buildup method.* You first identify all potential buyers for your product. Suppose your company is interested in estimating the total market potential for economy sedans. The market-buildup method is straightforward if you have access to all the required market information.

The first step is to identify all potential buyers of automobiles. Most corporations publish quarterly and annual reports showing sales volumes for their products. Car manufacturing companies are no exception. This information is readily available in a good public library or through market-research firms that specialize in providing this information to companies for a fee. You will have the option to obtain market-research information from a research firm that has been built into the computer game. An example of a market-research report is shown in Exhibit 5-1.

Let's review what Exhibit 5-1 is telling us about the market potential for economy cars. We know that consumers spent a total of $2,004,000 for all three types of cars in the previous period, and that $384,000 was spent for economy cars. Economy-car sales represented 32 percent of the total market. We also know that 42 luxury cars were sold by three manufacturers at an average price of $20,000 per car. Finally, you know that the three manu-

Car Type	Average Sales $	Number of Cars Sold	Potential New Sales %	Market Potential
Economy	$8,000	48	100%	$384,000
Midsize	$13,000	60	100%	$780,000
Luxury	$20,000	42	100%	$840,000

Exhibit 5-1. Market-buildup method using car sales from last month.

facturers sold a total of 150 cars, or an average of 50 cars per company. You could conclude that if you were to enter the car market as the fourth car company manufacturer with competitive cars, your sales would be one fourth of the total, or 38 cars (150 total cars/4 car companies = 38 cars).

Up to this point, we have been working with past history to determine how many cars consumers are willing to buy and what price they are willing to pay. This covers the information we needed in the first part of our market-buildup computation. We could conclude that consumers are consistent in their buying habits and that they will therefore choose to purchase the same number of cars in the next period.

But, as we all know, history does not always repeat itself. There are a number of factors that can influence consumer buying patterns from one period to the next. How can the principles of marketing be used to forecast future market demands?

Forecasting Future Markets.   Forecasting the market for most products and services is not an easy task. The few cases where forecasting is easy involve products that are considered essential. For example, water is required by everybody to survive and people use about the same amount every year. In most markets, product demands are not stable from one month to the next. Accurate market forecasting is difficult but it is an essential part of any successful marketing plan.

There are many alternative methods which can be used to develop market forecasts. One forecasting method is based on anticipating "what consumers say they will do." We want to anticipate what consumers are likely to buy, under a given set of conditions, over some period of time.

This concept suggests that the most useful source of information to provide us with the answers we need is the consumers themselves. Ideally, a list of all potential car buyers would be compiled. We would then approach all buyers and ask them if they were planning to buy a car next month. If they said "yes," we would ask them what type of car they plan to buy. Who will they buy it from? What price are they willing to pay for it? Armed with this information, we could forecast sales down to the exact car for each buyer.

Unfortunately, this method has several limitations. To begin with, the task of obtaining a prebuyer list would be difficult, if not impossible. Even if we assumed that such a list existed, would buyers freely divulge their intentions to buy a car? The value of this method would also depend on the extent to which the buyers have clearly formulated their intentions to buy cars, and then actually buy a car.

Buyer Surveys.   Buyer surveys can be used to help qualify buyer intentions. In its simplest form, a survey consists of a set of questions directed at a representative sample of potential buyers. The answers to the questions are carefully tabulated and analyzed. An example of a simple buyer survey questionnaire is shown in Exhibit 5-2.

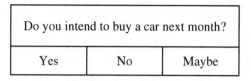

Do you intend to buy a car next month?		
Yes	No	Maybe

Exhibit 5-2. Simple buyer survey.

There are two problems with our simple "intention-to-buy" survey. Some consumers who answered "yes" or "no" may change their minds after the survey was completed. The second problem has to do with the "maybe" category. All we know from this response is that these people are potential buyers. For some reason, they cannot make a definite "yes" or "no" decision. If we knew something about their reasons, it might be possible to initiate a program that would motivate "maybe" buyers into becoming "yes" buyers.

We have added additional questions to our questionnaire to further qualify the market (see Exhibit 5-3). In addition, we hired a market-research firm to send our survey out to a representative sample of potential car buyers. A market-research firm has tabulated the results of the survey.

The number of questions we want to find answers for has been expanded

1. Do you intend to buy a car next month?		
Yes __	No __	Maybe __
2. If your answer was "yes," what type of car do you plan to buy?		
Economy __	Midsize __	Luxury __
3. If your answer was "no," please check the reason that caused you to make this decision?		
Already own a car __	Interest rates too high __	Car prices too high __
4. If your answer was "maybe," please indicate the reason why you are undecided?		
Interest rates too high __	Car prices too high __	Economy concerns __
5. If your answer was "maybe," what type of car might you buy?		
Economy __	Midsize __	Luxury __

Exhibit 5-3. Car buyer survey questionnaire.

from our original single question asking, "Do you intend to buy a car next month?" We are interested in knowing what type of cars people plan on buying for an obvious reason. We want to make certain that we have a supply of car models consumers want.

In addition, we want to know why a certain segment of potential buyers may or may not be interested in buying cars. If the "maybe" and "no" buyers indicated a concern about high interest rates, and the interest rates suddenly dropped after we had taken the survey, we may want to increase our sales forecast to include additional buyers.

Exhibit 5-4 shows the number of responses the research firm obtained

Question Number	Response I.D.	Number of Responses	Response percent
Q1	Yes	200	20%
	No	500	50%
	Maybe	300	30%
Q2	Economy	150	50%
	Midsize	100	33%
	Luxury	50	17%
Q3	Own Car	275	55%
	High Interest	75	15%
	High Price	150	30%
Q4	High Interest	200	67%
	High Price	50	17%
	Bad Economy	50	17%
Q5	Economy	225	75%
	Midsize	75	25%
	Luxury	0	0%

Exhibit 5-4. Tabulated survey results from 1000 potential buyers (total buyer population estimated at 15,000).

for each of the questions asked. In addition, the percent of the total response for each question was calculated. If we review the results from the first question, 20 percent of the respondents answered "yes" when asked if they intended to buy a new car next month.

In the second question, we can readily determine by percent the types of cars that these buyers intend to buy. The research firm has also told us that they surveyed a "representative sample" of 1000 potential cars from an estimated market that included 15,000 potential buyers.

We know from earlier discussions that consumers can change their buying intentions at any moment in time (i.e., owing to changes in economic events). If we know interest rates are falling and 200 of the 300 "maybe" buyers indicated a desire to buy cars if interest rates were lower, we may want to increase our forecast to include 200 "maybe" buyers. Following the same logic, we have completely ignored our "no" response buyers. Yet 15 percent of this group indicated an interest in buying cars if interest rates fall. Our revised computation for next month's car sales is shown in Exhibit 5-5.

Here is how we arrived at a total car sales number of 4800 units. A total of 15,000 potential buyers were surveyed. Twenty percent said they planned to buy a car. We reduced the percentage by 5 percent to adjust for consumers who would change their mind. Thirty percent of the survey group said they might buy a car. Of that group, 67 percent were concerned about high interest rates.

We know that interest rates will go down in the immediate future. We therefore believe that 15 percent of the "maybe" respondents will buy next month. The same approach was used to recalculate how many "no" respondents would change their minds because of the lower interest rates.

We have touched upon a couple of techniques market researchers use to analyze buyer surveys. No company can conduct its business successfully without estimating the actual size of present and future markets. Quantitative measurements are essential for the analysis of market opportunities and the development of a market plan.

Events That Change Markets

There are many marketing events that can affect a product's market at any one point in time. The occurrence of some events may be good for your market while others could be devastating. What are these events? How can you recognize them when they begin to occur? What kind of appropriate corrective action can you take.

Changes in the long-term growth rate of an industry can cause a number of different events to occur in the market. A strong upsurge in an industry's growth rate attracts new firms into the market. Competition runs wild as all

Yes Buyers = (Total Potential Buyers)(20% - 5% Anticipated Change)

= 15,000(15%)

= 2,250 Cars

Maybe Buyers = (Total Potential Buyers)(67% of 30% - 5% Anticipated Change)

= (15,000)((.30)(.67))-(.05)

= 15,000(.20-.05)

= 2,250 Cars

No Buyers = (Total Potential Buyers)(15% of 50% - 5% Anticipated Change)

= 15,000((.50)(.15))-(.05)

= 15,000(.07-.05)

= 300 Cars

Total Buyers = 2,250 + 2,250 + 300

= 4,800 Cars

Exhibit 5-5. Adjusted market survey buyer projections.

of the new entry companies aggressively attempt to capture their share of the market.

At the other extreme, a shrinking industry market can be triggered by product obsolescence. A glut of companies are left over trying to compete for a limited market. The marginal companies are immediately forced out of business. The surviving companies will enter into vicious competitive battles such as price wars to capture a dominant position in a dwindling market. Only a few will survive. The rest will leave the industry.

Shifts in buyer composition, preferences, and new ways to use a product can force changes in an industry's market strategy. A classic example is the computer industry. The entire industry was transformed by the surge of buyers' needs and wants for personal computers.

The demand for large mainframe computers had been the industry's standard for decades. The dinosaur mainframes started to die. New computer-literate consumers demanded technical service offerings which set a new standard for the industry. The companies that survived the transition were able to change their marketing strategies in time to capture a share of this shifting market.

Product and Market Innovation

Product innovation can broaden an industry's customer base. It can even rejuvenate the growth rate of an industry that may have been experiencing a dwindling market. Successful new-product introductions strengthen the market position of the innovating company at the expense of its competitors. Industries where product innovation has almost become a way of life include cameras, video games, computer software, and toys.

Advances in technology can dramatically alter the composition of an industry. This is particularly true if the new technology leads to new products that are unique or better than their counterparts. Technological change can also lead to changes in capital investments and plant sizes.

Market innovation occurs when a company successfully introduces a new way to market an old product. They are rewarded with a burst of buyer interest and an increase in the demand for their product at the expense of their competition.

Technical Diffusion

The diffusion of technical know-how is another element which can signal a change in an industry's marketing strategy. As the knowledge about the benefit of a particular manufacturing technology spreads, the original technical advantages to the company which held this knowledge erode. The diffusion of unique know-how about the process occurs through trade publications about the process, conversations among suppliers and customers, and the hiring away of knowledgeable employees.

It can also occur when a company's technical know-how is licensed to companies interested in fulfilling the role of supplier by using the sponsoring company's technology. Technical know-how is often a key reason why one company will acquire another company.

In recent years, technical know-how transferred across national boundaries has become an important force driving domestic and global competition. As more companies gain access to technical know-how, they upgrade their operations to compete head on against established companies. Ten years ago, only a few companies were capable of manufacturing personal computers. Today, there are hundreds of companies competing in the PC market.

Market Dominance

The entry of a major company into an industry always generates major industry shakeups. The sudden entrance of Toyota into the domestic car market 35 years ago is still causing shakeups to occur in Detroit today. The entrance of a major firm changes the industry structure by reshuffling the market leaders. If a major competitor decides to leave the industry, there is a rush by the remaining companies to capture the exiting company's market.

Domestic and International Markets

The increased international dominance of an industry can create events that will shift the competitive advantage between the international corporate players. The international movement starts when one company in the industry expands into the international market.

The new international player believes it can increase its market share and reduce its manufacturing cost by going international. They offer domestic products that are unique in foreign countries to increase their market share. At the same time, they may elect to manufacture part or all their product offerings in foreign countries to reduce cost. The cost savings can be substantial. For example, the labor rate in many of the Pacific Rim countries is one-fourth of U.S. rates.

A company's search for new international markets can cause a challenge among the leading companies in the industry. They, too, may not be satisfied with their share of the domestic market and will go after the lucrative international market. They are anxious to find out what the international market is doing to your cost line. They have also read Chapter 4 on economics and are accurately aware of the laws of economies of scale.

Price Leaders

Changes in a corporation's cost and efficiency structure used to undercut a rival's price can trigger major marketing changes. The cycle starts when a major competitor in the industry begins to realize economies of scale in their production process. Production efficiencies are applied to undercut the prices of the competition. As a result, the race for production growth dominates the industry.

The larger companies in the industry aggressively search for market strategies which will allow them to increase production and realize economies of scale. The smaller competitors suddenly find themselves in a position where they can no longer compete against the higher-volume producers. As a result, they'll drop out of the industry. Their market share gets gobbled up by the remaining corporations.

Buyer Preference

Changes in buyer preferences from a differentiated product to a cheaper "one-size-fits-all" product can affect the market. This situation occurs in the later stages of a product's life cycle. It happens when a mature consumer market realizes that the generic brand is just as good as the name brand. As a result, buyers shift patronage away from the sellers of the more expensive differentiated products to the sellers of the cheaper products.

If left alone, the smaller competitors aggressively leverage their standard products at the expense of the market share of the name-brand companies. The major firms in the industry are usually the ones that are put into a defensive position. At some point in the competitive battle, the majors realize that their brand-name products can no longer be sold at a premium price. Brand-name product prices are discounted down to standard-product price level in an attempt to eliminate standard product competitors.

The reverse of this scenario can happen in an industry dominated initially by standard products. The cycle starts when one or more of the companies in the industry introduce new features which differentiate their product from the standard product. The new features could include style changes, improved service offerings, added accessories, or image differentiation created through advertising. The market strategies of the entire industry change as rivals try to "out differentiate" each other.

Government Regulation

Changes in government regulations can force significant changes in an industry's practices and market strategies. Deregulation became a driving market force in the airlines, natural gas, banking, and the telecommunications industries.

Governments can also create entirely new markets. When the telephone companies became deregulated, consumers discovered that they no longer had to rent telephones from the phone company. Almost overnight, retail stores started selling telephones supplied by third-party manufacturers.

Emerging social issues influencing changes in buyer attitudes and lifestyles can have a powerful effect on an industry's product lines. The food industry is a perfect example. Consumer concerns about salt, sugar, nutrition, and chemical additives have forced the food industry to radically change their product offerings.

Safety concerns have influenced changes in the automobile, toys, and outdoor power equipment industries. The increased interest in physical fitness has created a new industry that specializes in making home exercise equipment. The specialized tennis and outdoor shoe market has exploded to cover every conceivable athletic activity.

We have covered a partial list of external forces that can affect the way products are marketed. The successful market strategy of today can and will become obsolete tomorrow. It must be subjected to constant refinement and change. The analytical task of marketing is to constantly monitor and evaluate all the forces that could potentially change the way a company is currently marketing its products.

Getting a Jump on the Market

What steps can you take to make sure you won't get caught off guard by a sudden change in the market? First, you have to identify events that could trigger changes in your market over the next several years. Look at both positive and negative scenarios. For example, if you are producing a consumer product that must be financed before it can be bought (i.e., automobiles), what happens if interest rates go up or down?

Next, access the implications, consequences, and benefits of each market event scenario. In the interest rate example, you know that if interest rates go up, you would probably sell less cars. If they go down, you'll sell more cars. How much will your sales go up or down based upon fluctuations in interest rates? This is where the analytical part of marketing comes into play.

You want to add marketing to your strategic plan. How do you quantify the potential impacts market events can have on your market? How do you develop market strategies to take advantage of positive events and neutralize negative events? You want a marketing plan you can pull "off the shelf" and implement immediately, the moment an event occurs. If you wait until after an event occurs to come up with a plan, you may be too late. The event may have passed by the time you create and implement your plan.

Here is an example of an "on-the-shelf" market strategy or plan. Let's assume that interest rates have been "bouncing all over the board." It's your number one marketing concern. You and your marketing team have determined that if new car loan rates were to jump 20 percent over current levels, your car sales would drop 10 percent. You asked your vice president of finance to negotiate a new car loan deal with the bank.

The deal goes something like this. You agree to pay all loan preparation fees to the bank for any of your customers that apply for a new car loan. On top of that, you agree to underwrite any bad debts that the bank may incur on behalf of your customers. In consideration for those two guarantees, you ask the bank to agree to a special new car loan rate for your customers. Let's say the bank agrees to the terms and signs the agreement.

Next, you tell your sales department to create a "dynamite" ad campaign that leverages the lower interest rates you can offer to your customers. The ad campaign complete with "ready-to-go" media copy is done. Negotiations with the bank and putting together the campaign take time. Two months later, all the parts of the plan are in place. You put the plan "on the shelf."

Four months later, interest rates jump 20 percent as a result of external economic events. You pull your contingency plan "off the shelf" and implement it within a week (not two months) after the rate hike was announced. You catch your competition by surprise. Your plan not only protects your market but you pick up market share at the expense of your competitors.

Strategic Market Planning

You want to incorporate marketing into your strategic plan. You've asked your marketing department to prepare an historical analysis to quantify the effect interest rates might have on your sales (see Exhibit 5-6).

Perhaps there is information in our buyers' survey that could be used to derive a marketing plan. Our original marketing goal was to develop a plan that would allow our company to realize a 10 percent growth in sales and maintain a 20 percent profit rate. From our competitive analysis, we have determined that we can make a 20 percent profit from the manufacture and sale of luxury sedans.

We know from our survey that 50 percent of the respondents indicated

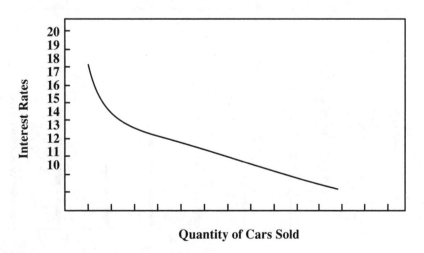

Exhibit 5-6. Number of cars sold at different interest rates.

they would buy a new car. Their car of choice was the economy car. This leads us to believe there is a strong future demand for economy cars. The trend is reinforced from our historical product data which show a continued increase in economy-car sales over the last four years (see Exhibit 5-7).

Your decision to manufacture and sell economy cars would appear to be logical, based on the research data. The marketing portion of your strategic plan can now be developed. Before you begin, you've got some important questions to answer. Is your competitive approach in place? Are you striving to become the low-cost leader in the industry? Can you differentiate your cars from the competition? Are you focusing on a specific customer group or market niche? Is your market plan clearly defined and understood by your entire organization? Is your product vertically integrated in the market? Do you have adequate geographic marketing and sales coverage? Are all functional departments covered in your strategic plan? This would include accounting, finance, marketing, sales, production, and manufacturing. You already know from your conversation with your vice president of marketing that you need to bring your sales organization into the plan.

But, you hadn't thought about your production and manufacturing departments. You realize you've got to make sure that your entire organization is "marching to the beat of the same drummer." You have got some work ahead of you to make that happen.

In addition, you know that it makes sense to constantly evaluate the logical consistency of your strategies. This will allow you to judge if any part of the marketing strategy is flawed. One of the best ways to determine if a company's marketing strategy is working is to analyze the company's recent performance over time. You decide to incorporate market trends and consumer preferences from the survey into your strategic plan (Exhibit 5-8).

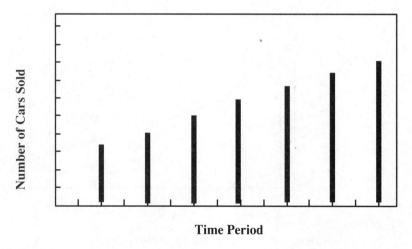

Exhibit 5-7. Economy-car sales over time.

Historical Sales Analysis				
Description of Plan Element	**Mon. 1**	**Mon. 2**	**Mon. 3**	**Mon. 4**
Forecast Car Unit Sales	52	48	45	49
Actual Car Units Sold	38	36	36	34
Forecast Less Actual Sales	14	12	9	15
Forecast vs. Actual % Delta	37%	33%	25%	44%
Forecast Car Unit Sell Price	$14,800	$14,100	$14,200	$15,100
Actual Car Unit Sell Price	$13,500	$12,900	$12,700	$13,100
Forecast vs. Actual $ Delta	$1,300	$1,200	$1,599	$2,000
Forecast vs. Actual Price %Delta	10%	9%	12%	15%
Economic Analysis				
Consumer Demand Unit Reduction Per $100 Increase in Sell Price	.10	.09	.12	.15
Market Survey Results				
Percent Yes Buyers				
Percent Maybe Buyers				
Percent No Buyers				
Percent Interest Rates Too High				
Bad Economy Concerns				
Current Events Data				
Leading Economic Indicators				
New Car Loan Interest Rates				

Exhibit 5-8. Sales plan for economy sedans.

Stability and consistency are the two critical factors required to assure the success of any marketing plan. You want to position yourself to make consistent improvements to the original plan. Radical and abrupt changes to the plan are a clear indication that the plan is not working.

Summary and Conclusions

No company can conduct its business successfully without attempting to measure the size of its present and future markets. Quantitative measurements are essential for the analysis of market opportunities and the planning of marketing programs. Current demand may be estimated for the market as a whole or for specific products. A company may use one or any combination of forecasting methods to determine future market demands.

We introduced you to three marketing concepts and showed you how to combine the best parts of each concept into a framework for a marketing plan. The next step was to develop a forecast of the market. We developed a questionnaire, solicited responses from the market, and tabulated the results. In the final analysis, we determined the market demand for economy cars.

Our discussion led us through some of the events that change markets. After arriving at a strategic marketing plan, you need to show it to your salespeople to make sure the marketing plan is in concert with the sales plan. You plan to meet with your sales department in the next chapter.

Game Assignments and Instructions

When you start the game for Month 4, you will notice that there is a new option on the Main Menu—Market Research Report (Exhibit 5-9).

You can now order a market-research report in a format similar to the examples used in this chapter (Exhibit 5-10). The report is not free. The current report price will be displayed before you place your order. If you choose to order a market-research report, it will provide you with marketing information about the current period of play. It will, therefore, not be available for you to review until the start of the next period of play.

When you select the Market Research Option, the submenu in Exhibit 5-11 will appear on your display. You order the reports selecting payment options (i.e., Charge to Accounts Payable). If you order the report this month, and return to this menu next month, it will include a new option—Review Last Month's Report. Your market report can be viewed and printed.

When you are done with Month 4, we recommend that you read the chapter on sales (Chapter 6) before you close out Month 4. Select the Exit and No Update option.

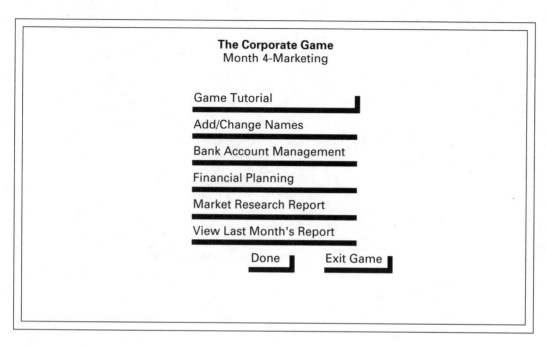

Exhibit 5-9. Month 4—Marketing menu.

The Corporate Game
Car Buyer Survey Questionaire - 1,000 Potential Car Buyers Surveyed

1. Do you intend to buy a car next month? Yes: 30%   No: 50%   Maybe: 20%

2. If your answer was "yes," what type of car do you plan to buy?
   Economy: 32% Midsize: 44% Luxury: 24%

3. If your answer was "no," please check the reason that caused you to make
   this decision. Already own a car: 26% Interest rates too high: 52%
   New car prices too high: 22%

4. If your answer was "maybe," please indicate the reason why you are
   undecided. Interest rates too high: 31%   New car prices too high: 30%
   Economy concerns: 39%

5. If your answer was "maybe," what type of car might you buy?
   Economy: 34% Midsize: 41% Luxury: 25%

Car average sell price and units sold this month by three auto companies:
Economy: 95/$15,500 Midsize: 88/$23,800 Luxury: 59/$28,994

F2 Print   F3 Return

Exhibit 5-10. Car buyer survey questionnaire.

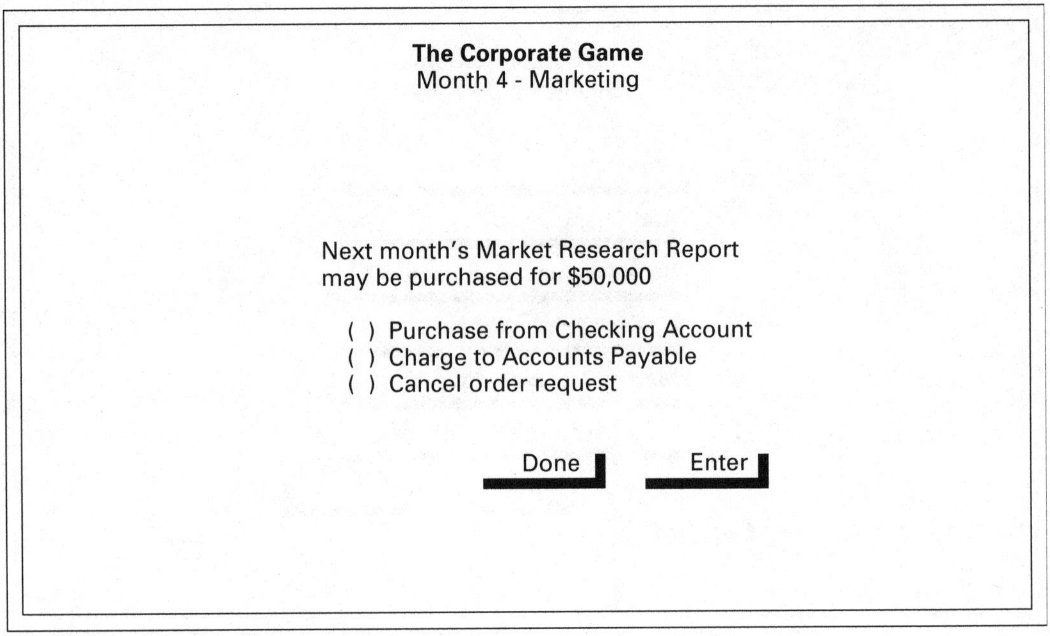

The Corporate Game
Month 4 - Marketing

Next month's Market Research Report
may be purchased for $50,000

( ) Purchase from Checking Account
( ) Charge to Accounts Payable
( ) Cancel order request

Done ∎   Enter ∎

Exhibit 5-11. Month 4—Market-research report order menu.

6

The Sales Game

Where the Rubber Meets the Road

All corporate planning sessions must have a sales forecast before they can get started. The reason is obvious. Projected sales revenues drive every element of the strategic plan. Projected total sales are used to determine the total amount of money available to meet planned expenses. Unit sales drive the production planning cycle.

For example, unit sales are used to determine the quantities of raw materials that must be ordered to produce the appropriate quantities of end products. The relationship between the sales plan and the elements inherent in the corporation's strategic plan is shown in Exhibit 6-1.

Cost of Overstating

The integrity and accuracy of the corporation's overall strategic plan are directly dependent upon the accuracy of the sales plan. The consequences of an overstated sales plan can have a devastating effect on the company. For example, if the sales plan is overstated by 25 percent, production runs will be overstated by 25 percent. At the end of the projected sales period, the corporation will have accumulated surplus product that nobody wants.

The cost associated with a 25 percent overstated sales plan can be tied directly to the cost of money. Assume 25 percent more product was produced than could be sold at a cost of $1 million. We have in effect tied up $1 million of cash assets. Inventoried product does not generate any interest or sales income. What is the bottom line cost of the overrun?

Let's assume that as an alternative, you could invest $1 million in certificates of deposits (CDs) that are returning 10 percent interest. If you have $1 million tied up in inventory, the corporation can't take advantage of the

Car Model	Unit Sales Forecast	Existing Car Inventory	Need to Produce (Cars)	Tons Steel per Car	Total Steel Needed	Parts per Car	Total Parts Needed
Economy	300	20	280	1.5	420	100	28,000
Midsize	150	10	140	2.0	280	280	29,400
Luxury	100	0	100	3.0	300	350	35,000

Exhibit 6-1. The effect of the sales forecast on raw materials and ending inventories.

CD investment option. The net effect would be a loss of $100,000 in annual interest income ($1,000,000 × 10 percent = $100,000/yr.). Worse yet, the loss of interest income comes right out of the corporation's profit line, because there are no costs associated with the generation of interest income.

The integrity of the sales plan is directly dependent upon the information and data that it receives from the other business disciplines. First, you must have a good accounting system in place to capture sales history for historical analysis.

The economic and marketing plans must also be in place to support the historical analysis process. To illustrate this process, let's assume we have historical economy-car sales information in our accounting system (see Exhibit 6-2). Historical sales are compared against the sales forecast over the past four months.

Description of Plan Element	Mon. 1	Mon. 2	Mon. 3	Mon. 4
Forecast Car Unit Sales	52	48	45	49
Actual Car Units Sold	38	36	36	34
Forecast Less Actual Sales	14	12	9	15
Forecast vs. Actual % Delta	37%	33%	25%	44%
Forecast Car Unit Sell Price	$14,800	$14,100	$14,200	$15,100
Actual Car Unit Sell Price	$13,500	$12,900	$12,700	$13,100
Forecast vs. Actual $ Delta	$1,300	$1,200	$1,599	$2,000
Forecast vs. Actual Price % Delta	10%	9%	12%	15%

Exhibit 6-2. The original sales plan for economy sedans.

The exhibit includes unit and dollar delta rows to show the difference between actual and forecasted sales. If you review the delta rows in the exhibit, you could conclude that we were not very accurate in our forecasting effort. Our sales forecast was overstated in all four months. Why were our sales forecasts off by so much? How can you improve upon the accuracy of your next sales forecast?

Economics and the Sales Plan

The principles of economics discussed in Chapter 4 might help us find answers to some of the questions. The concept of the consumer demand and production supply curves were covered in some detail. Exhibit 6-3 from Chapter 4 showed you how to estimate the economic impact of a change in the price of a car on units sold.

Given: A 1% reduction in price results in a 3% increase in the quantity demanded

Assumptions: Price and quantity demanded before the reduction was $10,000 and 1,000 cars

Then: The net increase in the demand for cars resulting from a 1% price reduction can be calculated

Sales before Reduction = (Price)(Quantity)

= $10,000 (1,000 Cars)

= $10,000,000

Sales after Reduction = Adjusted Price (Adjusted Quantity Demanded)

= (($10,000)(.99)) ((1,000)(1.03))

= ($9,900)(1,030 Cars)

= $10,197,000

Net Increase in Sales = (Sales after Reduction) - (Sales before Reduction)

= $10,197,000 - $10,000,000

= $197,000

Exhibit 6-3. Calculating the price elasticity of demand.

Let's assume you have instructed your economist, Harold, to maintain historical economic data. The information derived from the data shows the projected impact on the demand curve when the price of an economy sedan increased or decreased by $100. A $100 price increase in Month 1 would have resulted in a 10 percent decrease in unit sales. Demand continues to fall in Months 2 and 3. This information has been added to our sales history exhibit (Exhibit 6-4).

Does the added economic information offer any insights into our forecasting problems? Remember, we are concerned about the integrity and accuracy of our sales forecast. You are "under the gun" to project a new and more accurate sales forecast.

Let's analyze Exhibit 6-4 to see what happened over the past four months. To begin with, car sales had been on a steady decline. There was also downward pressure on unit prices. Prices consistently fell in Months 1, 2, and 3. For some reason, there was an upturn in the unit price in Month 4. What happened?

Historical Sales Analysis				
Description of Plan Element	Mon. 1	Mon. 2	Mon. 3	Mon. 4
Forecast Car Unit Sales	52	48	45	49
Actual Car Units Sold	38	36	36	34
Forecast Less Actual Sales	14	12	9	15
Forecast vs. Actual % Delta	37%	33%	25%	44%
Forecast Car Unit Sell Price	$14,800	$14,100	$14,200	$15,100
Actual Car Unit Sell Price	$13,500	$12,900	$12,700	$13,100
Forecast vs. Actual $ Delta	$1,300	$1,200	$1,599	$2,000
Forecast vs. Actual Price %Delta	10%	9%	12%	15%
Economic Analysis				
Consumer Demand Unit Reduction per $100 Increase in Sell Price	.10	.11	.12	.09

Exhibit 6-4. Modified sales plan for economy cars.

From our economic analysis, we were able to determine why our unit sales forecast was too high. Our economy cars were priced higher than what consumers were willing to pay, given the quantities we wanted to sell. This begs the next question. Why were consumers reluctant to pay our price? Let's turn to our marketing department for answers.

Marketing and the Sales Plan

In the chapter on marketing, we talked about how to use the market concept to integrate consumer needs and wants. There were two important components in the concept. First, we identified the needs of consumers. Second, we implemented a market-research program to identify what consumers wanted.

Let's assume that your vice president of marketing, Susan, had collected consumer market data over the past four months. For whatever reason, the information was not used to develop any of the sales forecasts. Today, you have decided to analyze the historical marketing information to determine if this information would have helped project more accurate sales forecasts.

You've invited Susan into your office to review the marketing information she collected. She conducted a consumer survey at the beginning of each month and collected competitive prices and car units sold for each of the months. The tabulated survey information is presented to you in Exhibit 6-5.

Let's analyze what the survey data are telling us. The first question in the survey asks consumers if they intend to buy a car. The percentage of "yes" respondents shows a steady decline over the four months. We could conclude that there may be a continuing decline or softness in the car market. But look at what was happening to the "maybe" respondents. The percentage increases over the same four months.

What's holding the "maybe" buyers back? Our attention turns to the reasons they checked in Questions 4 and 5. They were consistently concerned about high interest rates and the state of the economy throughout all four months. High car prices did not seem to be a major concern to them, as we had originally thought.

All this seems to make sense when we look at the responses to Question 5. Consumer preferences for buying economy cars increased each month. In fact, the trend is reinforced when we look at the number of economy cars our competition sold over the four months. The average economy-car price was competitive to ours. You decide to incorporate the economic, marketing survey, and competitive analysis data into your revised sales plan (Exhibit 6-6).

Question Number	Response Option	Response % Mon. 1	Response % Mon. 2	Response % Mon. 3	Response % Mon. 4
Q1 - Do you plan to buy a car next month?	Yes	20%	18%	17%	14%
	No	50%	52%	54%	58%
	Maybe	30%	30%	29%	28%
Q2 - If "yes," what type of car would you buy?	Economy	50%	52%	49%	55%
	Midsize	33%	29%	34%	23%
	Luxury	17%	19%	17%	22%
Q3 - If "no," what was your reason?	Own Car	55%	55%	57%	61%
	High Interest	30%	31%	30%	32%
	High Price	15%	14%	13%	7%
Q4 - If "maybe," what was your reason?	High Interest	27%	22%	29%	34%
	High Price	13%	15%	16%	17%
	Bad Economy	60%	63%	55%	49%
Q5 - If "maybe," what type of car would you buy?	Economy	75%	77%	68%	72%
	Midsize	25%	21%	29%	26%
	Luxury	0%	2%	3%	2%
Average Car Sell Price:					
Competition Price	Economy	$14,200	$14,900	$14,600	$15,800
	Midsize	$20,000	$17,900	$19,850	$19,435
	Luxury	$30,000	$27,000	$27,800	$28,900
Our Price	Economy	$14,800	$14,100	$14,200	$15,000
	Midsize	$19,300	$18,900	$19,100	$19,700
	Luxury	$26,400	$25,000	$26,700	$29,000

Exhibit 6-5. Tabulated survey results from potential car buyers.

Historical Analysis

Up to this point in our sales analysis, we have used historical data to analyze the needs and wants of our consumers. They appear to be placing a higher value on interest rates than on car prices. Our sales analysis has relied heavily upon historical accounting, economic, and marketing information. We built Exhibit 6-6 to tie all of the data and information together.

In the real world, we may use something more exotic like a computerized

Historical Sales Analysis				
Description of Plan Element	Mon. 1	Mon. 2	Mon. 3	Mon. 4
Forecast Car Unit Sales	52	48	45	49
Actual Car Units Sold	38	36	36	34
Forecast Less Actual Sales	14	12	9	15
Forecast vs. Actual % Delta	37%	33%	25%	44%
Forecast Car Unit Sell Price	$14,800	$14,100	$14,200	$15,100
Actual Car Unit Sell Price	$13,500	$12,900	$12,700	$13,100
Forecast vs. Actual $ Delta	$1,300	$1,200	$1,599	$2,000
Forecast vs. Actual Price %Delta	10%	9%	12%	15%
Economic Analysis				
Consumer Demand Unit Reduction per $100 Increase in Sell Price	.10	.09	.12	.15
Market Survey Results				
Percent Yes Buyers	20%	18%	17%	25%
Percent Maybe Buyers	66%	70%	71%	60%
Percent No Buyers	14%	12%	12%	15%
Percent Interest Rates Too High	16%	21%	22%	24%
Bad Economy Concerns	10%	8%	8%	8%

Exhibit 6-6. Sales plan for economy cars.

relational database to help us analyze the various sets of information. The important point illustrated in this exercise is how to use the principles of economics and marketing, supplemented with historical sales data, to develop an accurate sales forecast.

The Final Sales Analysis

The historical analysis was used to create a baseline for projecting future sales. The problem with relying totally on history is that it does not always repeat itself. Let's go back into *The Corporate Game*. We need to forecast our sales for the next period, Month 5. We know that consumers are concerned about interest rates and the state of the economy.

Suppose you had access to information that would give you some indications about where the economy was going in Month 5. In the real world, you do. It comes packaged in a variety of multimedia formats. You see and hear about the state of the economy every day in business journals, on the radio as you drive to work, or on the evening television broadcast. It may sound or read like this:

"CitiBank raises prime rate 2 points to 12 percent. . . . "

"Dow Jones industrial average dropped 35 points today amidst investor concerns about rising interest rates. . . . "

"The U.S. federal budget deficit jumped to an all time high. . . . "

"The government's index of leading economic indicators dropped by. . . . "

This is all current information available to you daily. Armed with strategic current events information, you can now complete the sales forecast for Month 5. Your final forecast is based on the assumptions and facts you extracted from the sales history figures and current events. Your sales analysis for Month 5 is based upon what you know from sales history and current news media information.

1. In the previous months, consumers were concerned about high interest rates and the state of the economy.

2. Your market survey showed that consumers preferred economy cars over the larger and more expensive models.

3. You sold 34 economy cars in Month 4 at an average price of $13,100 per unit. Your price was comparable to the average price of your competition.

4. The economic demand data showed that for every $1000 added to the selling price of an economy sedan, the number of units sold dropped by 0.02 units.

5. The prime rate has been increased to 12 percent. You assume that new car loans will follow suit and will increase from the current rate of 13 percent to 15 percent.

6. You perform a quick calculation to determine what the impact would be of adding 2 percent interest onto the average economy-car loan. It has the same effect as it would if you increased your price by $1000 per economy car.

7. Stock market concerns about higher interest and the rising federal budget deficits confirm your convictions. The economy will not improve in Month 5.

8. Based upon our market survey, we believe that consumers are primarily interested in buying economy cars.

Your new sales forecast is shown in Exhibit 6-7. You decide to add current events economic data to your sales plan.

You have decided not to change the price of your economy cars from the average sales price in Month 4 of $13,100. However, the projected increase in interest rates that is being publicized in the news media will have the same effect as a $1000 per car price increase. Your economic demand data show a 0.02 decrease in car units sold for every $1000 increase in price. You have, therefore, decided to reduce the unit sales forecast for Month 5 by 9 car units. Our calculations follow:

$$\text{Reduced forecast units} = (\text{Price elasticity factor})(\text{Month 4 actual sales}/\$1000)$$

$$= (0.01)(\$13,100 \times 34 \text{ cars}/\$1000)$$

$$= (0.02)(\$445)$$

$$= 8.9 \text{ car units}$$

The Sales Process

Our sales forecast was derived by using a customer satisfaction process rather than a goods-producing process. The process started by determining what the customer wanted. How many cars did they need? Marketing, economic, and business multimedia sources were used to refine our forecasts.

In a goods-producing process, the reverse happens. You first determine how many cars you can produce. Your sales force is then directed to go out and sell whatever the company produces. This approach is popular with capital-intensive companies.

Capital, once purchased, cannot be easily removed, manipulated, or modified to produce different products. The car industry is a classic exam-

Historical Sales Analysis					
Description of Plan Element	Mon. 1	Mon. 2	Mon. 3	Mon. 4	Mon. 5 Forecast
Forecast Car Unit Sales	52	48	45	49	40
Actual Car Units Sold	38	36	36	34	
Forecast Less Actual Sales	14	12	9	15	
Forecast vs. Actual % Delta	37%	33%	25%	44%	
Forecast Car Unit Sell Price	$14,800	$14,100	$14,200	$15,100	$13,100
Actual Car Unit Sell Price	$13,500	$12,900	$12,700	$13,100	
Forecast vs. Actual $ Delta	$1,300	$1,200	$1,599	$2,000	
Forecast vs. Actual Price %Delta	10%	9%	12%	15%	
Economic Analysis					
Consumer Demand Unit Reduction per $100 Increase in Sell Price	.10	.09	.08	.07	
Market Survey Results					
Percent Yes Buyers	20%	18%	17%	25%	
Percent Maybe Buyers	66%	70%	71%	60%	
Percent No Buyers	14%	12%	12%	15%	
Percent Interest Rates Too High	16%	21%	22%	24%	
Bad Economy Concerns	10%	8%	8%	8%	
Current Events Data					
Leading Economic Indicators					Down
New Car Loan Interest Rates					Up

Exhibit 6-7. Sales plan for economy sedans.

ple of a capital-intensive business. Other such industries include chemical companies, petroleum plants, steel mills, airlines, and railroads.

In recent times, capital-intensive businesses have become more responsive to the necessity of balancing their preoccupation with maximizing production. They are learning that the best way to accomplish their profit objectives is to pay more attention to the needs and demands of the consumer.

The change from a goods-oriented to a consumer-oriented process has been a slow and painful transition for corporate America. In the "sell whatever we make" sales mode, the burden was clearly on the sales force. Their mission was complicated by the fact that they had to know "everything there was to know" about their product line and their competitor's product line.

Salespeople were thrown into the consumer arena and required to find prospects. A lot of face-to-face selling was required. Salespeople became very adept at selling the benefits of their products to potential consumers. Learning about customer needs and problems became a secondary issue.

Mass-Production Myopia

Mass-production industries are compelled by a great drive to produce all that they can. They cannot resist the temptation to reduce unit cost by driving the production levels up. The profit possibilities look spectacular. However, as we saw in the Sea Kist story, just the opposite occurred.

Production output becomes so proliferous that all efforts are concentrated on trying to get rid of the product. A sudden glut of singing commercials and cut-rate price wars flood the market. Everybody wants to get rid of surplus product. Again, the sales department is told to sell everything by top management. Management concerns about profit become a secondary concern. Consumer inputs from the sales and marketing departments are ignored. Production has already dictated what consumers need and want.

The automobile industry provides a classic illustration of this point. The mass-production machines of Detroit were a famous and time-honored American tradition. For years, the automobile industry was committed to the relentless drive to change models each year. Consumer orientation to the new models was a critical element in the process. Detroit spent hundreds of millions of dollars on consumer research. They were convinced that consumers wanted big cars so that was what they made.

The fact that "little" foreign cars were suddenly entering the U.S. market and were immediately successful illustrates the failure of the mass-production myopia. Detroit's vast research network failed to reveal what consumers really wanted, i.e., economy cars. The U.S. auto industry was convinced that consumers wanted exactly what Detroit was offering. When they lost millions of customers to foreign small-car manufacturers, they finally decided to add economy cars to their product offerings. By then, it was too late. The foreign auto makers had already captured a major share of their market.

How could this unbelievable lag behind consumer wants and needs have been perpetuated for so long? Why didn't the researchers reveal the consumer small-car preference long before the hard numbers came in? The answer is simple. Detroit never researched consumer wants. All their research was designed to determine their preferences for Detroit products (i.e., large cars). All this started to happen in the late 1960s. Detroit is just now beginning to recover from the error.

The Ford Story

Henry Ford is credited with implementing mass-production techniques when he started producing Model-T Fords in the early 1900s. Ford was both a senseless and brilliant salesman. He was senseless because he refused to sell anything but black cars. He was brilliant because he developed a production system designed to meet the specific needs and wants of consumers.

We habitually celebrate him for his production genius. His real genius was in sales and marketing. His marketing genius told him consumers needed an independent mode of transportation. His sales genius told him what they wanted. They wanted a transportation machine that they could buy for $500. He sold millions of Model-A cars at that price.

Product Obsolescence

Every major industry at one time qualified for the magic appellation of a growth industry. In each case, the industry's assumed strength was anchored by the apparently unchallenged superiority of its product. As was the case with the early Fords, there appeared to be no effective substitute for them. Over time, even the mighty Ford became subservient to competing modes of transportation.

Thirty years ago, dry cleaning was considered to be an aggressive growth industry. Wool garments were "the in thing." Dry cleaning was a safe and easy way to clean wool garments. Today, the industry is in trouble. Wool is out and synthetic fiber garments are in. The use of chemical additives in the synthetics has dramatically reduced the need for dry cleaning.

When the light bulb came along, the kerosene lamp industry died. Water wheels and steam engines were the next to fall as soon as someone figured out how to make a good electric motor. Electric utilities have been considered the makers of the "no-substitute product" enthroned on a pedestal of invincible growth. The continued proliferations of electronic gadgetry in homes seem to have assured the continued growth of utilities. There appears to be no end in sight.

A second look is not so comforting. Scores of companies have been quietly developing powerful chemical fuel cells. If successfully developed, these cells could be easily installed in home closets and would provide all of the electric power a home needs. The electric lines that vulgarize so many neighborhoods would be eliminated. The endless demolition of our streets and service interruptions during storms would also end.

Will obsolescence kill the electric utilities? To avoid this prospect, they will have to develop fuel cells, solar energy, and alternate power sources. To survive, they will have to plot the obsolescence of the product that is the foundation of the utility industry.

There are a few of us still around who can remember the corner grocery store before supermarkets took over. Supermarkets first appeared on the scene in the early thirties. Nobody believed people would drive several miles to shop for food and sacrifice the personal service of the corner grocery store. Over time, a change in consumer preferences eliminated the corner grocery store.

Growth Industry Myth

There is no such thing as a perpetual growth industry. There are companies that capitalize on growth opportunities. Companies that think they can continue to enjoy perpetual sales growth will invariably go out of business. Every growth industry goes through the same product cycle of bountiful expansion followed by undetected decay. Four myths form the basic misconception of the perpetual growth industry.

1. Perpetual growth is assured by an expanding and more affluent population.

2. There is no competitive substitute for the growth industry's product.

3. Mass production and the ability to reduce unit cost as output rises will assure the profitable success of the growth industry.

4. The industry knows best how to satisfy consumer wants and needs.

The Future Sales Organization

What does product obsolescence have to do with the sales organization? As we move into the twenty-first century, the life of the average product is shrinking at an incredible rate. Product obsolescence is a fact of business life. You can no longer afford to train a sales force to sell products that may not be there six months or even two years from now.

This does not mean that we can eliminate the sales organization of the future; however, it will be dramatically reshaped. Sales and marketing will be merged into a single organization. The combined skills of these two groups will be sharpened to instantaneously recognize consumer demand changes.

The combined organization will know how to quickly translate consumer demands into product and service derivatives ahead of the competition. The new sales organization will know how to exploit and extend its product's life cycles. If this cannot be done, the company will simply go out of business.

Product Exploitation

Most salespeople are familiar with the concept of product life cycle. It's like the weather. Everybody talks about it but nobody knows what to do about it. In the Detroit story, the American auto industry didn't diversify into small cars until after the foreign competition grabbed 25 percent of their market. It took Detroit a long time to understand what product life cycles are all about. Today, they know how they work and how to deal with them.

If you truly understand what product life cycles are all about, you can put the concept to work to your advantage. In the balance of this chapter, we'll show you how to use the concept as a powerful sales instrument to establish competitive power. In the following discussion, we'll establish a common baseline for life cycle terms and definitions so that it will all make sense.

Historical Product Patterns

Every product's life story repeats a common set of recognizable stages. These stages are shown in Exhibit 6-8 and occur in the following order:

Market Development: This stage occurs when the product is first introduced into the market. There is no established demand for the product. As a result, initial product sales are low.

Market Growth: Consumer demand for the product begins to accelerate. The size of the total market expands rapidly as sales take off.

Market Maturity: Demand levels off because "everybody already has one." New sales come from replacement orders.

Market Decline: The product begins to lose consumer appeal. Market share is lost to new and more advanced products. Sales decline at a rapid rate.

How can the shape and duration of each life-cycle stage be predicted? How do you know what stage you're in? If you know the answers to these questions, you will have a significant sales advantage over your competition. Before we can answer the questions, we need to understand what happens in each of the four stages.

Market Development Stage

Introducing a new product into the market for the first time is fraught with unknowns and corresponding risks. If a demand for the product does not exist, it will have to be created during the initial market development stage. How long this takes depends upon the product's complexity, its degree of newness, the needs of the consumers, and the availability of competitive substitutes.

For example, the introduction of a proven cancer cure product would require no market development. The market already exists and there are no competitive products. The introduction of 3M's self-stick removable notes took longer. Although the product was unique, the consumers didn't know they needed it. A market for the product had to be created by using sales promotion and advertising techniques.

Most new products will either live or die during the market development stage. As a consumer, you only see the products that survive. The ones that didn't make it may have cost a company a lot of money, anguish, and maybe even a couple of careers during this experimental phase.

In today's tough economy, many disillusioned companies are adopting a "wait and see" policy before introducing new products. Being the first one on the block with a new product may not be the best strategy. Let the other

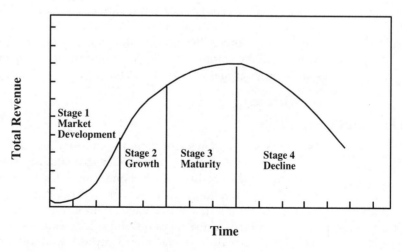

Exhibit 6-8. Product life cycle.

company be the pioneer and take the first arrow. If the idea works, others will jump in and quickly follow suit. For example, IBM was not the first company to offer personal computers to the home market. Apple and Tandy Corporation had PCs in the market, years before IBM. When IBM finally decided to "have one too," they sold a billion dollars of their PCs the first year they were introduced. Of course, IBM's name helped immensely during the introduction phase.

Market Growth Stage

A gradual and continuous rise in the sales curve must occur in the market development stage to assure the survival of a product during this stage. At some point in this stage, a marked increase in consumer demand occurs. The sales boom is on and the product advances to the growth stage. At this point, potential "wait and see" competitors (like IBM) jump in.

The first companies that entered into the market growth stage with an effective sales program generally do quite well. Some will enter the market with carbon copies of the originator's product, while others will actually make design improvements to the original product.

An ensuing fight for consumer patronage develops and poses a new set of problems to all participating companies. Intense competitive battles erupt. Product originators are faced with the new challenge of convincing consumers to prefer their product over competitive products.

As the rate of consumer acceptance accelerates, it becomes easier for the competitors to find new distribution channels and retail outlets. New product orders flood the industry's factories. As we discussed earlier, manufacturing managers have an innate desire to run operations at full capacity. They can do it during the market growth stage.

Growth-stage profit opportunities are exaggerated, which in turn attracts more entrants into the market. The market is flooded with surplus products. All this forces the industry into inescapable price wars and sets the stage for fierce competition. If this sounds like what happened in the personal computer market with the advent of the PC clones, you got it!

Market Maturity Stage

As the market becomes saturated, the industry moves into the market maturity stage. It is marked by the fact that almost everybody who originally wanted the product now has one. New sales are hard to come by and depend on population growth for new markets. Price competition becomes intense. All the players in this stage attempt to make finite differentiations in their product and services offerings. Extensive promotional campaigns are used to carry this message out to anybody who will listen.

Depending upon the product, new services and special promotional deals are often the clearest and most effective way to establish product differentiation. Advertising campaigns must be fine tuned to clearly communicate to mature consumers the specific product differentiation points. The maturity stage will continue as long as there is a continued level of product demand.

Market Decline Stage

The first decline in total product demand signals the start of the market decline stage. As demand declines, the excess production capacity that was built up during the maturity phase becomes a corporate anchor. It is very expensive to maintain idle production capacity. Only a few companies can weather the pending competitive storm that characterizes the decline stage. They all know it. However, most producers think that, with cunning management, they'll be one of the survivors. To hasten their competitors' exit from the industry, they initiate a variety of depressive tactics.

Prices and margins are severely cut. Mergers and buyouts are common. A few companies do weather the storm and survive. Production gets concentrated into the hands of the few survivors. And, life goes on in the corporate jungle.

Life-Cycle Planning

The first step in the planning cycle is to recognize that if your "perfect" product or service survives, it will pass through a life cycle of four stages. Your challenge will be to project the product's life-cycle profile. The time spent on this kind of advanced sales planning will reward you with big dividends later on. Initially, it will assure that a more rational approach is used in planning product introduction and promotional strategies.

A good product life-cycle plan can be used to create valuable lead time to make strategic and tactical moves as you travel through the life-cycle stages. The plan can be used to develop an orderly series of competitive moves. If properly implemented, it can extend a product's life cycle and support the process of phasing out obsolete products.

The duration of the four product stages is directly related to the uniqueness of the product and its features. That makes sense. If nobody has heard about your "better mousetrap," you've got an initial selling job ahead of you. The world has to be told about your product. Promotional forms such as coupons and discounts are common practices employed during the early stages. Consumers must clearly perceive the product as something they need and want.

The longer you're in the market development stage, the more it will cost you. Remember, you do not begin to realize significant profits until you enter the growth stage. Most products die before they ever get to the growth stage. You need to understand and be prepared to deal with this fact when you estimate the expected life of your product.

All these issues should be taken into consideration when you develop your life-cycle product plans. At a minimum, the plan would include worst-case and best-case scenarios covering the following product development issues:

1. Measure of the product's complexity level (e.g., high, medium, low).

2. Level of product's newness (e.g., never tried, similar to, and so on).

3. Estimate of the number of persons required to influence a buying decision (e.g., the more people required, the higher the introduction cost).

4. Degree to which product use will require consumers to shift away from their usual way of doing things to adopt the uniqueness of your product.

Pricing is another important consideration throughout all the stages. Do you set a high price to recoup your investment as quickly as possible, or do you set an artificially low price to discourage potential competitors and attract consumers? The answer assumes you know what the ultimate price should be. The price should include all present and planned production and capital cost. It should also include the full recovery of all research, development, and market introduction cost.

Now, armed with the total cost of your product, what price should you use when you introduce the product? You should stand firm on the price you need to recover all cost plus a profit. You don't cut it and you don't raise prices in the initial introductory stage. One of the hurdles that you must clear in this stage is the price hurdle. You must determine if consumers are willing to pay the price that you must ultimately get for your product to make a profit.

The fact that everybody will buy it at a 50 percent discount doesn't tell you anything if you can't make money at the discounted price. If consumers are not willing to pay the full price, then ask yourself the hard question: Can you make any money on this product? If the answer is "no," you kill the product, and move on to the next corporate game.

Summary and Conclusions

The slogan we adopted for this chapter is "where the rubber meets the road." No organization can survive without having a viable sales organization and a dynamic sales plan that is fully integrated throughout the corporation. An accurate sales plan sets the tone for establishing the integrity of the corporate strategic plan.

At the start of the chapter, we built the first part of the sales plan by using historical data derived from the accounting and financial systems. From our analysis of the data, we questioned the accuracy of previous sales forecasts.

In our search to find out what went wrong, we turned to our economics department for some answers. Historical product demand data were added to our sales plan. Our analysis of the economic data showed there was a softness in the demand for our products in all of the historical periods.

We wanted to know more about why the market was soft. We consulted our marketing department for some more answers. We analyzed market surveys and competitive price data. When we added these data to our sales plan, it told us that consumers were not buying our product because of their concerns about the state of the economy. They were particularly worried about high interest rates. Our price analysis showed that our product was competitively priced.

We were challenged with the task of developing a new sales forecast for the next sales period. The historical data that we now had access to told us a lot about what had happened in the past. But they begged the question about what could happen in the next sales period. We turned to multimedia current events to complete our analysis. In the end, we arrived at a new sales forecast that had considerably more integrity in it than any of our previous forecasts.

We built our sales plan using a process called the *consumer-satisfaction* process. It is based upon the premise that we must carefully analyze consumer needs and wants. Our revised sales forecast was based upon that analysis.

Our attention was then turned to an alternative process which we called the *goods-producing process.* In this process, a company produces all the products it can make, given its level of production capacity. The sales force is directed to go out into the market and sell whatever the company produced. The "love affair" that corporate America has had with the goods-producing process is changing rapidly. The reasons for the change are covered in several examples.

There was one key ingredient not covered in the scenario when we built our original sales plan. Product life-cycle planning was left out. To establish a baseline, we defined what product life-cycle planning is all about and why it's important. Next, we identified the four stages that all products pass through in their life cycles.

We showed you how to develop a product life-cycle plan. How this is accomplished within each of the four stages was covered in some detail. In the end, we talked about many of the tough issues and decisions that corporations must make in the product life-cycle planning arena.

Game Assignment and Instructions

When you load the game disk into your PC, the Main Menu for Month 4 should appear on your display if you elected to not close out the month as we suggested in the previous chapter. When you are done with Month 4, close out the month by selecting the Done option. The Main Menu for Month 5 will appear on your screen (Exhibit 6-9).

This is an important month and we would suggest that you read Chapter 7 first before you close out the month. It is the first month in the game when your company can start producing and sell cars. The new menu option (Order Manufacturing Resources) allows you to acquire all the resources needed to build cars.

Ordering Manufacturing Resources

Select the Order Manufacturing Resources option and we will show you how it works. Exhibit 6-10 should appear on your display. The left side of the menu shows you the current inventory of manufacturing assets your company either owns or rents. The right side of the menu shows the current purchase and rental prices for the various assets.

Orders for manufacturing assets are placed by entering order informa-

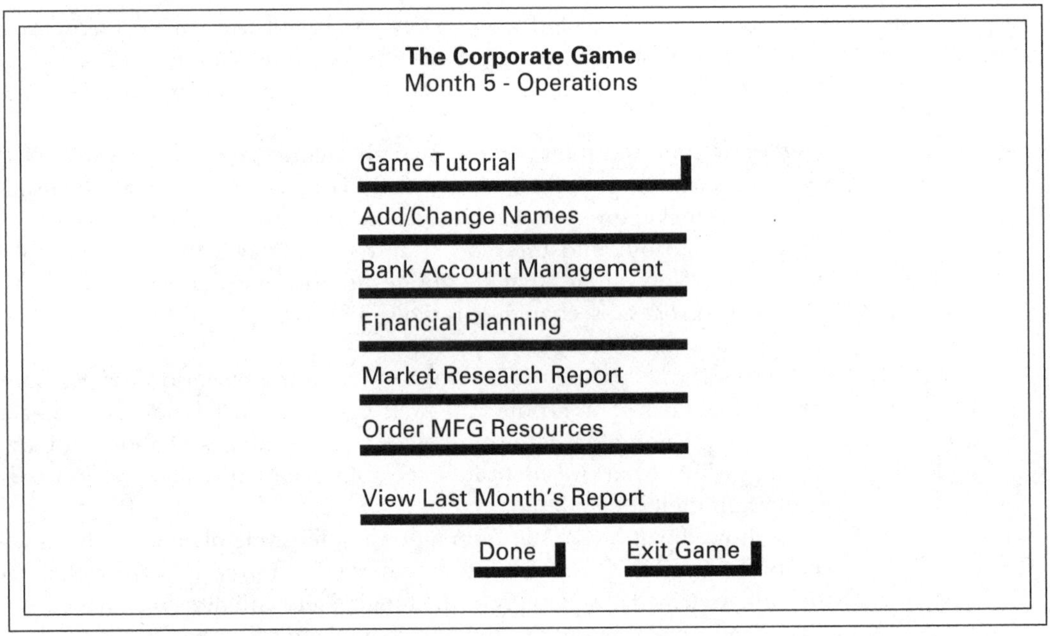

The Corporate Game
Month 5 - Operations

Game Tutorial

Add/Change Names

Bank Account Management

Financial Planning

Market Research Report

Order MFG Resources

View Last Month's Report

Done   Exit Game

Exhibit 6-9. Month 5—Operations menu.

The Corporate Game
Month 5 - Operations
Acquire Manufacturing Resources

– – – – Current Inventory – – – –   – – – – Purchase Resources – – – –

	# OWNED	# RENTED	# to BUY	BUY PRICE	# to RENT	RENTAL PER MONTH
Type-A Machine	0	0	0	$ 275,000	0	$ 28,645
Type-B Machine	0	0	0	$ 325,000	0	$ 32,500
Type-C Machine	0	0	0	$ 375,000	0	$ 43,750
Type-D Machine	0	0	0	$ 975,000	0	$ 121,875
Floor Space (1000s sq ft)	0	0	0	$ 12,500	0	$ 1,500

	Hired	Add	Per Month	Cancel
Work Crews	0	0	$ 2,500	
	Owned	Buy	Per Ton	Done
Tons of Steel	0	0	$ 1,200	
	Owned	Buy	Per Part	Enter
Parts	0	0	$ 10	

Exhibit 6-10. Month 5—Manufacturing resources menu.

tion on the left side of the menu. For example, you can select one of four types of machines (Types A, B, C, or D) to either purchase or rent. If you enter a "1" in the rent column of machine Type A, you will have rented one Type A machine. You buy or rent factory space by using the same approach.

Raw materials (i.e., steel and electronic parts) are purchased by entering the order quantity in the appropriate field. Labor crews are hired by entering the number of crews you want to hire. There are 100 labor-hours per month in each crew you hire. All orders that you enter into the Order Manufacturing Resources menu become firm or final orders when you exit and update the month.

Tutorial

The Tutorial includes a production control table that you should review to determine the number of manufacturing resources you'll need to build different mixes of cars (Exhibit 6-11).

As you page down through the Tutorial, you will come across a business newspaper called *The Fast Street Journal* (Exhibit 6-12).

It is published on the first day of the month (i.e., May 1) and includes all kinds of business, economic, and competitive information about the game's business world. Use it to fine tune your corporate strategies.

The Corporate Game

Production Requirement	Economy Sedan	Midsize Sedan	Luxury Sedan
Steel (tons/car)	1.0	2.0	3.0
Parts per Car	750	1,000	1,500
A-Type Machine Capacity	20	15	16
B-Type Machine Capacity	40	30	24
C-Type Machine Capacity	50	37	40
D-Type Machine Capacity	80	60	64

Three (3) labor crews required to run one A-Type machine
Nine (9) labor crews required to run one B-Type machine
Nine (9) labor crews required to run one C-Type machine
Twelve (12) labor crews required to run one D-Type machine
One labor crew is equal to 100 hours at $25/hr.
One A-Type machine requires 75,000 square feet of factory space.
One B-Type machine requires 125,000 square feet of factory space.
One C-Type machine requires 100,000 square feet of factory space.
One D-Type machine requires 225,000 square feet of factory space.

F2 Print   F3 Return

Exhibit 6-11. Production requirements menu.

The Corporate Game
The Fast Street Journal

May 1st Edition

Steel Makers Trim Loses

For the steelmakers, the prospect of continued price discounting dims
hope for a third or fourth quarter return to profitability. "There has never
been a price like there is today", complained one marketing executive.

Major Bank Lifts the Prime Rate 1% to 11%

The Great American Bank move comes amid forecasts that interest rates will
continue to increase. The nation's other major banks are likely to follow.

Detroit

Automakers plan to boost output 3% this month. The Demon Auto Company
announced that it will close its Atlanta assembly plant for the next two weeks
to adjust inventories. The plant assembles economy sedans.

F2 Print   F3 Return

Exhibit 6-12. *The Fast Street Journal* example.

Producing Cars

You must tell the game how many cars you want to produce, based upon the level of manufacturing resources you acquire. You do this by selecting the Financial Planning option from the Main Menu. The number you enter in the Cars to Make column is what the Game assumes you want to produce (Exhibit 6-13).

If you enter more cars than you have resources to produce, the game will proportionately allocate your production request down to a production level that matches your available resources. If you do not have a sufficient quantity of a critical resource (i.e., no steel), then you will not be able to produce any cars.

Selling Cars

You must also tell the game how many cars you want to sell and the minimum sales price you will accept for each model offered. You do this by selecting the Financial Planning option from the Main Menu. The number you enter in the Cars to Sell column is what the game assumes you want to sell (Exhibit 6-14).

The Corporate Game
Month 5 - Operations
FINANCIAL PLAN & MASTER BUDGET

Type of Car	# Cars to Make	Cost to Produce	# Cars to Sell	Minimum Sell. Price
Economy	10	$120,000	0	$ 0
Midsize	15	$130,000	0	$ 0
Luxury	5	$ 80,000	0	$ 0

Estimates of Month End Account Balances

CHECKING	SAVINGS	ACCTs PAYABLE	NOTEs PAYABLE
$ 0	$ 0	$ 0	$ 0

Estimate the value of your:

FLOOR SPACE	PLANT EQUIPMENT	RAW MATERIALs	INTEREST INCOME
$ 0	$ 0	$ 0	$ 0

NEW--------INVENTORY

'OTHER' INCOME	COST	SIZE	DONE	ENTER
$ 0	$ 0	0		

Exhibit 6-13. Month 5—Financial planning menu.

<table>
<tr><th colspan="5">The Corporate Game
Month 5 - Operations
FINANCIAL PLAN & MASTER BUDGET</th></tr>
</table>

Type of Car	# Cars to Make	Cost to Produce	# Cars to Sell	Minimum Sell. Price
Economy	10	$120,000	5	$ 14,000
Midsize	15	$130,000	10	$ 16,000
Luxury	5	$ 80,000	5	$ 20,000

Estimates of Month End Account Balances

CHECKING	SAVINGS	ACCTs PAYABLE	NOTEs PAYABLE
$ 0	$ 0	$ 0	$ 0

Estimate the value of your:

FLOOR SPACE	PLANT EQUIPMENT	RAW MATERIALs	INTEREST INCOME
$ 0	$ 0	$ 0	$ 0

NEW--------INVENTORY

'OTHER' INCOME	COST	SIZE	DONE	ENTER
$ 0	$ 0	0		

Exhibit 6-14. Month 5—Financial planning menu with entries.

Be careful with this option because mistakes can be costly to your company. For example, let's say that you enter 10 as the number of economy cars that you want to sell but you forget to enter a sales price for economy cars. The game will assume that you literally want to give 10 economy cars away to charity. That is exactly what will happen, and your ending inventory for economy cars will be reduced by 10 cars.

Market-Research Report

If you elected to order a market-research report last month, you can view or print the report this month. Select the Market-Research Report option from the Main Menu. The submenu in Exhibit 6-15 will appear on your display.

Assuming that you ordered the report, the Review Current Report option will appear on your display. Select this option to view or print the report. You can also order the report for next month by selecting one of the two payment options.

```
┌─────────────────────────────────────────────────────┐
│ ┌───────────────────────────────────────────────┐   │
│ │              The Corporate Game                │   │
│ │             Month 5 - Operations               │   │
│ │                                                │   │
│ │                                                │   │
│ │            Review Current Report ▉             │   │
│ │                                                │   │
│ │         Next month's Market Research Report    │   │
│ │         may be purchased for $50,000           │   │
│ │                                                │   │
│ │            ( )  Purchase from Checking Account │   │
│ │            ( )  Charge to Accounts Payable     │   │
│ │            ( )  Cancel order request           │   │
│ │                                                │   │
│ │                                                │   │
│ │            Done ▉          Enter ▉             │   │
│ │                                                │   │
│ └───────────────────────────────────────────────┘   │
└─────────────────────────────────────────────────────┘
```

Exhibit 6-15. Month 5—Market-research review report.

Final Recommendation

Again, we recommend that you exit this month *without* updating the files for Month 5. Read Chapter 7 before you complete and close out Month 5. The chapters include numerous examples and advice on how to acquire and use manufacturing resources.

7

Controlling the Production Process

Covering Your Assets

Production control is one of the least understood and least appreciated business disciplines on the list. Most executives don't understand it. As a result, they delegate the production responsibilities down to a lower level in the management chain.

IBM's Tom Watson, Jr., was one of the exceptions. He started his career as a salesman of sewing machines, pianos, and organs. He had no production and manufacturing background and, indeed, little formal education. By the time he joined IBM under the watchful eye of his father, he understood the importance of production control and its influence on cost and product development.

When the first transistors came out in the 1950s, Watson reasoned that they would be a cost-effective replacement for the vacuum tubes that were used in IBM's computers. As an added benefit, the transistor replacements would dramatically increase the processing speed of computers. Watson made the decision to move IBM into the transistor age. This decision alone moved IBM's production cycle ten years ahead of its nearest competitors.

Your success will, in part, depend upon your understanding and appreciation of production control. A successful production plan depends on accurate product data and consumer demand projections from the company's economic, marketing, and sales departments. All the strategic plans come together in the production plan.

Production influences cost more than any other function in the corporation. Fortunes are made or lost based upon the accuracy of production esti-mates. How you control the production process to assure the success of your company is what production control is all about. You have just hired Susan, your director of production. She knows how the production process works. You plan to meet with Susan later to discuss how production control will fit into your strategic plan. You want to learn everything you can about production control before the meeting.

Production Control Objectives

The primary objective of production control is to maximize the efficient use of the company's production facilities to produce high-quality products at a competitive price. Production control manages the orderly movement of goods through the entire manufacturing cycle. There are three steps in the production control process: (1) routing, (2) scheduling, and (3) dis-patching. Routing and scheduling are the planning steps. Dispatching is the action step. Scheduling determines when the work is to be done. It sets the timing for when specified products will be produced.

Routing determines how the work will be done to produce products. Every detail of how a product is to be made is covered in the routing proc-ess. It includes designating the machines and materials used to manufac-ture the product.

The dispatching function issues production orders at the correct time, a function similar to dispatching trains at a railroad station. Dispatching starts by notifying the production facilities when materials and labor are needed to support the production schedule.

Scheduling, routing, and dispatch may at times function independently of each other, but they all depend on one another. A breakdown in any one function or step can seriously disrupt the entire production control process.

For example, if production scheduling wants to produce ten (10) auto-mobiles and dispatch fails to provide the manufacturing materials at the right time, the entire manufacturing process comes to a complete halt. Any disruptions that occur in production can be very costly. Not only will your company lose profits from the car that it could not produce and sell, but it may incur added expense. Idle resources such as labor crews that are "standing around" waiting for materials to arrive are an example of added expenses.

Production Costs

One of the most telling signs of a company's financial health is its competi-tive cost position. Cost comparisons are particularly important in industries where intense price competition exists. The low-cost producers usually con-trol the industry. Even in industries where product differentiation exists, competing companies have to keep their cost in line with rivals or risk losing their competitive advantage. The cost to produce comparable products will vary among competitors. Some of the reasons for cost disparities are listed as follows:

- There are differences in the prices paid to suppliers for common items such as raw materials, parts, utilities, and capital leases.

- There are differences in cost based upon the technology levels used and the age of a company's plant and equipment. The technology issue is concerned with the overall efficiency of a plant. Older plants tend to be less efficient. However, older plants may enjoy lower depreciation expense levels than their newer rivals.

- Economies of scale may contribute to lower cost. Different operating costs are associated with different production volumes, plant sizes, overhead expenses, and administrative and development costs. We'll talk more about economies of scale later in the chapter.

- There are differences in marketing, sales, and advertising cost. These services are tailored to the unique requirements of a company.

- Distribution cost and retail markup policies differ between competitors. Distribution costs include the cost of transporting products to retail distribution points. Retail markup covers price breaks offered by different companies.

Given the numerous reasons for cost variances between companies, your company must be on the "cost alert" to survive. You need to know what the cost categories are and how to control them. You know your competition is concerned about the same costs as you are. To put all the costs into perspective, we have built a cost activity chart (see Exhibit 7-1). It identifies major cost categories and the primary expenses contributing to each category.

The exhibit includes a buildup of costs that adds value at each stage of the product's production cycle. Every cost function must pay for itself by adding value to the product. In the competitive world, cost functions must either add value to the end product or be eliminated. Value-added examples include processes that increase the product's price, lower manufacturing cost, or improve product quality.

Variable Cost

There are two types of costs that are an integral part of the production process: (1) variable costs and (2) fixed costs. Fixed costs are relatively stable over time and do not change with the level of production output. Variable costs change with the level of production output.

Let's assume your company buys a $50 battery from a supplier for each

Purchasing and Material Planning	Production and Manufacturing	Sales and Marketing	Support Services	Wholesale, Distribution, and Retail
Raw materials	Facilities and equipment	Sales force operation	Accounting and finance	Distributors
Component parts	Production processing	Advertising and promotion	Legal services	Wholesalers
Energy	Assembly and packaging	Market research	Public relations	Dealers
Inbound shipping	Labor and supervision	Dealer relations	Executive and management	
Materials handling	Maintenance	Order processing		
	Product design	Service Department		
	Quality control			
	Inventory management			

Exhibit 7-1. Corporate operations cost chain.

car it produces. The total variable cost of batteries would be $50 times the number of cars produced. The variable cost-behavior for batteries is shown graphically in Exhibit 7-2. Other variable-cost examples include most materials and parts, direct labor, and sales commissions.

Fixed Costs

Fixed costs are sometimes called *period costs* because they are related to the passage of time. Examples include rent, lease payments, plant, and equipment payments which are typically paid monthly. The fixed-cost behavior for plant and equipment is shown graphically in Exhibit 7-3. Fixed cost remains the same as the quantity of cars produced increases.

Marginal fixed cost is an important characteristic of fixed cost. If we divide fixed cost by various production quantities, we get a very different cost relationship than what we had before. We used the numbers from Exhibit 7-3 to build Exhibit 7-4.

Marginal fixed cost decreases in direct proportion to increases in the quantities produced. This relationship can result in significant cost savings for large producers. It also forms the basis for economies of scale. The larger the scale of an operation, the lower are its marginal fixed costs. We can show this relationship in Exhibit 7-5.

The fixed-cost curve slopes down and to the right. As production output

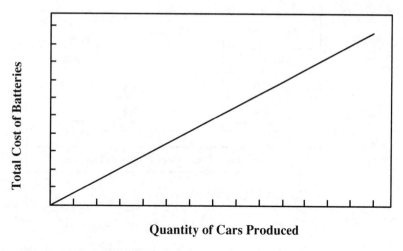

Quantity of Cars Produced

Exhibit 7-2. Variable cost of batteries.

increases, fixed cost per unit decreases. The production process is experiencing the advantages of economies of scale.

Total Costs

Total costs are calculated by adding fixed costs to variable costs. The combined fixed and variable costs are plotted in Exhibit 7-6. If total revenues exceed total costs, then a profit is made. Or conversely, if total revenues fall below total cost, the company is in a loss position.

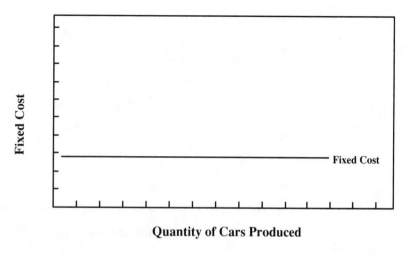

Quantity of Cars Produced

Exhibit 7-3. Fixed cost of building and equipment.

Fixed Cost	Units Produced	Marginal Fixed Cost
$10,000	1	$10,000
$10,000	2	$5,000
$10,000	3	$3,333
$10,000	4	$2,500
Marginal Fixed Cost = Fixed Cost/Units Produced		

Exhibit 7-4. Marginal fixed cost.

Production managers are constantly faced with decisions about what to produce based upon selling prices and variable and fixed costs. They must decide how to acquire and use resources economically to meet corporate profit objectives. Inadequate costs and sales forecasts will cause undesirable or even disastrous results to the company's profits.

Cost can change at any moment in time. Therefore, production decisions are often made and often change over short time periods. How many cars should we manufacture this month? Should we buy just enough materials to cover our production schedule for the month? These questions are examples of short-term decisions affecting variable costs. Decisions to buy or rent a factory or capital equipment are long-term in nature. Once long-term fixed-cost decisions are made, they become difficult to change quickly.

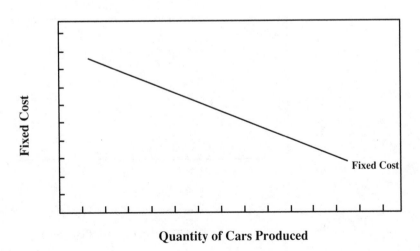

Exhibit 7-5. Changes in marginal fixed cost when output changes.

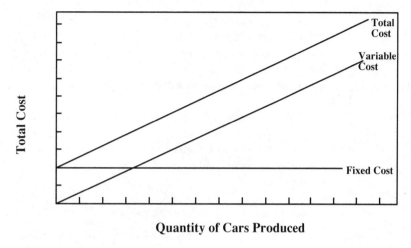

Exhibit 7-6. Total cost of cars.

The Breakeven Point

All corporations want to make money. To do so, they must exceed their company's breakeven point. The breakeven point is the point in the production cycle where total revenues equal total costs. It is the point where zero profits and losses are incurred.

Total revenue depends on consumer demand and the prices consumers are willing to pay for a product. Total costs vary with the number of units produced. Thus, the breakeven point varies with the number and cost of units produced and the number and price of units sold. We can show this relationship in Exhibit 7-7.

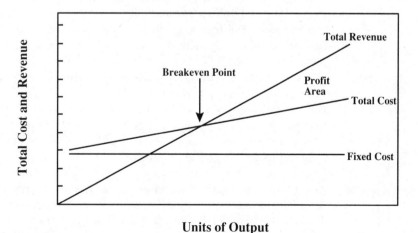

Exhibit 7-7. Breakeven chart.

Profits are made when you move above the breakeven point. Losses are incurred when you move below the breakeven point. The objective of performing a breakeven analysis is to find the optimum profit point. This is the point at which profits will be the highest. To determine the location of this point, all costs associated with various levels of demand and prices must be considered.

To illustrate the breakeven point, suppose you plan to sell economy cars for $19,000 each. Your variable cost per car is $15,000. You have decided to rent your factory space and equipment at a total fixed cost of $20,000. How many cars must be sold to break even? The solution to the problem is calculated as follows:

$$\text{Let X} = \text{Number of cars to be sold to break even}$$

$$= (\text{Fixed cost}) / (\text{Price} - \text{Variable cost})$$

$$= (\$20,000) / (\$19,000 - \$15,000)$$

$$= (\$20,000) / (\$4,000)$$

$$= 5 \text{ cars}$$

Contribution to Margin

Contribution to margin is the excess of sales over variable costs. In the previous example, each car sold would generate a contribution to margin of $4000 ($19,000 − $15,000). Hence, the sale of five cars contributed $20,000 ($4000 × 5) of margin to the company, which was exactly what we needed to cover our fixed expenses and break even.

Contribution to margin is used frequently in this chapter. It may be expressed in total dollars, production units, sales units, or as a percentage. In our example, the total contribution was five cars multiplied by $4000, or $20,000. The unit contribution was $4000 per car, and the percentage contribution was $4000 divided by $19,000, or 21 percent.

The contribution percentage is used in cost-volume-profit analysis where breakeven results are expressed in dollars instead of units. In the example, the breakeven point in sales dollars can be easily computed by multiplying five cars by the $19,000 sales price to obtain $95,000. However, the breakeven point may also be obtained by using another equation.

Recall from our earlier discussion that the breakeven point is the point where profits are zero. We know our company would prefer to make a profit rather than just break even. How can we determine the total contribution in units and dollars we would require to cover our costs and make a profit? The profit percentage must be consistent with the company's 20 percent profit goal. Our same basic equation can be used to find the answer if we add desired profits to our original formula (see Exhibit 7-8).

Cars Produced	Car Sales Price	Variable Cost/Car	Fixed Cost/Car	Profit/Car	Total Profits
20	$9,000	$5,000	$1,000	$3,000	$60,000
40	$9,000	$5,000	$500	$3,500	$140,000
50	$9,000	$5,000	$400	$3,600	$180,000
80	$9,000	$5,000	$250	$3,750	$300,000

Exhibit 7-8. Cost and profit analysis per car.

Production Control and Profits

The control of production cost can have a significant effect on corporate profits. As we have seen, production costs are affected by many factors. Product pricing, the mix of products produced, and the efficient use of production resources such as labor and equipment are examples of factors influencing production cost.

Breakeven analyses are based on assumptions made about the estimated levels of sales, cost, and volume. A change in any one estimate will alter the breakeven point. If the contribution to margin is known, the change in profits resulting from a change in sales or production volumes is easy to calculate.

Exhibit 7-9 shows what happens to profits when production volumes change. We could have changed any one or all the variables affecting contribution to margin to calculate the subsequent impact on profits. This con-

	4 Cars Sold	5 Cars Sold	9 Cars Sold
Total Sales	$36,000	$45,000	$81,000
Less: Total Variable Cost	($20,000)	($25,000)	($45,000)
Contribution to Margin	$16,000	$20,000	$36,000
Less: Total Fixed Cost	($20,000)	($20,000)	($20,000)
Total Profit (Loss)	($4,000)	$0	$16,000

Exhibit 7-9. Profits resulting from changes in sales volume.

tribution concept is useful for analyzing problems or developing corporate production strategies.

For example, if your company is operating at a loss, the contribution percent will indicate how much the loss will either increase or decrease with each dollar change in one or more of the variables. A high contribution percent will cause greater profits than a smaller percent as sales dollars increase above the breakeven point. The opposite holds when sales volume falls below the breakeven point where the higher the percent, the greater the losses as sales volume decrease.

Changes in Variable Costs

Both the contribution to margin and the breakeven point are altered by changes in the variable costs. In the earlier examples, if the cost of labor went up by $2000 per car, variable cost would increase from $15,000 to $17,000 and the contribution to margin per car would fall from $4000 to $2000. The breakeven point increases from five to ten cars. Had our cost decreased from $5000 to $4000, our contribution would have increased to $5000 per car, giving us a new breakeven point of four cars.

Variable costs are subject to various degrees of control at different volumes of production. When the automobile business is booming, you may become preoccupied with producing all the cars that you can at all costs. You know that each car produced will generate a profit. When business is slack, you may want to "ride herd on" all costs.

As we have stated before, the real-world economy and the economy that has been built into the game are not very forgiving. Sudden decreases in sales volumes are often accompanied by increases in selling expenses and lower selling prices. To illustrate the point, let's examine all the variable-cost components it takes to produce economy cars. There are two variable-cost elements to consider: (1) labor and (2) materials. Exhibit 7-10 shows the number of labor-hours required to produce cars at various volumes.

Two important concepts are illustrated in Exhibit 7-10. First, there is a point where no additional cars can be produced, regardless of how much extra labor is added. In fact, car production actually falls when labor is added. This happened when we went from 70,000 to 80,000 labor-hours. Car production fell from 575 to 525 units.

This concept is called the *law of diminishing marginal return*. The law states that if equal increments of an input (e.g., labor-hours) are added, and the quantities of other inputs (e.g., production equipment) are held constant, then the resulting output (e.g., cars produced) will decrease at some point. If your company has only acquired enough machines to manufacture 575 cars, then that will be all the cars that you can produce, regardless of how much labor you add.

If your factory will only accommodate a labor crew of 70 workers, produc-

Labor Hours	Cars Produced	Number Hrs/Car	Labor Cost/Car	Marginal Productivity
10,000	100	100	$2,500	0
20,000	220	91	$2,275	120
30,000	340	88	$2,200	120
40,000	420	95	$2,375	80
50,000	500	100	$2,500	80
60,000	575	104	$2,600	75
70,000	575	121	$3,025	0
80,000	525	152	$3,800	(50)
90,000	490	184	$4,600	(35)
Note: Labor costs are $25/hour				

Exhibit 7-10. Marginal productivity of labor to produce cars.

tion output can diminish when additional labor is added. Workers, feeling crowded, would begin to get in each other's way, disrupting production.

The second point illustrated in Exhibit 7-10 is called the *marginal productivity of labor.* Different efficiency levels of labor are reached at different volumes of production. We determined that 10,000 labor-hours were required to produce 100 cars (100 hours per car). If we know that the hourly rate for labor is $25, we can calculate the cost of labor per car at this production level (100 hours × $25 = $2500). As production increases, we begin to realize improved efficiencies from our labor force. There is perhaps less idle time, and our equipment is more fully utilized. Our average labor cost per car drops accordingly to its most efficient productivity point (88 hours per car).

The marginal productivity tells us the number of additional cars we can produce each time one additional component of labor is added. We know 100 cars can be produced with 10,000 hours of labor. If we use 20,000 hours of labor, 220 cars can be produced, which would represent a marginal productivity increase of 120 cars (220 − 100 = 120). When the marginal product becomes zero, we have reached the point of diminishing returns.

Material costs are another example of variable cost. The quantities of materials used to manufacture cars change in direct proportion to production volumes. If 3 tons of steel are required to manufacture one car, then 6 tons are required to make two cars. However, production volume can influence the unit cost of material. Suppliers of raw materials are often willing to provide price concessions to companies who buy materials in large quantities. For example, the discounted cost for steel is shown in Exhibit 7-11 and graphically illustrated in Exhibit 7-12.

Our cost per ton of steel will continue to decline if we order up to 60 tons. Beyond this point, the steel mills will not allow further price concessions. We can assume that at 60 tons, the mills have reached their break-even point. Any further reductions in unit prices would result in a loss for the steel mills.

Now, let's assume you are an astute production manager. You know it takes 1.5 tons of steel to make one economy car. You can expand the steel price exhibit to develop another exhibit showing the variable cost of steel required to produce economy cars at different volume discount prices (Exhibit 7-13).

We can now estimate variable costs for any predetermined production run by using the data from Exhibit 7-13. Our example shows what it would cost to manufacture 100 economy cars.

If you are playing the PC side of *The Corporate Game*, you can order raw materials at different price and order quantities. To simplify the material requirements process, there are only two categories of materials used to construct a car: (1) steel and (2) electronic parts. Material discount tables similar to the ones shown here are displayed in the game menus.

Order Quantity (tons)	Cost/Ton
1-10	$500
11-20	$450
21-30	$425
31-40	$410
41-50	$405
51-60	$400
over 60	$400

Exhibit 7-11. Current price quotes for steel.

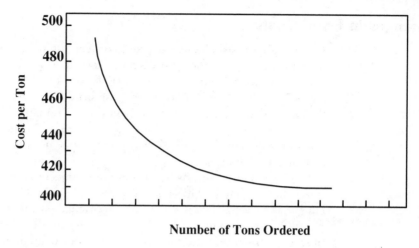

Exhibit 7-12. Price per ton of steel.

Cars Produced	Steel Cost/Ton	Steel Cost/Car	Total Steel Cost
4	$500	$1,500	$6,000
8	$450	$1,350	$10,800
12	$425	$1,275	$15,300
16	$410	$1,030	$19,680
20	$405	$1,215	$24,300
24	$400	$1,200	$28,800
28	$400	$1,200	$33,600
Note: Three tons of steel required per car			

Exhibit 7-13. Cost of steel at different car production volumes.

Changes in Fixed Costs

Like variable costs, changes in fixed cost can alter the breakeven point. If we return to the economy car example, look at what happens to the break-even point when fixed costs change (Exhibit 7-14). If the rental cost of the factory increased by $4000, fixed cost would increase from $20,000 to $24,000. Assume variable costs and sales prices remain unchanged.

The breakeven point would increase from 5 to 6 cars. Our original formula for calculating the breakeven point can be used to show the results of a change in fixed costs.

Unlike variable costs, fixed costs are not subject to control when production volumes change. Let's assume you decide to build a manufacturing facility that costs $24,000 per month in mortgage payments. The new facility has sufficient capacity to produce 80 cars per month. When the automobile business is booming, and you are running your plant at maximum capacity, you have nothing to worry about. You would be producing cars at the lowest fixed cost possible. This example assumes that you can sell every car you produce at a profit (80 cars/month).

Suppose the economy takes a sudden turn for the worse. There is high unemployment which causes consumers to cut back on their demands for new cars. Your company can now only sell 40 cars per month. As we have seen from our previous discussion, you can take immediate steps to reduce your variable costs. But what happens to your fixed costs? Fixed costs re-

---

Sales Price = $19.000/car

Variable Cost = $15,000

Fixed Cost before Increase = $20,000

Fixed Cost after Increase = $24,000

Breakeven Point Calculation = Fixed Cost/Sales Price - Variable Cost

Breakeven Point before Increase = $20,000/$4,000

= 5 cars

Breakeven Point after Increase = $24,000/$4,000

= 6 cars

Exhibit 7-14. Breakeven analysis when fixed costs change.

main unchanged at $24,000 per month. The mortgage payment on your plant is due each month. You cannot change the physical size of the plant to a smaller, less expensive facility to accommodate the lower production volumes. This scenario is illustrated in Exhibit 7-15.

Production or output in car units has decreased from Point *B* to Point *A* in the exhibit. As a result, we move up the fixed-cost curve to the higher fixed cost per unit point. Two important fixed-cost characteristics are illustrated. First, total fixed costs do not change when we change production volumes. However, as we showed in our earlier discussions, fixed costs per car change dramatically when production volumes change. Fixed costs per car decrease as production volumes increase.

This makes sense because we have built a plant capable of producing a maximum of 80 cars per month. If we produce 80 cars, each car produced absorbs the least amount of fixed costs possible ($20,000/80 cars = $250/car). This particular characteristic of fixed costs directly affects profits and assumes that there are no changes in the sales price or variable costs.

You could choose to play the game by using a conservative approach. You could develop a manufacturing strategy that minimizes most risks. For example, you may conclude that the risks of building a large plant with an 80-car production capacity is too risky for the profits you would realize on each car sold. Hence, you may decide to build a smaller plant with a 40-car production capacity and reduce total fixed costs and risk.

However, this strategy may ignore the total profit objectives of the company. The Total Profits column in Exhibit 7-8 indicates that up to $300,000 in profits can be generated when 80 cars are produced. You need to con-

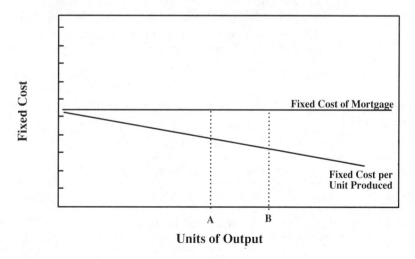

Exhibit 7-15. Mortgage cost when output changes.

Machine Type	Car Production Capacity	Factory Square Ft Required	Factory Rent per Month	Crew Size
A	20	5,000	$10,000	40
B	40	7,000	$11,000	75
C	80	10,000	$15,000	80
D	80	10,000	$15,000	80

Exhibit 7-16. Alternate-machine economy-car production capacities.

sider both the marginal profit you can make from each car produced and the total profits you can realize when you develop profit and risk strategies.

There are two components of fixed cost that have been built into the game: (1) the monthly payment for your factory, and (2) monthly rent payments for capital equipment. The combination of equipment and the size of the plant are the key factors for determining plant capacities. The alternate production capacities of mixing plant floor space with equipment and crew size per machine are shown in Exhibit 7-16.

Maximizing Profits

Let's assume that you want to use breakeven analysis to maximize total profits. Total profits (TP) will be the amount left over after you deduct total fixed and variable cost. Your marketing department has just completed a sales survey of economy cars and has sent the results to you in Exhibit 7-17.

Price per Car	Cars Sold	Total Fixed Cost	Total Variable Cost	Total Cost	Total Sales	Total Profit
$12,000	32	$180,000	$192,000	$372,000	$384,000	$12,000
$15,000	25	$180,000	$150,000	$330,000	$375,000	$45,000
$17,000	21	$180,000	$126,000	$306,000	$357,000	$51,000
$19,000	17	$180,000	$102,000	$282,000	$323,000	$41,000

Exhibit 7-17. Total profit at different sales volumes and prices.

You want to determine the price that will maximize your profits. The exhibit shows that you would maximize profits if you charged $17,000 for every economy car sold.

Profit-maximization analysis is used by production management to compare the effect of different prices and costs on profits. The comparison helps establish product pricing strategies. As we have seen, pricing decisions are influenced by many other factors including competitive conditions. All these factors must be taken into account when you set your prices.

The Strategic Production Plan

You've set up a meeting with your production director, Susan, to discuss how production fits into your strategic corporate plan. You're comfortable with the accuracy and integrity of your sales plan. It's been reviewed by your economics, marketing, and sales departments. The sales price for each car model will assure you of achieving a 20 percent profit. If you meet your profit objective, you're going to be in "bonus city" come the end of the year.

Before you start counting all your money, you've decided to show the plan to Susan. After all, it's her department that is going to have to meet the "cost bogies" to get you that 20 percent profit margin. As scheduled, Susan enters your office and announces herself with her favorite expression, "What's up, boss?" You like that. "Susan, I want you to take a look at the cost numbers in our strategic plan. Perform one of your sanity checks to make sure we can meet the cost numbers."

After a few minutes of contemplation, Susan comes back with an answer that sends you to the floor. "We cannot hold to those numbers. Our costs of materials have increased since those costs were originally put together. Let me show you what I am talking about." She hands you a graph (Exhibit 7-18) that brings to light the reality of the situation.

Susan continues with her explanation. "Based upon the revised numbers and the current cost of materials, the best we can make will be a 10 percent profit." The tan color in your face begins to change to white. You have already tipped your hand and told the board of directors that you were going to deliver a 20 percent profit margin. They all slapped you on the back, congratulated you, and said they would start working on your bonus compensation package. You're going to be "dead meat" if you have to go back and tell them that you made a slight error . . . like you missed profits by only 50 percent.

Susan is quick to pick up on your dilemma. "What's wrong, boss? Your face has turned white. I think I can solve our cost problem!" What would Ross Perot have said? "I'm all ears," you tell her. "If we implemented a JIT system, I know we could bring our cost back into line with our profit objectives."

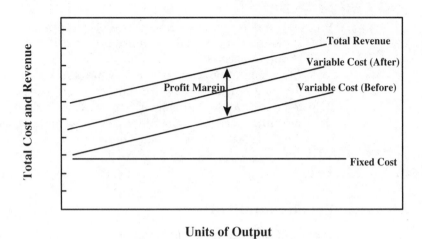

Exhibit 7-18. Affect of changes in variable cost on profit margins.

"What's a JIT system?" you ask. "It stands for *just-in-time*. It's a methodology that has been successfully used by companies around the world to dramatically reduce production and manufacturing costs. I have been working with the manufacturing staff to put together a JIT plan for your review. Why don't you read the material in the next chapter that covers the JIT concepts? We can meet with you at the end of the chapter to show you our plan." With a sigh of resignation, you agree. "You're looking better, boss." Susan leaves your office.

Summary and Conclusions

In the real world, a manufacturing company is influenced by many factors. We emphasized the important role production plays in controlling total manufacturing cost. This led us into a discussion about variable and fixed costs. Each cost category expresses a different behavior when production quantities change. We showed how to derive total cost by adding variable and fixed costs together. From there, we combined total cost with total revenue to create a breakeven chart.

Techniques for tracking all production variables on a breakeven chart and using contribution to margin calculations were also illustrated. Several charts and computations were used to provide a framework for our analysis and as a technique for evaluating production performance. The following points were covered:

- A change in either the selling price or cost rates alters the breakeven point and the contribution to margin ratio.

- If the sales price is greater than the breakeven price, the contribution to margin ratio will be high, resulting in greater profits.

- A low contribution to margin ratio necessitates increases in the sales volume to obtain an increase in profits.

In the final analysis, we showed you how to pull all of the production control costs and concepts together to maximize corporate profits. All related production costs were recorded in an Exhibit and compared against various revenue options to determine the production point that generated maximum profits. Now, it's on to the next chapter to learn all you can about just-in-time manufacturing.

Game Assignments and Instructions

If you followed our advice in Chapter 6, you did not close out Month 5. When you load the game, the Main Menu for Month 5 should appear on your screen. Fine tune your Financial Plan with the car units you want to produce. Make sure you enter the car units that you want to sell by model and establish the minimum sales price that you will accept for each unit.

The instructions in the Game Tutorial will walk you through each of the decisions that you must make to conclude the play for this month. You will have the option to order equipment and raw materials, hire a labor force, and commit yourself to the size of factory that you want to build or rent. Refer to the tables included in the Tutorial and the Order Manufacturing Resources options to determine material order quantity, equipment and factory space, buy or rent requirements, and the number of work crews to hire.

All the financial and planning commitments that you will make in this chapter will go into effect when you close out the month. You have met with your senior management team to review your business strategies for the month. You know that whatever decisions you make today will go into effect tomorrow. Therefore, treat this game assignment as a test of everything that you have learned up to this point.

After you have entered your last decision into the computer, the game will move forward to Month 6 (Exhibit 7-19). The game assignments in the remaining seven sessions (June through December) are identical to what we have covered in Month 5. Make sure you read the *Fast Street Journals* that will appear in the Tutorial option of the Main Menu.

Each journal presents a variety of articles relating to the state of the economy for the designated month of play. As you read the articles, look for clues and hints about what could happen or has happened to the game's economy. Adjust your business strategies and plans accordingly to improve upon the success of your company.

If you order one or more of the machine types (i.e., Type A, B, C, or D)

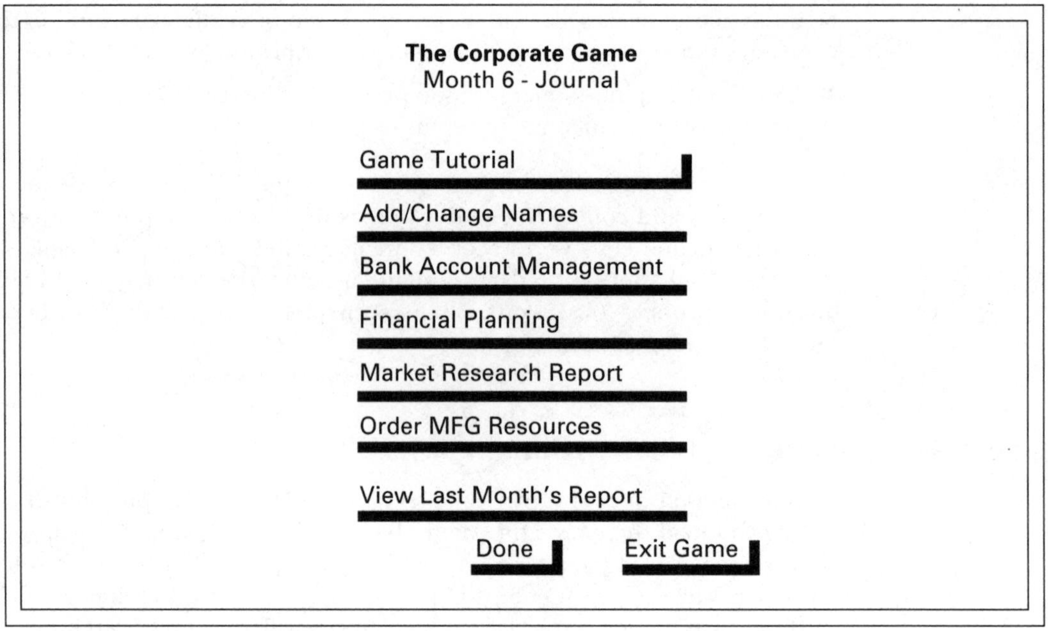

The Corporate Game
Month 6 - Journal

Game Tutorial ▌

Add/Change Names

Bank Account Management

Financial Planning

Market Research Report

Order MFG Resources

View Last Month's Report

Done ▌   Exit Game ▌

Exhibit 7-19. Month 6—Journal menu.

and you want to use the same machine to produce multiple models of cars, the machine's capacity will be allocated to accommodate your production mix. Exhibit 7-20 provides you with an example to show you how the game determines machine production capacities for the different car models.

When you are finished with Month 6, close the month out and complete the play for Month 7. Close Month 7 out and exit the game using the Exit and Update option. Return to the book and read Chapter 8. When you are finished with the chapter, complete Month 8 in the game. The remaining chapters and months are now in sequence (i.e., Chapter 9 = Month 9, and so on). Good luck!

Maximum Production Capacity = 20 economy cars or 20 production units
Production Units Required to Produce Each Model Using A-Type Machine
One Economy Car = 20/20 or 1 production unit
One Midsize Car = 20/15 or 1.33 production units
One Luxury Car = 20/16 or 1.25 production units
Capacity Check to Produce 8 Economy, 3 Midsize, and 4 Luxury Cars
Capacity Used Calculation = (Maximum machine capacity) - (Desired number of cars to produce)(Production units required to produce each car) = Remaining machine capacity
8 Economy Cars = 20 - (8)(1) = 20 - 8 = 12
3 Midsize Cars = 12 - (3)(1.33) = 12 - 4 = 8
4 Luxury Cars = 8 - (4)(1.25) = 8 - 5 = 3
Unused Machine Capacity = 3 production units

Exhibit 7-20. Calculations for determining car capacity production mix using one A-type machine.

8

Manufacturing
Just-in-Time

Just Enough to Win

Just-in-time (JIT) manufacturing is a popular manufacturing planning concept. In a JIT environment, you acquire just enough raw materials and manufacturing resources just-in-time to support a production plan driven by market demand. JIT avoids having excess raw materials or excess manufacturing resources to produce what is needed. It is used as a driver to reduce manufacturing cost to the lowest possible level without compromising quality.

The JIT concept is not new. In the early 1970s, a man by the name of Olie White came up with the original JIT concept. At the time, Olie called it manufacturing resource planning (MRP). As MRP evolved over the years, it became known as JIT. Both concepts were driven by the same efficient use of manufacturing resources principles.

This chapter covers JIT in detail and explains why this approach is critical to the corporation's strategic plan. If you're in the manufacturing business, you must have a good JIT system to survive in today's increasingly competitive market. We'll show you how to implement a JIT system. There are several examples included that demonstrate how JIT can be used to:

1. Improve the efficiency of the production process
2. Reduce material, labor, and capital costs
3. Streamline the entire manufacturing process
4. Integrate manufacturing into the other business processes

A number of books have been written about JIT. Many of them cover what you need to do to sell executive management on the idea. We do not include an executive sales pitch in this book. One only needs to look at what our international competitors have done to American industry to find out why JIT is so important. Our foreign competitors have become experts at using JIT to produce high-quality, competitively priced products. Although we Americans created JIT and we taught it in our colleges and universities, we didn't use it. Our JIT knowledge was exported overseas to our competitors so that they could use it to effectively compete against American companies. As a result, international competition from countries like Japan has taken over many of our key industries.

Many believe that "made in America" manufacturing has reached a critical turning point. Are we converting our manufacturing industry into a service industry just to survive? We can certainly see evidence of this in the huge trade deficits that we have built up over the years.

An Integrated Approach

As a company expands and contracts in dynamic marketing environments, operational adjustments are needed. Old requirements change and give way to new market-driven requirements. New procedures must be developed and added to the manufacturing process to remain competitive.

Historically, U.S. manufacturers have not integrated manufacturing changes into their strategic plans. This was in part owing to the fact that many manufacturers operated without strategic plans. Changes were implemented on a departmental basis, without regard to the company's overall strategic plan.

As a result, companies became embroiled in a patchwork evolution that begged for improvement. They missed hundreds of opportunities to significantly reduce their overall manufacturing cost. In the process, they failed to make any real contribution to their bottom line.

The primary objective of JIT is to improve the performance of all the functions of manufacturing. In the process, it relies heavily on the integration of the various business systems to make it all work. The common goal of JIT is to eliminate all corporate functions that burden the company with unnecessary cost, and to continuously improve upon the quality of manufactured products.

JIT Misconceptions

Historically, management has tended to ignore the concept and ideals of JIT manufacturing. Quite frankly, we don't know why, because JIT makes good business sense. Perhaps some of the apprehension is caused by misconceptions about the concept. One of the biggest misconceptions is that JIT is an inventory-control system. That makes it easy for corporate management to say "I don't know anything about inventory because I'm a marketing type. Let the inventory guys implement JIT. I like to fish. I'm off the hook."

Inventory control is an important part of JIT, but it is just one of many system components. At the least, JIT insists that you manage inventories at minimum levels to control costs.

The second misconception is that JIT is a grand quality-control program. Therefore, it belongs to the QC organization. Certainly, JIT emphasizes quality control throughout the program. But, like inventory control, producing defect-free products is only one part of the program.

Another misconception is thinking that the purpose of JIT is to force the material-handling function back to the suppliers. Suppliers are required to handle the inventory problems and reduce the corporation's material cost at the same time. For JIT to work, a team relationship must exist between the corporation and its suppliers. Forcing hardships on suppliers will not get the job done.

The term *trust* is used throughout JIT terminology. It's not the kind of trust where you say "I'm the buyer and you need my orders. Therefore, you have no choice but to trust me." It's the kind of trust you earn "the old-fashioned way" with honesty, openness, and respect. Mutual trust is vitally important to make JIT work.

Cost Advantages

There are a number of areas where JIT can reduce bottom-line costs. First, the cost savings are typically realized from improvements in material-handling procedures. Case study books are filled with documented testimonials about companies that have reduced material cost and handling by 30 to 50 percent using JIT techniques. Here are some examples to show how they did it:

1. They reduced the number of suppliers they dealt with by selecting their best performers. Their purchasing departments were able to negotiate better unit pricing by placing larger orders with fewer suppliers.

2. They reduced the number of service contracts by switching over to long-term contracts, which contractors typically prefer. They are willing to grant better terms and conditions for long-term contracts.

3. Certain companies were able to eliminate expediting, which resulted from a shortage of supplies owing to late deliveries. The few remaining suppliers now had a bigger piece of the action and were better motivated to meet committed delivery dates.

4. The need for receiving and inspection departments was eliminated. This was where the trust factor came into play. Again, because suppliers were highly motivated to keep long-term contracts, they conducted their own receiving and inspection functions (i.e., quality verification). Suppliers knew the company was conducting spot audits to keep everybody honest. But the spot audits cost a fraction of what they were previously paying for full receiving and inspection functions.

5. Material inventory levels were drastically reduced. As soon as a company became comfortable with the integrity of supplier-committed delivery times and dates, the need to maintain a backlog of emergency raw materials dropped dramatically. Inventory carrying charges were significantly reduced.

The second major area where cost savings can be realized is in the manufacturing area. It generally starts with a JIT goal to achieve a perfect production run with no quality defects. At the same time, manufacturing resources are used at 100 percent of capacity. When these levels are achieved, the savings come from a number of areas.

1. Products are easier to manufacture. They tend to have a longer life cycle.

2. The goal of 100 percent defect-free products reduces the cost of internal inspections.

3. Capital equipment is used at 100 percent of capacity, which increases the return on assets.

4. There is no loss of materials resulting from production mistakes or spoilage.

Achieving cost savings is an inherent philosophy in JIT. It assumes that no matter how perfect your manufacturing processes are today, there is always a better way to do it. Your 100 percent goal today will not be good enough tomorrow. As a result, JIT improvements become moving targets. That is what makes this part of *The Corporate Game* challenging. You are constantly implementing JIT to make it better.

There are indirect JIT benefits that help the sales and marketing organizations. When production schedules stabilize, salespeople can commit to delivery dates to customers with a high degree of confidence. In addition, when production steps are eliminated, such as final inspection, you shorten the lead time it takes to get products to customers.

Overall product cost reductions translate into more competitive prices. JIT price advantages can be used strategically to move the company to a new position on the supply curve. If competitors can't match your cost, your company dominates the market (Exhibit 8-1).

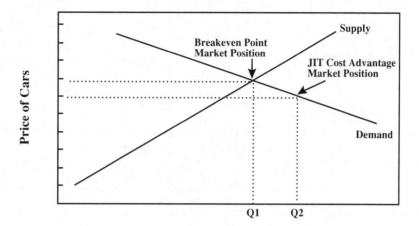

Quantity of Cars Supplied And Demanded

Exhibit 8-1. JIT market advantage.

How JIT Works

Before we proceed with some of the finer points of JIT, let's construct a manufacturing scenario. We'll build on the scenarios we established in the previous chapter to show how everything fits together.

In the previous chapter, we concluded that the consumers wanted economy cars. To arrive at this conclusion, we relied heavily on data that were fed to us by the accounting, finance, economics, and marketing departments. You're convinced that economy cars is the business to be in for now.

You've arranged a meeting with your directors of production (Susan) and manufacturing (Bill). You've told them of your intent to start building economy cars. You want to produce a high-quality economy car at the lowest price possible.

The meeting starts with Susan speaking first. "All our manufacturing equipment has been designed to produce either midsize or luxury cars. We don't have the capital equipment to build economy cars." Your eyes begin to narrow. Susan quickly recognizes the symptoms and cuts back in. "But we can get the equipment we need." Using the overhead projector, she displays Exhibit 8-2.

You take note of the various production options. Should you buy or rent the capital equipment you need? From a production efficiency standpoint, what is the best option? You now turn to Bill and ask the next question. "How are we going to build this car? We need a quality product at a price that will blow the socks off our competition."

Bill has just read a book on JIT manufacturing. He's convinced that JIT is

Machine Type	Car Production Capacity for Economy - Midsize - Luxury			Factory Sq. Ft. Required	Factory Rent/Mo.	Machine Depreciation Expense	Crew Size Required
A	20	15	16	5,000	$28,645	$41,250	40
B	40	30	24	7,000	$32,500	$49,050	75
C	80	37	40	10,000	$43,250	$56,250	80
D	80	60	64	10,000	$121,875	$146,250	80

Exhibit 8-2. Alternative production capabilities.

the way to go. He projects Exhibit 8-3 on the screen to show you what the material requirements are to produce an economy sedan.

"I've talked to the sales and marketing departments. We have reviewed, in detail, how many economy-car units we can sell over the next six months. We believe that if we can deliver an economy car at a price 10 percent below our competition using JIT, we can increase our market share by 60 percent. Our analysis of the market is shown in Exhibit 8-4."

Your next leading question follows. "That's all fine, but how are you going to get that price? I need a 20 percent profit to get the board of directors off my back. And what will this JIT stuff do for us?" Bill starts into the second half of his presentation. "Based upon our marketing and sales analysis, we need to produce on average 40 economy cars per month over the next six months."

"There are four types of machines we can buy or rent to produce economy cars. If we elect to purchase the machine, the average capital, labor, and factory cost to produce economy cars using the various machine options is shown in Exhibit 8-5.

"We have the option of renting the capital equipment we need to pro-

Material	Units Required per Car	Current Material Cost per Unit
Steel	1.5 Ton	$1,200/Ton
Parts	750	$10 Each

Exhibit 8-3. Economy-car material requirements.

Average number of economy cars sold per month =	100 cars
Our current market share (25% of total) =	25 cars
Average economy car retail price =	$13,500
Economy car demand elasticity =	.02*

Our Projected Market Share after Price Reduction

Our revised market share =	(Current market share) + (% of remaining market)
=	(25 cars) + (20% of 75 cars)
=	(25 cars) + (15 cars)
=	40 economy cars

* A 1% price reduction will result in a 2% increase in units sold. Therefore, a 10% price reduction will result in a 20% increase in units sold.

Exhibit 8-4. Economy-car market share analysis.

duce economy cars. If we elect to rent, the average capital, labor, and factory cost to produce an economy car is shown in Exhibit 8-6.

"Based on our revised sales forecast, we need to produce 40 economy cars per month. The total factory cost to accomplish that rate of production using the various machine options is shown in Exhibit 8-6. Based upon my analysis of the purchase or rent equipment options, I would recommend that we rent a Type C machine.

Machine Type	Machine Purchase Price	Depreciation Expense per Month	Labor Hours Required	Factory Space Required	Economy Car Capacity	Total Cost per Month	Cost per Car
A	$275,000	$41,250	300	75,000	20	$123,750	$6,187
B	$327,000	$49,050	900	125,000	40	$196,550	$4,914
C	$375,000	$56,250	900	100,000	50	$178,750	$3,575
D	$975,000	$146,250	1,200	225,000	80	$401,250	$5,015
Labor Cost = $25/hr. Factory Space Cost = $1/sq. ft. Depreciation Cost/Month = 15% of machine purchase price							

Exhibit 8-5. Cost to produce economy cars if capital equipment is purchased.

Machine Type	Machine Rent Price/Month	Labor Hours Required	Factory Space Required	Economy Car Capacity	Total Cost per Month	Cost per Car
A	$28,645	300	75,000	20	$111,145	$5,557
B	$32,500	900	125,000	40	$180,000	$4,500
C	$43,250	900	100,000	50	$165,750	$3,315
D	$121,875	1,200	225,000	80	$401,250	$4,710
Labor Cost = $25/hr. Factory Space Cost = $1/sq. ft.						

Exhibit 8-6. Cost to produce economy cars if capital equipment is rented.

"Referring to Exhibit 8-6, the cost per car ($3315) is substantially lower than the other equipment options. This option would allow us to lower our economy-car prices by 10 percent to capture the additional market share that we need.

"The current cost of materials (steel and parts) is shown in Exhibit 8-7. The total amount and cost of materials to produce the economy cars are projected over the next six months (see Exhibit 8-8)."

Order Size for Steel	Price per Ton
Less than 45 tons	$1,200
45 or more, but less than 100 tons	$1,140
100 or more, but less than 200 tons	$1,128
200 or more tons	$1,116
Order Size for Parts	**Price per Part**
Less than 11,250 parts	$10
11,250 or more, but less than 22,500 parts	$9.50
22,500 or more, but less than 33,750 parts	$9.40
33,750 or more parts	$9.30

Exhibit 8-7. Material cost at different order quantities.

"Our monthly raw material requirements do not qualify us for volume purchase discounts offered by the steel and parts suppliers. If we were to order all the steel and parts we need to satisfy our material requirements for the next six months, we would qualify for the volume discounts.

"However, we don't have warehouse space to store six months of materials inventory. The option of renting outside warehouse space would cost more than what we would save from the discounts. However, our accounting and finance departments have become very creative, just in time.

"What if we approached our key steel and parts suppliers with an alternative offer? We would negotiate a contract to buy 240 tons of steel and 180,000 parts on a guaranteed minimum-buy purchase order over the next six months. We would tell them we need six monthly deliveries of materials on specified dates and times. Now, would we qualify for volume order discounts?"

You contemplate what Bill has just suggested. If you were the supplier, would you accept the terms of the order? You get on the telephone and ask the purchasing department to find out. They call you back in five minutes and tell you the answer you wanted to hear: "The contract with our material suppliers has been negotiated at the volume discount price." The total material costs before and after your purchasing department negotiated the contract are shown in Exhibit 8-8. You're starting to become impressed with this JIT concept.

Bill cuts in with a leading statement that gets your instant attention. "Let me show you how we can use JIT to instantly increase our productivity rates by 10 percent." He presents Exhibit 8-9, showing the before and after labor savings that will be realized over the next six months.

Bill proceeds to explain the exhibit. "The plant takes two 15-minute breaks every day. When we take a break, we all take it together. That means that we have to stop all movement on the lines. If the breaks were staggered, we could keep the lines moving. This would add a full half hour

	Month 1	Month 2	Month 3	Month 4	Month 5	Month 6
Total Cost Before	$380,000	$380,000	$380,000	$380,000	$380,000	$380,000
Total Cost After	$323,640	$323,640	$323,640	$323,640	$323,640	$323,640
$ Saved	$56,360	$56,360	$56,360	$56,360	$56,360	$56,360
% Saved	15%	15%	15%	15%	15%	15%

Exhibit 8-8. Cost before and after JIT to produce 40 economy cars.

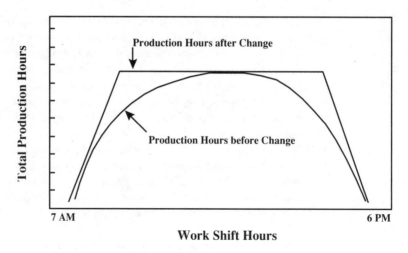

Exhibit 8-9. Effect of shift change on production hours.

more to production each day at no additional cost. It would save us an additional $300 per car."

At this point in the presentation, everybody is excited, including you. Your team has done an excellent job of answering your original question; "What's this JIT stuff all about?" They have covered a lot of ground. The numbers show how they are going to reach the company's cost and profit goals. You ask the final question. "Show me one chart that summarizes everything you have presented so far." They do and it all comes together in Exhibit 8-10.

You're impressed with this JIT concept. Your team has presented you with a compelling case that will allow you to introduce economy cars into the market and save a "whopping" $1 million over the next six months. You

	Before JIT	**JIT Savings**	**After JIT**
Sales Price per Car	$12,150		$12,150
Cost per Car	$10,900	$1,709	$9,191
Profit %	10%	15%	25%
JIT Savings = Labor + materials or $300 + $1,409			

Exhibit 8-10. Economy-car profit analysis before and after JIT.

congratulate Bill and Susan on a job well done. "I knew JIT was the way to go. Just wanted to see if you had done your homework on the subject. Let's implement the program as presented." The meeting is over and you head to the local library to read everything you can find about JIT.

JIT Leadership

Who's the leader of JIT? One person. The top executive is responsible for championing the leadership of JIT. Without leadership focus, JIT will drift into one of the endless chasms that gobbles up all those other programs that never get off the ground. Strong leadership will be required to redirect the corporation's physical and mental attitudes from how business was done to how it will be done under JIT.

All too often, senior management assigns the responsibility for implementing JIT to a single department. It may be quality control, production, or manufacturing. This approach is doomed to failure. The selected department does not have the power or authority to pull everything together. The support needed to make JIT work comes from the other departments. No one department carries that much power to assure the participation and cooperation of the supporting departments.

Again, the responsibility for implementing JIT belongs squarely with senior management. The following true story illustrates the point. Several years ago, I was working for a company that was attempting to implement JIT. One of the JIT team members was responsible for the corporation's data processing organization. Because JIT systems can rely heavily on support from data processing, data processing was given the mission to implement JIT.

Every department in the company was involved in the implementation plan. None of them could agree on a consolidated plan, let alone a common JIT approach. Accounting wanted a set of numbers to track, which was completely opposite from what finance wanted. Sales and marketing were at total odds on how to resolve consumer demand issues. Production control and manufacturing were so far apart on their issues that they weren't talking. To make a long story short, the implementation of JIT was getting nowhere.

The executive vice president who ran the division heard about the problems we were having and decided to pay us a visit. We were all called into a meeting room for what turned out to be a very brief but productive meeting. He started the meeting with a bang.

"I understand you people are having problems implementing JIT. Let me set the record straight. Effective immediately, I am taking over the responsibility of seeing to it that JIT gets implemented. Therefore, it will be fully implemented within six months from today. I will know that it has been implemented because I will be back out here in six months to see a "full up" JIT demonstration. If it has not been implemented by that time, then you will all be fired. Are there any questions?"

There were no questions and our beloved executive vice president left the meeting room. The JIT team now had a common goal and objective. We all understood how important JIT was to our corporation. As you would guess, we successfully implemented JIT within the allotted six-month time period. And yes, the executive vice president did pay us a visit six months later. He was pleased with the JIT demonstration. Nobody got fired.

Implementing JIT

Production Control

Production control works closely with product engineering to assure the development of a marketable product. They are also concerned with the company's ability to manufacture the product. They must have a production process in place to produce quality products. It must also be flexible so that it can be revised to accommodate design changes.

To achieve JIT performance, all aspects of the production process must be controllable. Production must work closely with engineering to establish how each process will be used to produce product.

Production also has a responsibility to the sales and marketing department. It must develop a master schedule that supports the sales plan. Customer demand for product "pulls" the production schedule. You no longer produce product and then turn it over to sales to see if they can sell it. You produce just enough product to meet sales commitments.

Sales and Marketing

Integrating sales and marketing into JIT is essential to the production and manufacturing processes. Accurate sales projections drive the manufacturing engine to produce the right product mix at the right time. JIT demands a stable customer base with reasonable customer commitments that can be met by manufacturing. Timely sales and marketing information must be fed into the production plan to assure customer satisfaction.

It is the responsibility of the sales and marketing organizations to sell customers on JIT advantages. The ability of manufacturing to keep delivery commitments is certainly one of the major advantages. A stabilized manufacturing environment may result in a number of cost-reduction advantages to the JIT company. The customer benefits if cost savings are passed on in the form of lower prices.

Sales and marketing must establish a firm customer base that is anxious to take advantages of the proposed features of JIT products. Advertised features may include higher product quality and reduced order lead times. Customer commitments under JIT must be met at all costs to maintain credibility.

JIT manufacturing depends on firm customer orders and very accurate short-term sales forecasts. Accurate forecasting is a requisite for reducing excess overhead and last-minute master schedule changes.

Purchasing Responsibilities

The functions and responsibilities of purchasing will change significantly when JIT is implemented. The traditional function of purchasing is to acquire the goods and services the company needs to operate. That part doesn't change. What does change is the supplier base. JIT requires a small and very reliable supplier base. Purchasing is responsible for establishing a supplier base that meets the JIT criteria.

In the process, purchasing must also improve upon the quality of goods and services acquired, reduce order lead times, and negotiate cost reductions whenever possible. Cost reduction covers two areas of opportunity. First, the reduction in the supplier base reduces internal acquisition cost. Second, the consolidation of suppliers leads to larger orders being placed with fewer suppliers. This leads to volume discounts and preferred customer opportunities. In the overall JIT purchasing process, an emphasis is placed on continuous improvements in customer/supplier relations.

Accounting

In a non-JIT environment, accounting's involvement with suppliers is routine. They simply receive supplier invoices and pay them, based upon a predefined accounting schedule. This approach changes under JIT. Creative payment schedules become an important part of contract negotiations and long-term supplier relations.

For example, a contract may require a supplier to deliver materials every nine days. Payment for delivered materials may be due on delivery or three times a month. If the accounting system is set up to pay invoices once a month, it has got to be changed. Accounting must participate in the contract negotiations and agree to any special terms that affect accounting.

Quality Control

In the early days of manufacturing, quality control was not a separate function. It was controlled by individuals responsible for maintaining their own quality. The advent of larger and more complex manufacturing processes gave rise to separate and distinct quality-control organizations. These groups were responsible for defining and controlling quality throughout the manufacturing process.

In recent times, the trend has been to consolidate quality control back into the manufacturing organization. JIT advocates generally endorse this trend for obvious reasons. The only way that you can continuously produce defect-free products is to control product quality at every turn in the manufacturing process. JIT relies on in-process control rather than end-product inspections to catch product defects. Finished-product inspection functions are eliminated under JIT.

Quality-control checks must be in place to assure that the output of the production process meets or exceeds established quality standards. By applying the principles of process control to each step of production, the integrity of the total process can be dramatically improved.

Receiving and inspection functions can be eliminated. Supplier quality control has been assured through contract negotiations and improved supplier relations. All product quality-control responsibilities are consolidated into the production processes. JIT moves quality control to the closest point where the product defect can be discovered and fixed on the spot.

The JIT quality-control organization is given a new mission. They perform process improvement studies, quality audits, JIT educational sessions, failure analysis, and reliability studies. JIT moves quality into functional areas where there is more "bang for the buck."

Material Control

Material control is responsible for the selection and requisition of quality raw materials that support the manufacturing process. In some companies, this may be a specialized function under its own department. In others, the materials functions are consolidated under the purchasing department.

As we discussed earlier, our JIT goals are to reduce the supplier base, consolidate orders, and push material control back into the hands of our trusted suppliers. As soon as JIT starts, it becomes a relatively simple process to initiate a request for materials. Long-term supplier contracts are in place and timely material deliveries are assured. All this will have the favorable effect of reducing the internal work load on the material-control group.

JIT also changes the priorities by which materials are purchased. Typically materials contracts are negotiated based on price, delivery, and quality. The order gets reversed in a JIT system: quality, delivery, and price. Why? The impact of a quality defect in materials on a JIT production line can have a devastating effect.

Defective materials can shut the line down. Because there is no surplus product flowing through the line, the restart and catch-up cycle can prove to be very difficult. Hence, a cheaper price for a lesser-quality material may be a poor investment.

Inventory Control

Inventory control is responsible for controlling the levels of inventory at a variety of locations. In a non-JIT environment, inventory tends to be maintained at higher levels to cover what is often referred to as safety stock. Safety stock inventory is used to cover potential errors in the projected inventory levels required to support manufacturing. JIT inventory control eliminates the need to maintain safety stock and inspect inventories. Customer return-goods inventories are minimized or eliminated.

The lack of good inventory-control practices can hide a multitude of problems. Companies that rely on the buildup of excess materials and products ignore fixing the problems causing the excess buildup. The cost of the excess is often significant.

In a JIT program, just enough inventory is allowed into the production cycle to support the exact requirements of the cycle. Inventory-control problems in this tight environment quickly surface and must be resolved at the source. There is no safety stock that can be used to patch the problem. As a result, the number of inventory turnovers increases, which results in further cost savings.

Inventory turns are a measure of how efficiently a company is using its materials. These are measured by dividing the total amount of material processed or used in a year by the average level of inventory maintained. JIT companies typically enjoy inventory turns that are ten times better than non-JIT companies.

The Workers

Historically, production workers have not been given the option to point out inefficiencies in their respective work areas. Any attempt to do so was considered to be paramount to political suicide. Identified deficiencies pointed directly at management who created the process in the first place. If the process of continued improvement is to work, this attitude must change. Continued improvement is basic to the ongoing success and to the real payback of JIT.

The responsibility of making sure this happens falls squarely on the management team. Incentives for employee participation must be developed and implemented at the outset of the program. Employees must be convinced they are a part of the JIT team and that their identification of process improvements is not a threat to future employment. In fact, they need to understand that JIT is the way to secure their future employment. Job security is enhanced as the company becomes more competitive under JIT. Employee education and honest commitments from all levels of management are essential to get employees to buy into JIT.

A senior executive once approached me and told me that he was sold on JIT. "Where do we start?" He didn't like my answer. "Everywhere." But it was a true answer. I could not think of a single function or department within a company that is not affected in some way by the full implementation of JIT.

In the early planning stages, you conduct a complete evaluation of every function and system in the organization. How do these functions fit together within the framework of the current system? How are they performing and what baselines or benchmarks are you using to measure performance? This information is essential to establishing JIT expectations and for monitoring the success of the program.

Developing a JIT Model

When you complete your evaluation of the company's current functions, systems, and baselines, begin developing a hypothetical JIT model that will work for your company. Start by playing the "what-if" game with your JIT implementation team. Concentrate initially on lead times, inventory levels, and quality levels.

Create a flow diagram that identifies all of the steps necessary to bring raw materials into the facility. Determine how long each step takes. Can you eliminate any steps? What if you consolidate your material orders and have your suppliers deliver materials directly to the manufacturing floor? Would these actions reduce lead time?

Where are your inventory-control areas and how much inventory are you maintaining? How many times are you turning your inventory on an annual basis? What is it costing you to store inventory? How much would you save if you reduced your inventory levels to just what you needed to support the next day's manufacturing run?

Where are your quality-control points? What is it costing you to control quality at each of those points? How many defects are being identified for each quality-control dollar spent? What if you contracted with your suppliers to perform the same quality checks that you're currently performing? Would your quality-control cost increase or decrease? If you implemented this process, would you be able to reduce lead time?

Developing a working model for your company raises many questions that demand tough analytical answers. You may not be satisfied or comfortable with all the answers that you come up with. But that is all part of the JIT game.

Implementation Schedule

How long does it take to implement JIT? You probably won't like the answer when we say "forever." But consider the good points of our answer if, on the first day of the JIT implementation schedule, success is shown and continues to be shown throughout the implementation cycle. The cycle never ends and your cost savings will continue to increase, forever! If you go back to our discussion on continuous improvement, you continue to identify process improvements. The JIT system becomes a way of life for every employee in the company.

Summary and Conclusions

Establishing a JIT company requires a commitment from every department. All departments are focused on a common set of goals. Goals are actively supported from the senior executive on down through the management chain. We started the discussion by defining JIT. Several common misconceptions were dispelled. We then proceeded to explore several JIT cost advantages.

From there, we created a JIT scenario to show how JIT works. Numerous illustrations and examples were presented to reinforce the concept. Departmental responsibilities were identified along the way.

Game Assignment and Instructions

When you load the game disk, the Main Menu for Month 8 should appear on your display (Exhibit 8-11). For this reason, the instructions included in the on-line tutorials are no longer required. The tutorials now include an expanded version of *The Fast Street Journal*. Read the *Journal* before you develop your business strategies for the month. Analyze the information and data contained in the *Journal*. Make sure you understand where you are or are about to go in the game's economic and business world before you close out the month.

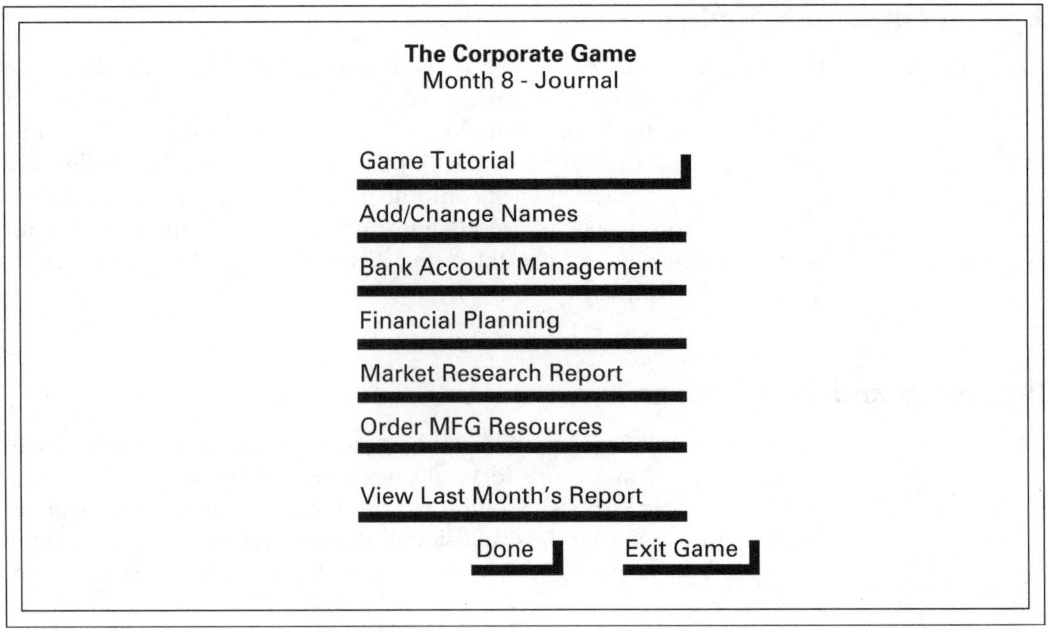

The Corporate Game
Month 8 - Journal

Game Tutorial

Add/Change Names

Bank Account Management

Financial Planning

Market Research Report

Order MFG Resources

View Last Month's Report

Done   Exit Game

Exhibit 8-11. Month 8—Journal menu.

9

Perfection Isn't Good Enough

Fine Tuning People Assets

We have talked about all the ways you can fine tune the corporate machine. Together, we developed a strategic plan that was fully integrated into all the business disciplines. We proceeded to develop a production plan that supported the manufacturing operation and a JIT system. All capital resources of the corporation were utilized at 100 percent of capacity. Who could possibly ask for anything more? But we forgot about our people!

Managers tend to spend more time managing the capital assets of the company than they do managing their people assets. The reason is simple. It's easier! A piece of capital equipment on the factory floor doesn't talk back. People do!

Have you ever gone through the process of getting your company to approve a $10,000 capital equipment expense request? Chances are you spent $5000 just to complete the paperwork showing how productive the new machine would be. Then it was on to the executive review board for approval. That process probably cost you another $5000. So, you broke even.

When you hired a worker for $25,000 a year, the whole process was probably done in a few hours. No productivity reports or executive approvals were required. Until recently, labor productivity wasn't important in this country. It's a hot item now. In this chapter, we talk about techniques you can use to assure that the productivity of your people assets complements the productivity of your other corporate assets.

The Human Asset

In the past, it was considered bad form for an employer to refer to an employee as an asset. The asset distinction carried the connotation that people were slaves. Fortunately, conventional wisdom of modern-day management has eradicated many of the human asset misconceptions.

New paradigms have come into play that view labor as an expense item. Labor's value-added contribution lies in its cost being minimized or its productivity being maximized. The paradigm isn't unique. From the very beginning, labor has been treated as an expense item on the profit-and-loss statement.

The human capital asset theory, on the other hand, sees the employee as an asset valued in much the same manner as computers and inventories. Does that mean that we add a line item to the balance sheet called "human assets" and create a second line called "depreciation of human assets?"

There are interesting and controversial implications if we add human assets to the balance sheet. Do you depreciate human assets as they get older? If you do, would that be considered age discrimination? Maybe human assets appreciate as they get older. The older you get the smarter you get . . . right?

Any further extrapolation of this discussion can only cause controversy. The point is that you've got to come up with a way to get more out of your employees if you want to survive in the corporate game. The challenge is to figure out a way to increase employees morale as you squeeze them for more productivity. That shouldn't be any problem. You're the CEO and that's why they are paying you the big bucks. We'll help you put together an employee productivity program that works in the balance of this chapter.

America's Fading Work Force

"Layoffs undermine loyalty. Puny pay raises turn some off. Wanted: creative managers." This headline appeared in *The Wall Street Journal* (Exhibit 9-1). Shortly after the article was published, the Japanese added some salt to the wound. Their political leaders blasted America's work force as being "lazy and unmotivated." Is the work drive in America sputtering like an old Hudson?

The statistics on American's labor force suggest that the Japanese may be wrong. Americans are working as many hours today as they did decades ago. Absenteeism is down. In fact, the average hours worked by a family is up significantly. Working families and couples are common today.

However, the statistics may not be telling the whole story. Just because Americans are showing up for work doesn't mean their hearts are in it. What if they are all showing up with a minimum of absenteeism because they are afraid of losing their jobs? Maybe their spouses have to work just to

> # Employee Ennui
> # If the U.S. Work Ethic
> # Is Fading, "Laziness"
> # May Not Be the Reason
>
> ## Layoffs Undermine Loyalty,
>
> ## Puny Pay Turns Off Some,
>
> ## Union Rules Protect Sloth
>
> ## Wanted: Creative Managers

Exhibit 9-1. *The Wall Street Journal,* February 7, 1992.

make ends meet. Suppose workers are disenchanted with both their jobs and the companies they work for?

What if this attitude is present in your company? Let's face it. We have all been in this situation at one time or another. If this situation exists in your company, the cost in lost productivity could be staggering. So, what can you do about it? How can you prevent it from happening?

Where Do You Start?

Let's get back into *The Corporate Game* and continue our story. You suspect you've got people problems. Nobody seems to be motivated and you can't seem to get anybody excited about the new just-in-time manufacturing system you're implementing. To make matters worse, things are tough in the auto industry. Sales and profits are down. You had to limit employee raises to ridiculously low levels.

You decide to call your trusted golf buddy and confidant, Dan, to solicit his advice. "Dan, I am having problems getting my people off dead center.

Nobody wants to hustle and I know it's costing me a lot in lost productivity. What do you think I should do?"

There's a long pause at the other end of the line before Dan speaks. "You need to hire a specialist. Get yourself an industrial psychiatrist who will come into the plant and conduct a half-day motivational seminar. That will do it." What a great idea. You thank Dan and hang up the phone.

It doesn't take you long to find a "name-brand" industrial psychiatrist who has worked miracles for other companies. So what if he wants $5000 a day plus expenses? You're probably losing more than that in a single complaint session at the water fountain.

The big day of the motivational seminar arrives. Everybody is present and accounted for in the auditorium. You know they all really want to be there even though you told them that they had no choice. If you're going to pay this guy $5000 to make a speech, then everybody better attend this session.

Your motivational expert steps up to the podium and begins to speak. Within the first five minutes of his presentation, he has cracked enough company jokes to have everyone rolling on the floor with laughter. You think to yourself, "This guy is great. He sure knows how to loosen up an audience."

He has laid the groundwork for the theme of the presentation—employee motivation and productivity. At the end of the presentation, you want every employee to walk away with a renewed feeling of enthusiasm. Team building will be the "watch word" of the day. Employee productivity will surely increase.

At the appropriate time, your expert speaker asks the group a simple question, which is the focus of his entire talk. "What is the vision of your company?" No one raises a hand. The speaker, thinking everybody might be shy, gently encourages your employees to give him an answer. The auditorium grows deadly silent. Everyone is looking at someone else and a lot of them are just looking at the floor.

Your expert speaker has a sinking sensation in his stomach. "Your company does have a vision, doesn't it?" A few people shrug and a few more shake their heads. He is dumbfounded. How could any company achieve any goal without a vision? He excused himself to go to the men's room. That was the last time you ever saw him.

What's a Vision?

If you want to truly motivate your people, you need to create a corporate vision, which is a statement of how the organization will look in the future. A vision is designed to:

Tap into deep corporate concerns and needs

Assert where the corporation wants to go

Project a theme that is worth going after

Provide meaning to the work performed by employees

Direct dedication to quality and productivity

Excite enthusiasm and the drive for achievement

There are two types of visions: realistic and illusionary. Corporations are only interested in the realistic visions necessary to drive forward thinking and to achieve measurable progress. The degree to which knowledge is applied to create a corporate vision determines the degree to which it is real. Visions created without knowledge fall into the category of daydreaming.

Visions get started by examining the past and present. Somewhere in the analytical process, the vision creator derives sufficient wisdom to accurately project into the future. In the process, the vision begins to take shape (see Exhibit 9-2). It incorporates a dissatisfaction with what currently exists with a desire to set a direction that will lead the corporation into a better set of conditions.

Visions are prerequisites to long-term planning. As we have demonstrated in the earlier chapters, long-term planning is basic to the corporation's strategic plan. It allows the organization to operate in a state of action rather than reaction due to unanticipated change. With vision, you control the path of change with complementary actions. Without a vision, change

A vision is a statement of how an organization will look in the future and will:	
Engage the heart and spirit of the organization	
Tap into embedded organizational concerns and needs	
Assert what the organization wants to create	
Represent something that is worth going after	
Provide meaning to the work of the employees	
Be based upon human needs for quality and dedication	
Tips on Creating a Vision	
Project goals 2 - 5 years out	Written in present tense
Focus on customer requirements	Express quality and teams
Compelling and motivational	Expresses hope and possibilities

Exhibit 9-2. Key elements of a vision.

just happens. You end up implementing offsetting actions in an attempt to control the direction of the change, after the fact.

The Chrysler Vision

Several years ago, Chrysler Corporation was in serious financial trouble. They were about to go out of business and this would have cost hundreds of thousands of jobs. At the eleventh hour, two significant events occurred. Lee Iaccoca was named CEO of Chrysler and the federal government agreed to underwrite Chrysler's multibillion-dollar recovery loan. Nobody expected Chrysler to survive.

In spite of the pessimism, a miracle started to happen at Chrysler. To everybody's amazement, the company began to show signs that it might survive. What did Lee do to turn Chrysler around? He created a vision, mission, and goal statement that every employee at Chrysler could relate to.

His vision statement was simple. "We have got to produce a better car if we want to keep our jobs." Let's explore the meaning of Lee's vision statement. Anybody could come up with a vision statement that said "we have got to create a better product." But hold on! Lee was just getting started.

Everybody knows that corporate America has to produce better products and services to survive in today's tough international market. What Lee added to the formula was the second half of his vision statement: "if we all want to keep our jobs."

Suddenly, in his simple vision statement, he captured the imagination and attention of every Chrysler employee. "I've got to build a better car if I want to keep my job." Employee motivation began to set in. But it raises the next question: "What can I do as a Chrysler employee to support Lee's vision?"

Lee, in his infinite wisdom, gave them the answer they were looking for. He created a mission statement that supported his vision statement. "We must build a car equal to or better than a Toyota Celica." At the time, nobody in Detroit owned a Toyota Celica, or even knew what one looked like. Lee solved the problem by placing a Celica in front of every employee entrance into the Chrysler plants. He put a "cap" on his mission statement by adding a goal statement. "Let's do it in a year."

Did Lee's employee vision strategy work? Did Chrysler survive and in fact pay off the federally insured loan early? Is Chrysler still a viable corporation today? The answer, as you already know is "yes, yes, and yes." Did Lee's vision, mission, and goal statements solve Chrysler's long-term problems? Again, the answer is "yes." If your employees don't know where you want your company to go, they can't help you get there. Chrysler employees knew exactly where Lee wanted them to go and they were highly motivated to help him get there.

Creating a Vision

How do you create a meaningful vision that will work for your company? First, establish a vision of why your company exists. In the vision statement, state the purpose of the company. State the direction the company needs to follow. Identify the benefits that will be realized by all the employees as the company moves toward the vision.

To pull it all together, actively seek input from every level in the organization. Use your management team to solicit inputs. Listen, coach, and analyze everything that comes in. In the end, it's up to you as the CEO to compose and publish the final corporate vision statement.

A vision statement demands total support from your employees. If you use participation to create your vision, you end up with a vision that has been mutually developed by your entire organization.

Once established, the vision almost replaces the company logo. The communication and reinforcement of the shared vision are a continuous event. It's shown and explained to new employees. It appears on company bulletin boards and in newsletters. It's a popular subject at meetings throughout the organization.

The next step is to understand the relationship between a vision, mission, and goals (Exhibit 9-3). A vision statement is like a lighthouse. Its purpose

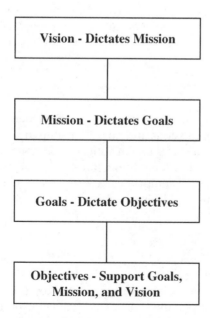

Exhibit 9-3. The elements of establishing a corporate purpose.

If we don't satisfy you 100%, we won't take your money.

You don't owe us 1 penny until all pests on your premises have been eradicated.

If you are ever dissatisfied with our service, you will receive a full refund, plus fees for another exterminator of your choice.

If your facility is closed down due to the presence of bugs, we will pay all fines, lost profits, and $5,000.

Exhibit 9-4. "Bugs" Bug Killer guarantee.

is to give direction. Building a better car or cleaning up the environment are examples of simple vision statements.

Visions are viable for the life of the current form of the company. Only a major reorganization or refocus will necessitate changes in a properly developed vision. An example of one company's reinforced vision statement is shown in Exhibit 9-4. After reading Bug Killer's vision statement, would you buy their product? Wouldn't you be proud to work for a company with a 100 percent customer satisfaction vision statement?

Mission and goal statements can be boring, mundane, and noninspirational. You can't get away with that when you create a vision statement. Vision statements must be dynamic and inspirational. They provide the energy, power, and passion to achieve missions and goals.

Missions and Goals

The viability and even the life of the corporation depend on the success of actions taken to meet missions and goals. Missions and goals are made up of clearly identified objectives that are short- or long-term in duration. If a short-term objective is detrimental to a long-term objective, the viability of the corporation's vision is compromised. The same is true if long-term objectives are not synchronized with short-term objectives.

Mission Statements

Mission statements point to the corporation's vision. It's a statement of how the corporation will move forward progressively toward its vision. Think of it as a strategic implementation plan. Chrysler's mission was to build a car equal to or better in quality than a Toyota Celica. "We need to increase profits by 50 percent" is another example of a mission statement. Missions are based on:

A special duty or function

A task with a purpose

Specific operations to support a higher operation

Most progressive corporations have multiple missions. Each functional group may have a mission that focuses on its specific role. All group missions must roll up to support the visions of the corporation. For example, the group that is responsible for assembling the engine for the Chrysler car may have its own mission. This mission may be to control defects at a specified level to achieve engine quality standards comparable to or better than a Celica.

Goal Statements

A goal is one step, which when completed, moves the corporation closer to its vision and mission. Goals have relatively short time durations and always have beginning and end dates. Goal statements are very concise and state a desired end result and the benefits of the result. For this reason, they are task oriented and are based on:

A need to accomplish something

Assuring measurable results

Creating a specific focus

Providing direction

Past experience

The Chrysler workers were given a one-year goal to build a car that was better than a Celica. Another example of a goal would be to reduce engine rejects by 10 percent by the end of next month.

Corporations will typically have a number of goals in place at any one moment in time. Individuals from different functional areas may be working together on teams to accomplish single or multiple goals.

Objectives

Goals may be supported by multiple objectives. Like goals, objectives state a desired action, the timing of the action, and the expected results to be achieved when the action is complete. If a goal is supported by five objectives, then the successful completion of all five objectives completes the goal.

Reward Excellence

All vision statements share one common attribute. They are a very important part of the company's value system. Work to find a way to reward employee behavior that supports the shared vision. Encourage your employees to focus on the corporation's value system. If employees go the extra mile, reward them.

Constructively confront negative behavior that is in conflict with the corporate vision. Most negative behavior stems from an employee's lack of skill, knowledge, or miscommunication about the vision. In a vision-driven company, management is challenged with the task to constructively change negative behavior. Motivate your people to change because they want to and not because of a fear of losing their jobs.

Promote Change

Some people shudder at the very idea of change. It represents the unknown to them and they are generally not prepared to handle it. In today's corporate world, change is a part of the new reality. It demands effective problem analysis and the quick implementation of a change to permanently fix problems.

In order for that to happen effectively, you have got to encourage your people to take risks. Without a reasonable level of risk, positive changes will never become a reality. My uncle used to tell me about a man who never made a mistake because he never made a decision.

Make failure analysis a positive part of the process. Encourage your people to learn from their mistakes. In the process, they'll improve upon their odds for long-term success.

Continuous Improvement

Continuous improvement is becoming a way of life in corporate America. Our just-in-time system relies heavily on continuous improvement to achieve ongoing efficiencies in the manufacturing process. The basic underlying principle of continuous improvement is the recognition that there is always a better, undiscovered way of doing something.

Undiscovered is the key word. You need as many people as you can get to work at discovering better processes. That is where your employees can really help. They know more about your current processes than anybody. As a result, they are better equipped to discover improvements.

A detailed action plan for excellence is an integral part of the corporation's continuous improvement plan. Each action plan should address significant and specific problems and it must be based upon the most complete information available.

If you know that one of your production processes is twice as slow as your competitor's, nominate it as a hot candidate for improvement. Work with your people to do something about it. Get them to create goals and set objectives. Tell them you don't care who created the process in the first place. Just fix it!

Set Priorities

To reach a shared vision, senior management must identify the priorities needed to get there. Don't just sit there and say, "Well, my people will figure out what the priorities are sooner or later." It will probably be later rather than sooner. You may not be able to afford the later scenario.

Don't allow your employees to waste company time trying to second guess what the priorities are. Tell them what the priorities are so they can work on solving the problems that are standing in the way.

Empowerment

Now that your people understand what the company's vision, missions, goals, and objectives are all about, how do you get them to move in the right direction to solve the problems? You empower them. Empowerment is the process of moving responsibility and authority down into the organization. The employees who have expertise about a process are given the authority to make decisions to improve the process.

Empowerment is a progressive process. It requires knowledge and understanding of the goals of the corporation. The primary objective of empowerment is to promote continuous improvement activities by:

- Moving the decision-making process to the lowest level possible
- Allowing management more time to focus on its own levels of improvement
- Increasing ownership, pride, and responsibility throughout the organization

It is unrealistic to dump decision-making responsibility onto people who have neither the skills nor the information to take on empowered responsibility. Empowerment is a sequential process. It must be implemented progressively as employees gain the knowledge and ability to take on new responsibilities.

Part of the progression must focus on the availability of information. Nobody can be empowered and expected to make meaningful and timely decisions without access to accurate information.

Empowerment Misconceptions

A basic empowerment misconception is that you are either empowered or you're not. There are different levels of empowerment that evolve as the process matures. As people begin to learn more about their responsibilities, they will take on different levels of empowerment. When do they become fully empowered? If you buy into the concept of continuous improvement, empowerment is a continuous process as well. Hence, the target of becoming fully empowered is a continuous process without an end.

Another misconception is that empowerment only applies to employees and not to management. Empowerment applies throughout the organization. No one should be excluded from being empowered. It's in the best interest of the corporation to have everyone empowered.

Thinking that empowerment creates chaos is another common misconception. As long as each person knows and understands the vision, missions, and goals of the company, this should never become a problem.

Each level of the organization will require training in skills such as decision making and solving problems, before employees at that level can begin to become empowered. This is a requisite before any manager or employee can be empowered in a controlled environment.

The last misconception is that managers will lose power and control when their employees become empowered. This is a major obstacle to empowerment. It ignores the fact that managers, as well as employees, are a collective part of the empowerment process.

Management must be actively involved in implementing all phases of empowerment. As the need for training evolves, management must determine how best to apply training mechanisms. In addition, management must participate in the development and implementation of the systems needed to support the important processes. Corrective actions from the analysis of data can be initiated by management or implemented by empowered employees. If anything, management's responsibilities and power increase as a result of having empowered employees.

The Empowerment Process

If empowerment is a self-motivated improvement process, how do you get it started? You begin by strategically assessing your organization. What are the empowered needs of your people? Where do they reside? Where should empowerment be implemented to have the greatest positive impact on the company?

Are information systems in place to support empowerment? What are the training needs of your employees and managers? Once you have the answers to these important questions, you can begin to implement empowerment.

The reactions of your employees will be mixed when you begin the implementation process. Some of your lower-level employees will openly welcome empowerment as an opportunity for advancement. Some will perceive it as corporate scheme to cut costs and jobs. The job jeopardy concern and any other concern can severely cripple the implementation effort. Address and eliminate any barriers as soon as they are discovered.

Empowerment is a cooperative system based upon open communication. Managers and employees must work together to define the boundaries of empowerment that satisfy the employee's need to progress and management's need to control risks. As the system develops and mutual trust is established, the boundaries can be widened.

Empowered Teams

Team building becomes a natural offspring of the empowered organization. Employees are motivated to collectively identify innovative ways to improve the efficiency of the company. They will start to form teams to tackle all kinds of difficult problems. Management is quick to pick up on the value-added effect of empowered teams. If they are smart, and they usually are, they will do everything they can to clear obstacles from the path of the teams.

Let's step back for a moment and review what we have covered so far. We've put together a vision statement that all of your employees can relate to. They have bought into the program because, for the first time, they believe in it. The overall level of employee enthusiasm is beginning to increase as a result of your new empowerment program.

You don't want to let go while you're ahead, so you move swiftly to implement missions, goals, and objectives that supplement the company's vision. Action plans are in place. Everybody is hysterical with optimism. Your just-in-time system is finally beginning to gel.

Once a team becomes empowered, the probability for success increases dramatically. Teams go through various stages of evolution in the empowerment process, as we have illustrated in Exhibit 9-5. Once fully empowered, the team becomes so strongly knit in their purpose that the risk of defeat is reduced to an insignificant percentage. Trying to manage an empowered team becomes a real pleasure and a challenge at the same time.

Empowered teams move so fast that most of management's time is spent trying to clear obstacles out of their way before the team runs over them. They don't need to be managed in the traditional sense and they certainly don't need to be motivated. Is it really possible for an innate thing called a corporation to motivate people to accomplish superhuman feats?

It's happening every day. You may not be aware of it. Maybe you're having problems competing with your competitors. What are they doing that you

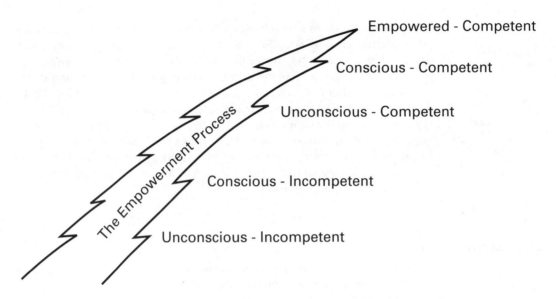

Exhibit 9-5. The empowerment process.

are not doing? Are they using empowered teams? You come home and start
reading the sports section in the evening paper.

The headlines read as follows; "Yankees down 9 - 0 in the bottom of the
9th. They pull off 10 home runs to win 10 to 9." Wow! How did they do that?
Then it hits you. The Yankees, like every other baseball team, is a corporation, just like yours.

The only difference is that they have one team and your company has
many teams. But the results of an empowered team are the same. Your JIT
team and the Yankee team had a common goal—improve their overall level
of productivity. The Yankees pursued it with enormous energy and won.
What about your team?

Symptoms of Empowerment

You got lucky. You ended up with an empowered JIT team before you even
knew it. You want to create more empowered teams but you're not sure how
to identify one after it's been created. The first change you notice is that
there is no turnover or absenteeism among the team players. If a meeting is
called, they are all there exactly on time. No one is late because of the importance of the team's time. Time is considered a cherished team commodity.

The team is totally focused on accomplishing its mission. The remote
thought of failure has been totally removed from each employee's vocabu-

lary. Team members have a strong sense of identity. They often exhibit a cocky team attitude, which can be an annoyance to people who are not on the team. Team members often come up with a team name to distinguish themselves from others, like "The Dolphin Team."

There is a definite feeling of ownership for any by-products created by empowered teams. Team members like to have their names grouped together and placed under their accomplishments for all to see. You will often see their group picture posted on company bulletin boards. The final sign of an empowered team is the obvious enjoyment that members take in their work.

Team Obstacles

We have talked about empowered teams and discussed some of their unique attributes. Several examples were given to show how teams work and why they are an important productivity resource. What are some of the obstacles that can hinder or impair teams?

Let's play out the following corporate game scenario. You have just put a team of your best players in place to tackle a very tough problem. In fact, the problem must be solved soon or it could cost you that promotion you're bucking for. You trust your team, but what happens if the team fails? You need a backup plan to cover your bets, so you create a second team to work on the same problem.

That makes good defensive management sense in many situations—with the exception of team building. Any defensive measures taken to guarantee success in spite of the team will severely cripple both teams. They will never succeed at their mission. You will have effectively removed the component of trust that all teams must have to succeed.

Bureaucracies are another team killer. Empowered teams hate paperwork and consider it a waste of time unless it directly contributes to the success of the team. You will often hear team members say, "I can't do my real work until I get this paperwork out of the way." It is not uncommon for a team to be given direct access to an executive who assists team members in eliminating any bureaucracy that may get in their way.

Picking the Right People

We all know that if you have the right people, you will succeed. One bad apple can cause a disproportionate amount of grief and agony. Your vision, mission, goals, and all your action plans depend upon having good team players. What can you do and how can you improve your odds of selecting the right people for your company?

Think through the assignment first before you start looking at people candidates. We're not talking about the job description. If the task is to select a new sales manager, what's at the heart of the assignment? If you need someone to recruit and train new salespeople in a new territory, then that requires a certain type of person.

If the assignment is to establish a market presence for the company's new line of products, then a different type of person may be required. In the first example, your emphasis might be placed on a candidate's people-handling skills. In the second example, you may want a salesperson with strong marketing skills.

The next step is to begin identifying candidates who fit the assignment mold. As you begin to assemble candidate resumés, ask yourself the following questions: "What are this person's strengths and are they the right strengths for the assignment?"

Discuss candidates with several people who have worked with them. One person's judgment is not enough. You need to get several other opinions to verify the answers you get. If you get conflicting answers, get another opinion.

You've done your homework and now have a qualified list of viable candidates. It's time to begin the interview process. Make sure the candidates understand the job assignment. The fact that they may have been in sales management for the past 20 years doesn't cut it if their past assignments don't match what you are looking for.

Ask them very specific questions which apply directly to the assignment. You cannot expect to get definitive answers back on every question, but it should give you a feel for how well these individuals will be able to move and think on their feet.

Summary and Conclusions

This chapter started off with a discussion about human assets. They are often forgotten or ignored when companies strive to improve overall productivity. People are a critical part of the productivity process. How do you motivate your people into playing the corporate game? You start by creating a corporate vision statement. We showed you how to do this and provided you with several examples.

Next, we showed you how to develop corporate missions and goals to support the vision statement. Numerous examples were given. People motivation was an important part of our development plan.

We showed you how to implement and use objectives to support goals. Along the way, we talked about change and how to motivate your people to promote change. This is essential to our continuous improvement strategy.

We talked about employee empowerment and how to use empowerment to accelerate the continuous improvement process. Several of the misconceptions about empowerment were exposed. The discussion about employee empowerment led us into a discussion about team empowerment.

Empowered teams were an added bonus to the empowerment process. We showed you how to recognize an empowered team and how to keep the team motivated. As you move into the next chapter on total quality management, you will see how critical empowered people are to achieving the next step of perfection, a total quality company.

PC Game and Instructions

When you load the game on your PC, you should be starting Month 9 (Exhibit 9-6). This is an interesting month to play. See if you can tell why by reading the September issue of *The Fast Street Journal*. We recommend that you read the *Journal* before you set your corporate game strategies in motion.

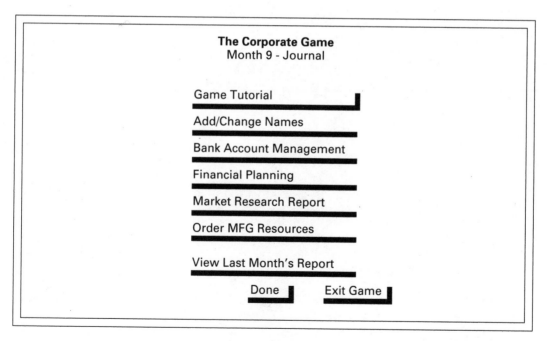

Exhibit 9-6. Month 9—Journal menu.

10
The Total
Quality Game

In the Race for Quality, There Is No Finish Line

A number of articles and books have been published criticizing the quality of products and services offered by U.S. companies. All kinds of quality get-well schemes are being offered to get corporate America back into the swing of things. Why is there a sudden surge in emphasis on quality in this country?

Have the quality standards of U.S. products been slipping over the past decade? We do not believe that they have. What has happened is that the quality of competitive international products has been steadily improving. American companies have been complacent in keeping their quality standards at status quo levels. The end result is an ever increasing trade deficit as we continue to lose market share to higher-quality products.

Just a few years ago, quality was considered an insignificant business function. A couple of quality-control people would be stationed at the end of a production line, looking for defects in finished products. Defects had to be significant before they were caught. The philosophy was, "Let the customer find the defects and we'll see what we can do about it later."

This philosophy is undergoing rapid changes. An increasing number of American companies are making quality a top priority. Quality recognition has been reborn and dressed with a new set of priorities. It's becoming a part of strategic planning just like finance, marketing, and production control. Today, quality control is called total quality management (TQM), which has distinct implications across all business disciplines.

The new TQM concept is global in its focus and attempts to integrate quality throughout all business processes. TQM recognizes the market as the single source of the corporation's income. It recognizes that the customers who make up the market are the final product arbitrators. They ultimately determine what product quality levels are needed and what prices they will pay for products.

Quality Is Obvious

Every manager believes in quality. They'll all hold up quality banners and say, "You bet we believe in quality. Let's put more of that quality stuff into our operation." A lot of it is lip service. Only a few appreciate and understand the important role that quality is playing in today's market. Fortunately, the list of quality converts is beginning to grow.

The need for higher quality is obvious. Customers have to be satisfied with the quality of your products and services if you expect to capture repeat business. You need to constantly monitor customer quality expectations to stay ahead of the game. If all of this quality stuff is so obvious, then why are we encountering quality problems throughout the United States? Perhaps we have not yet learned how to put common sense into common practice.

Before any serious quality program can begin, senior management must clarify what is expected from the quality program. And, senior management must practice what it preaches on a day-by-day basis. You cannot talk about improving customer services without talking to customers. You cannot preach teamwork and then refuse to attend a team meeting. You cannot tell the guy who holds the screwdriver to implement a quality program and assume that the job will get done.

The History of TQM

In 1987, the U.S. Department of Commerce initiated a TQM program to help American companies regain world-class recognition for U.S. product and service offerings. The program is anchored by the Malcolm Baldrige National Quality Award (see Exhibit 10-1). The award recognizes service and manufacturing businesses that can demonstrate exemplary quality in their practices and in the quality of their products.

There is a comprehensive set of award criteria used to evaluate applicants. Since the program's inception, the criteria have evolved into a set of TQM standards that companies throughout the United States are using to implement their own TQM programs.

Each year, the Commerce Department processes over a quarter of a million requests for the Baldrige Award Guidelines. The program is catching

Exhibit 10-1. The Malcolm Baldrige
National Quality Award.

on. It's hard to find a major company that's not familiar with the program.
A copy of the application guidelines is available by writing to the following
address:

United States Department of Commerce
Technology Administration
National Institute of Standards and Technology
Route 270 and Quince Road
Administration Building, Room A537
Gaithersburg, MD 20899

The balance of this chapter follows the Baldrige TQM guidelines. The
intent is not to show you how to apply for the award, but rather to focus on
quality attributes that make up a world-class TQM organization.

Let's return to *The Corporate Game* and get started. You just received a
phone call from Tom, your director of quality control. He wants to meet

with you and tell you about a new TQM program that he has just learned about. He's piqued your interest. You've done some reading on the subject and you know you need to somehow get your people involved in quality. You ask Tom to join you in your office.

Tom enters your office armed with a stack of presentation foils. He starts the conversation with an appropriate introduction. "In the past few months, our company has made some significant progress. Look at what we have accomplished. We have a dynamic financial plan that is fully integrated into our economic, sales, and marketing plans. All our strategic plans support our production and manufacturing processes. We are moving full speed ahead with the implementation of just-in-time manufacturing and our employee morale is on a definite upswing. But, we are missing one thing. We don't have a total quality management plan. Let me tell you why we need one." He shows you his first chart (Exhibit 10-2).

Tom proceeds to explain the chart. "There are seven categories covered by a TQM program. Think of them as though they are an umbrella covering the entire company—all of its departments and people. If you review what each category is looking for from an excellence standpoint, it can give you interesting insights on what our company is doing. What are our

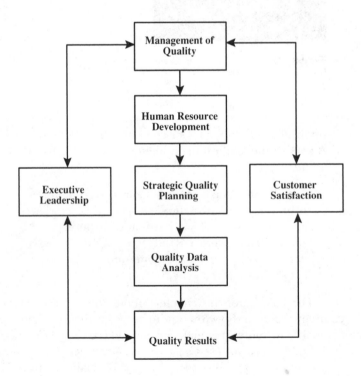

Exhibit 10-2. Total quality management framework.

strengths and weaknesses? How do we focus our resources on a continuous improvement program? We talked about the important role the continuous improvement process plays in a JIT environment. Exhibit 10-3 illustrates the concept from a TQM perspective."

You're intrigued, but the last thing you want to do is to endorse some kind of TQM sabbatical or utopia program that goes nowhere. You know Tom is a hard-working and dedicated team player. You don't want to discourage him from what could be a good idea. But, you also want to be honest with the man.

"Tom, I need time to review some information about TQM. Before we go any further on the subject, I want to be able to talk about TQM with some level of knowledge." You ask Tom to prepare an outline covering each of the seven categories and their performance criteria.

You also ask him to summarize how each of the criteria would be used to help improve the company's performance. "Let get back together in about a week after I get your material. We'll see if it will fit into what we are doing with our strategic plan."

Without any hesitation, Tom hands you the material that you just requested. You're impressed! You had figured that it would have taken him at least a couple of weeks to put all of that TQM stuff together. The meeting is over and you start to read what Tom gave you. Tom's material starts off with a brief description of the seven TQM categories:

Leadership—deals with how senior management provides TQM leadership and involvement to maintain an environment of quality excellence throughout the organization.

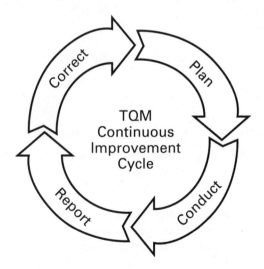

Exhibit 10-3. TQM continuous improvement.

Information and analysis—covers how the company's data and information are used to plan, manage, and evaluate quality.

Strategic quality planning—describes the company's quality planning process to achieve TQM status.

Human resource utilization—covers the company's overall human resource management effort and its quality objectives.

Quality assurance—shows how the company improves upon the design of its products and services to achieve higher-quality results.

Quality results—summarizes trends in quality improvement and current quality levels for products and services.

Customer satisfaction—describes how the company determines and satisfies customer requirements.

Leadership

The level of quality leadership in a TQM company is based on how management creates and sustains clear quality values throughout the organization. What management systems are in place to guide all the company's activities toward quality excellences? What quality role does management play in the community to demonstrate its commitment to quality? How does the company integrate its public responsibilities into its internal quality values?

You begin to understand what quality leadership means from a leadership perspective. Your senior managers need to be intricately involved in the company's TQM effort. Are they practicing what they preach and prescribe? Can you show specific ongoing examples where your management team spends a large percentage of its time in quality-related activities? Tom has included several examples that illustrate how quality leadership can be demonstrated:

- Hard evidence that the entire management team is involved in the quality effort
- The amount of quality-specific training that each manager receives annually
- Quality-related teams and task forces that management participates in
- Specific quality-related community programs management participates in

Quality Values

The company's quality values must be projected in a consistent manner (see Exhibit 10-4). A clear process must be in place for the adoption, implementation, and reinforcement of those values throughout the organization to achieve TQM status.

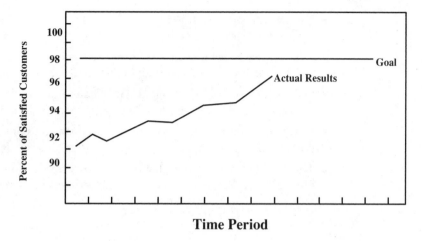

Exhibit 10-4. Customer satisfaction goal versus actual.

Are those values incorporated into your vision, mission, and goal statements? How are those values communicated throughout the company? Tom's examples of quality-value indicators follow:

- Use of different media to communicate quality values to all employees
- Existence of a systematic process for evaluating and adopting quality values
- Existence of formal and informal employee recognition programs that reinforce the importance of quality values

Management of Quality

All employees in TQM companies are accountable for quality. A hierarchy exists showing the quality-value measures that are in place and who is responsible for what, based upon level, function, and position. How these values are integrated into the daily management of the company is an essential part of TQM.

All quality-value measurements tier up. Individual measures form the basis for their supervisor's measures, which in turn roll up through the management chain to the senior executive. Quality accountability examples include:

- All job descriptions identify quality indices that can be controlled by the individuals covered by the job descriptions.
- The responsibility for all quality indices is clearly defined.

- A clear path showing how indices are tracked from the lowest to the highest employee level is in place.

- The degree to which all employees are measured on quality factors, which contributes to the overall quality goals of the company, is defined.

- Quality measurement systems and procedures are in place. All employees are encouraged to accomplish quality goals across functional lines.

- It can be demonstrated that the quality measurement systems are producing favorable results.

- The measurements are evaluated and corrective action is taken to assist units that are not performing according to the company's quality goals.

Information and Analysis

The information and analysis category covers the scope, use, and management of the information that supports the company's TQM plan. What types of quality-related data are collected and how are the data examined to make decisions?

Most companies collect quality data in some form. How are these data being used? Do they end up as data in reports that no one reads because the information is not needed to make day-by-day decisions? A true quality-conscious company has a specific set of criteria it uses to select the data it collects. The data are required to track key measurements that are important to the company and its customers.

For example, a steel mill might measure the amounts of dirt and oil that are present on finished rolled steel. There may be strict quality standards in place to identify acceptable levels of dirt and oil before shipping steel to customers. If the steel gets dirty in transit, as it usually does, and is subsequently cleaned at customer receiving docks, what purpose is served by the preshipment quality program?

Another important factor to consider is the objectivity of the data collection process, which may, in fact, be influenced by the people who collect the data. Your customer service department is tracking customer satisfaction with survey cards. The same department is responsible for tabulating survey results. You could question the objectivity of the tabulated results.

Collecting data and tabulating the results are only one part of the TQM management process. What do you do with the results? How is the information passed down to the people who are responsible for those results? What actions have been taken to improve upon the results, and is there a clear indication that the results are improving?

The next issue has to do with standardization in the reporting techniques. For example, there was a company that had 20 departments independently tracking quality measures. Each report was in a different format. On close analysis, it was discovered that over half the departments were reporting on the same data. The redundancy of the data being collected raised an issue. Was the company's quality program truly integrated, as it had advertised? The fact that none of the numbers matched raised a question of data integrity.

Data Comparisons and Benchmarks

Collecting data and reporting on results for internal review and improvement programs are an important part of the quality management process (Exhibit 10-5). But, how do the data compare with the results being achieved by your competitors or industry standards? If your quality objective is to become a world-class producer, then you have to define what that means. What are your quality targets?

A defense contractor contended that it could not get benchmarks from its competitors because the data were considered to be "competition sensitive." It was suggested that the contractor take another look at the industry. According to a military customer, it was common knowledge that nobody in the industry was meeting their commitments to customer delivery dates. If the defense contractor established benchmarks to meet 100 percent of its committed customer delivery dates and achieved the goal, the contractor would by default become the world-class leader in the industry.

Benchmarks do not have to come from companies that are in the same business or industry as yours. Let's say you are a computer manufacturer and you know you have major inventory-control quality problems. The automobile industry is known for having one of the best inventory-control programs in the country. Your benchmarks could subsequently be patterned after what is being achieved in another "best-of-breed" industry.

Customer Requirement	Process Capabilities	Competitor Data	Benchmark Data	Supplier Data
Focus Group	Computers	Demon	Motorola	IBM
Surveys	New Orders	Ford	NCR	Various

Exhibit 10-5. Quality data used in the planning process.

Analysis of Quality Information

If your company systematically analyzes all quality data collected to identify trends, problems, and opportunities for improvement, you are on your way to becoming a TQM company. There is a hidden agenda behind the word systematically. Let's break it down into its component parts.

When we say systematically, TQM assumes that you are analyzing quality-related data on a recurring and timely basis. The analytical process involves all levels of management. All the data are analyzed, which means that they have been filtered to include only relevant nonredundant data.

Problems and opportunities are clearly identified as a significant value-added by-product of this analytical process. In fact, you can identify tangible and intangible benefits coming out of this process on a recurring basis. The payback to the corporation is so significant that it gets top management attention.

In the traditional company setting, a manager's quality charts are posted for everyone to see. All the graphics on the charts point in only one direction. The numbers are good and they are always getting better. Only on a rare occasion will you see a quality chart where the numbers are bad and getting worse. But, that's where the action is. We would much rather see an honest manager who is willing to display a tough quality problem than one who is only willing to show good news.

Managers with tough quality problems probably have an aggressive action plan in place to fix the problem. They know what TQM is all about. The other managers with the perfect charts stand on the sidelines watching the parade go by and wonder what's happening.

Strategic TQM Planning

If your quality plan is a stand-alone document developed by one organization (i.e., Quality Control), then it is nothing more than a quality plan. By definition, the focus of a quality plan is limited to the scope and authority of the group that created it.

A strategic TQM plan covers the company's complete planning process for achieving and retaining a quality leadership position. It is created and maintained by all the major functions within the company (see Exhibit 10-6). Short- and long-term quality goals are clearly identified and fully integrated down to the lowest level of the company.

The TQM plan addresses, in detail, how your company will pursue market leadership by providing superior products and services. You're using a systematic approach for setting quality goals that ties directly into your quality objective to become a leader in your target markets. All major functions in the organization participate in the goal-setting process.

TQM

Customer
Satisfaction

Corporate Vision

Corporate Mission

Quality Goals

Quality Objectives

Exhibit 10-6. Total quality management foundation.

Your goals must be reasonable and relevant to customer expectations. What certain customers want and expect may not be feasible. Look at what other companies in your industry are offering for competitively priced products in order to establish your competitive standards.

Once established, the TQM plan is integrated into the strategic plan. In many companies, the strategic plan isn't shared with the employees. They may have participated in preparing one of the subsets of the plan, but they don't know what the total plan is all about.

This leads to conflicting goals and lack of direction. Although it may not be necessary to share the entire plan with all employees, they do need to know the general direction the corporation is taking and what their role is to help make it happen.

Many companies produce excellent TQM plans that appear to be fully integrated into the strategic plan. Only a few successfully translate these plans into actions that are systematically carried out during the year. Most companies deposit their plans into a file cabinet where they sit until the year-end review rolls around.

TQM companies have mechanisms in place to assure that their plans do not gather dust in file drawers. Their plans are continuously reviewed by all levels of management and are actively discussed with all employees. All corporate goals and objectives contribute directly or indirectly to the plan.

Major quality goals and the principal strategies for achieving these goals are in place. Goals are broad enough to relate to all segments of the business. For example, one goal may be to increase the reliability of your economy cars to help you reach a stated objective. You want to increase your market share by 10 percent over the next 12 months.

The important point to emphasize is that TQM and strategic planning are not done in a vacuum. The planning process starts by using information collected from outside sources. It starts by identifying customer needs and requirements. Many companies develop strategic plans without ever considering customer requirements. They think they already know what customers want. If they are wrong, the entire plan can move the company down the wrong path.

When quality goals are firmly in place, you deploy the TQM plan. How do you propose to accomplish your goals? What resources are committed to work on specific goals? Resources may include budget dollars, people, equipment, and support from your suppliers.

Statements like "By increasing the quality of our products, we will increase our market share" are far too general and vague. Quality goals should produce quantifiable improvements that show up in business success factors like profit, sales, and market share.

Human Resource Management

TQM is also concerned with how a company's overall human resource management program and strategies support quality objectives. How are human resource plans derived from the quality plans, goals, and objectives? Plans and improvement activities include:

Programs for promoting cooperation between employees

Initiatives to promote management cooperation with employees

Use of employee recognition systems

Education and training initiates that support TQM objectives

Human resource plans should demonstrate a clear and logical relationship between quality plans, goals, and objectives. For example, if you need more knowledge about ignition systems to improve the quality of your cars, your resource plan might include training to improve employee knowledge in this area. Your plan may also cover strategies for recruiting ignition experts from the outside.

Next, devise a means that will allow all your employees to contribute effectively to the company's quality objectives. In the previous chapter, we talked about how to use employee empowerment to motivate employees to accomplish key corporate objectives. We also talked about teamwork. The use of effective teams, staffed with empowered employees, is one of the best ways to assure employee involvement and participation in the company's TQM plan.

Product Quality Assurance

Product quality assurance is the part of the TQM program that examines the systematic approaches used to assure that product and service quality goals are met. It's also integrated into the company's continuous improvement processes. Quality development starts with the gathering of information about customer needs and requirements. TQM companies have processes in place for translating customer information into product features and standards.

The process begins by gathering information about specific components of the products that you produce. For example, suppose you asked your customers to make a list of the five characteristics they considered important about car ignition systems. The characteristics are prioritized and passed on to design engineers for incorporation into the new ignition design criteria.

All too often, companies fail to incorporate external product requirements into the design process. They end up with "white elephants" that nobody wants. Ford produced an Edsel motor car without seeking customer input at a time when nobody wanted big cars. That mistake cost the company billions of dollars.

Customers are only one source to tap for product requirement information. Talk to the employees who will be involved in marketing, producing, or servicing your products. You need their input early in the design process to verify customer requirements.

Quality-Control Plans

A quality-control plan is used to assure that all aspects of the end-product quality have been covered. It's a detailed plan that identifies the important manufacturing processes and specifies the indices by which each process will be measured. Indices are indicators derived from data collected throughout the process to determine if product quality goals are being met.

Here is how to create a simple quality-control plan. First, identify all of the processes involved in the production of your cars. For clarity, present this information in a matrix similar to the one in Exhibit 10-7.

The processes to produce an economy car are listed along the left side of the exhibit. The horizontal axis identifies who owns each process. The quality indicators that are in place to measure process quality levels, quality indicator goals, and actual indicator results are shown on the matrix.

What do you do if your quality plan goes out of control? Your actual indicators are outside the bounds of your quality goals. You implement what the quality control professionals call a *cause analysis process*. Exhibit 10-8 shows how this process works.

Manufacturing Process	Process Owner	Quality Goals	Quality Results
Door Assembly	Dept. TF1	1:10,000 defects	1:25,000 defects
Engine Assembly	Dept. AD6	50,000 hrs.	25,000 hrs.

Exhibit 10-7. TQM process goals.

An empowered quality improvement team meets to identify the root cause of the quality problem. A solution to the problem is identified and implemented. The problem is closely monitored over an appropriate period of time to verify that the corrective action plan worked.

Continuous Improvement Process

The cause-analysis process can also be used to improve upon processes that are meeting current quality goals. For example, suppose you heard about innovations in plating technology that would allow you to tighten the tolerance on bumper installations. Your marketing people have told you about customer complaints in this area.

Once again, you activate a quality improvement team to figure out ways to make the current process even better. This is an example of directed improvement. The improvement is coming from management and not from the employees. Although it's an important stage in the implementation of TQM, full implementation occurs when your employees start making continuous quality improvement recommendations. It becomes a part of their day-to-day operational responsibility.

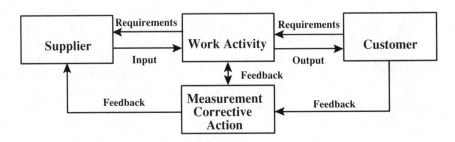

Exhibit 10-8. TQM improvement process.

Supplier Quality

We talked about the importance of supplier quality in the just-in-time process. We didn't cover how you measure and control suppliers to assure that they meet your company's TQM expectations. What processes do you have in place to assure and improve upon the quality of supplier delivered materials and services?

You first have to identify the quality requirements for delivered goods and services. If your company is heavily dependent upon a large network of suppliers, you may want to establish a priority list beginning with your most critical suppliers. Next, identify the quality requirements for the top-priority suppliers (Exhibit 10-9).

When you implemented JIT, you negotiated agreements with your suppliers to provide materials and services that are in line with the company's quality goals. Although you trust your suppliers, you want to put in place certain measurements and indicators to monitor supplier performance. Key checkpoints in your supplier quality-control program include:

- Identification of critical suppliers

- Identification of supplier agreed-upon quality indices and indicators

- Implementation of an effective system for communicating quality standards, requirements, and deviations from negotiated standards with suppliers

It's important that you have a well-defined approach for ensuring that your suppliers are fully aware of the role that they play in your TQM program. The effort that your company puts into ensuring quality from its suppliers should be directly dependent upon the degree that your TQM program relies upon supplier support. Key supplier quality programs should include:

- The amount of effort that the corporation devotes to assure supplier quality is meeting required levels

- Adequate definition and communication of expected supplier quality standards

Supplier	Quality Indicators	Quality Requirements
Federal Systems	Deliver when promised	99% of time
Western Assembly	Defect free switches	less than .005 rejects

Exhibit 10-9. First two entries in a prioritized list of suppliers.

- Deployment of systems to measure supplier performance on a recurring basis
- Supplier continuous improvement processes are in place showing a record of progressive improvement over time

Quality Results

Quality results are the bottom line of the TQM program. It puts to the test everything we have implemented up to this point. All the previous discussions concentrated on the implementation of TQM processes and activities. Quality results show evidence and facts that the TQM effort has produced favorable results.

The quality results process is shown in Exhibit 10-10. Four different points are measured: inputs, processes, outputs, and satisfactions. All corporations have inputs, processes, and outputs. Outputs can be products and services, which are sold to consumers who ultimately register some level of satisfaction or dissatisfaction with the product or service.

As you begin to build up your database over time, you will be able to identify important quality trends, whether good or bad. If you use an exhibit similar to the one shown in Exhibit 10-11, a great deal of information can be shown in a limited space.

Graphs like the ones in Exhibit 10-12 can be used to illustrate and track key quality rating information. A good rule to follow when using graphics is to include a goal line on each graph. Goal lines establish how well you are performing over time.

How do you establish quality goal lines? Was it a line arbitrarily set at some point to make the quality trend look good? TQM companies will establish goal lines that are at higher-quality levels than their competitors. They go after the best products in the industry.

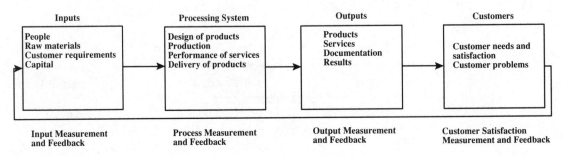

Exhibit 10-10. The customer satisfaction process.

	1990	**1991**	**1992**	**1993**	**1994**
Repeat Business %	18%	23%	28%	36%	44%
Car Failure Reports	10	15	44	18	11
Inspection Failures	8	33	3	4	0

Exhibit 10-11. Demon Car Company summary of quality data.

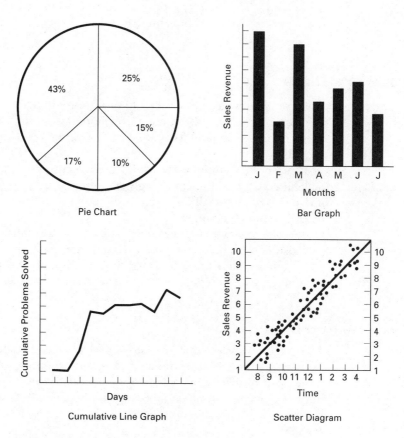

Exhibit 10-12. TQM chart measurement alternatives.

Customer Satisfaction

The final TQM category is customer satisfaction. It's the bottom line of the TQM program. You can do all of the quality items that we have been talking about, but if your customers still think your product is average or inferior, then your company will remain average or inferior to your competition.

Advertising and market promotion can be used to influence customers to buy the product the first time. Product quality is what keeps them coming back and feeds the customer referral system. You may buy a new car because of its great styling and price. You will never buy another one if the quality is poor.

How does a company determine current and future customer expectations and requirements? The chapter on marketing showed you how to use questionnaire surveys to help establish the needs and wants of potential customers. Another good source of data is new customers. Surveying new customers to find out why they selected your product can provide valuable information. The same approach could be used to survey lost customers so that corrective action can be initiated.

Customer Relations

Most companies have processes and procedures in place to effectively manage customer relations. If done correctly, it can be one of the best ways to solicit customer comments (good or bad) on the company's products and services.

A variety of techniques is used to solicit customer input. You have to make it easy for customers to register comments. Customer service or hotline toll-free numbers have become quite popular. Comment cards are another common technique.

How often you measure customer satisfaction is another important factor to consider. Conducting a survey once a year generally won't get the job done. The frequency and thoroughness that you employ to gather current customer satisfaction data are what drives a successful TQM program.

Analyzing Customer Relations Data

A TQM company will analyze customer-related data to determine if shifts in its market strategies, corporate policies, and resource allocations are warranted as a result of the analysis. For example, if you found that a majority of the buyers for your economy cars is in the 25 to 35 single male category, you may decide to tailor your advertising plan to reach this specific market segment.

Hyatt Hotel distributes customer comment cards in all of their hotel rooms. As a result, it was discovered that a large number of their weekend hotel guests did not like the Sunday noon checkout policy. They wanted to spend Sunday afternoon in the area shopping, golfing, and playing tennis. They also wanted to take a shower before returning home. Hyatt instituted a late checkout policy for all weekend guests.

Customer Commitment

Commitment to customers is what companies offer to promote trust and confidence in their products and services. Commitments may include guarantees, warranties, or other implied understandings with customers. When Chrysler introduced a 7-year/70,000 mile warranty, it was saying a lot about its belief in the quality of its products.

The strengths of your TQM plan grow substantially if you can show how your customer commitments have increased in the form of repeat business as a result of continuous improvements in your products.

Complaint Resolution

It is always easier to process the customer compliments as opposed to the complaints. Unfortunately, continuous improvement demands complaint input. How your company handles complaint information should be an important part of your TQM program.

Most companies have systems in place for recording letter and phone complaints. These types of systems only cover the "hard" complaints—such as the customer who is mad and will take the time to talk to anybody about the problem. Most customers who have a problem will not take the time to resolve it. Instead, they'll just stop buying your product for reasons you'll never know.

What TQM procedures can you put in place to capture data on these kinds of complaints? You need to have a system in place for documenting all written and verbal comments made by customers about your products.

For example, Blanchard Laboratories processes laboratory specimens and distributes test results to physicians by way of couriers. Every courier has been trained to listen and record any comments relative to the customer's perception of the lab's services. Any complaint-oriented comments are immediately reported to sales managers for problem resolution within 24 hours. Couriers are rewarded for submitting timely and properly documented complaints.

Measuring Customer Satisfaction

All TQM companies have various techniques in place to measure customer satisfaction. Although we have talked about feedback cards and questionnaire surveys as methods of obtaining customer feedback, they only provide you with a part of the story.

The problem with surveys is that most people won't take the time to fill them out. It they are pressured to fill one out, they will do it quickly without much concern for accuracy. They tend to rate everything average or above average.

One of the more effective ways to measure customer satisfaction is to examine their behavior. The fact that a high percentage of your customers continuously trade their old models in for your new models says a lot about customer satisfaction for your cars (see Exhibit 10-10). The amount of repeat business is one of the best satisfaction indicators you can have.

You also need to address how your level of customer satisfaction compares to your competitors. You can pick up some information from your surveys by asking your customers what they think about your competitors.

There are market-research firms who specialize in measuring consumer satisfaction across an industry. They use the same measuring techniques to assure the consistency of the data collected. They can also identify the key features that customers want from product groups. Because customer satisfaction is the most important TQM measurement, TQM companies are constantly assessing customer satisfaction levels.

Customer Results

TQM companies can demonstrate how levels of customer satisfaction have improved over time due to specific quality programs. World-class companies can present data showing that their customers are more satisfied than any of their competitors.

In the final analysis, the TQM results are translated beyond the customer satisfaction indicators. The company's employee morale factors are up. People like their work and their company is compensating them for "going the extra mile."

The company is in a healthy financial position, which keeps the stockholders happy. The management team likes TQM because it offers them a challenge to find ways to continuously improve upon the business processes. There are no reasons to get bored when you work for a TQM company.

Your Meeting with Tom

You finally finish reading the TQM material that Tom gave you. There is a lot more to TQM than you had originally thought. How do you tie it all into your strategic plan? Tom is on his way to your office. He enters and you thank him for providing you with the background information on TQM.

You start the conversation with a question. "Tom, can you reduce all of the pieces and components of TQM into a single chart? How does it fit into what we are already doing in our strategic plan?"

Tom places a foil on the overhead projector and displays the chart you requested (Exhibit 10-13). He starts his explanation by saying "TQM is nothing more than the umbrella that covers our strategic plan."

"It provides the company with all the checks, balances, and controls it needs to assure that the strategic plan moves the corporation forward in the right direction. That is why the strategic plan is in the middle of the chart. It's the heart of TQM."

"The corporate vision, missions, and goals form the top tier of TQM. They provide continuity and direction to the overall planning process. Customer needs and requirements preside on the left side of the plan. Every-

Exhibit 10-13. The total quality management cycle.

thing that we do must ultimately be in concert with the expectations of our customers."

"The right side of the exhibit covers the functional areas of the company and what they must do in conjunction with our suppliers to assure that the principles and concepts of TQM are met." You thank Tom for his truly brilliant explanation.

You bait Tom for an answer by asking him a question. "There is one thing that we are missing." Tom asks, "What's that?" You respond, "We need more data and information about our operations if we really want to get serious about TQM. Let's read the next chapter on information technology to see if we can get some ideas about what to do in this area."

Summary and Conclusions

The chapter began with a general discussion about quality, where it's been, and where it's going in this country. We introduced you to The Malcolm Baldrige National Quality Award, America's national effort to get back into the international quality race.

You met with Tom, your director of quality control, and learned about TQM. As you began to study the process, you realized that there were a number of similarities between the TQM program and the other programs that you had implemented. Continuous improvement and strategic planning were two recurring examples.

TQM seemed to offer you a way of combining all your strategic plans together into one integrated package. And, the program certainly had the right focus. Customer satisfaction is the name of the game, as far as you're concerned. Without it, no company can survive.

You and Tom both agree to implement TQM. However, you realize that you're going to need access to more information to support a successful TQM program. Tom has assured you that the information you're looking for is in the next chapter—The Power of Information. You read on!

PC Game Assignment and Instructions

When you load the game, you should be in Month 10 if you have been following our recommendations (Exhibit 10-14). You've only got two more chapters in the book to complete.

The Corporate Game
Month 10 - Journal

Game Tutorial

Add/Change Names

Bank Account Management

Financial Planning

Market Research Report

Order MFG Resources

View Last Month's Report

Done   Exit Game

Exhibit 10-14. Month 10—Journal menu.

11

The Power
of Information

Bullets for Corporate Guns

The old adage that information is power is still true today. It's been the underlying theme of this book. Every decision that we have made up to this point in *The Corporate Game* has been based upon information derived from each of the business disciplines.

Our entire strategic plan was built on an information base. Information from our accounting and financial systems formed the initial base of the plan. We added economics, marketing, and sales information to improve upon the integrity of the plan.

Production control and manufacturing were brought together to build our new just-in-time (JIT) manufacturing system. JIT is generating its own set of information that gets fed into the company's continuous improvement processes. All this information is now incorporated into the total quality management (TQM) system.

That's a lot of information to use and control. If information can be used as "bullets for corporate guns," you're not going to run out of ammunition. You wonder if you really need all this information.

Information Technology

Information technology is moving at a record pace, which has, in turn, driven the price of computing down to ridiculously low levels. Every company can now afford computer hardware and software. Have all these advances really changed the essence of what managers need to know to do their jobs well?

Processing information correctly to make the right decision can mean the difference between surviving and going out of business in today's tough economic environment. To illustrate the point, suppose you lost a $20 gold coin on a dark street one night. Would you look for the coin where you think you lost it or under a street light, where the lighting is better?

It depends on what information you have. If you have information that indicates the coin was lost on the dark side of the street, you would look on the dark side. If no such information is available, looking under a street light is an intelligent strategy. The coin is just as likely to be there as any place else, and with the benefit of the light, your chances of finding the coin are dramatically improved.

The story provides the underlying theme of this chapter. Information is nothing more than a management tool, which, if properly applied, reduces the inherent risks when any decision is made. We are not concerned about what tools (e.g., computers and software) you use to process information. That's the easy part. What we are concerned about is how you deal with the flood of solicited and unsolicited information that you receive every day. How do you filter out irrelevant information to get at the facts you need to make the right decision?

The Way It Was

Just a few short years ago, there were stable domestic markets throughout corporate America. As a result, there was no pressure to be innovative. A new product might remain largely unchanged for years or even decades before it became obsolete.

Companies could produce enormous quantities of the same products by using routine automated processes to realize significant economies of scale. As production volumes increased, unit cost dropped, and profits rose accordingly. For obvious reasons (i.e., profits), top management tightly controlled the use of routine production procedures.

New workers could be taught in a few hours how to perform a typical mass-production task. They were given the career option of performing this simple task for the rest of their lives or they were simply replaced. Trade unions became a thing of the past in this country.

Over time, the truly skilled worker became a dinosaur. Only a few people in manufacturing understood what they were doing. One worker would be responsible for inserting the bolt. Another would tighten the nut. The pride of craftsmanship and the desire of the American worker to learn gave way to the ultimate in automation. A spirit of fatalistic "I don't give a darn" resignation passed over America's work force.

Corporate management knew exactly what was happening. But they didn't care. They were thriving on increased output and profit margins were soaring through the roof. When computer-controlled manufacturing became available in the late 1960s, these same companies were quick to jump on the bandwagon. They quietly began to replace workers with automated systems.

By the mid 1970s, global competition entered the country through the back door and began to put a damper on America's rising automation spiral. Asian and European companies started to capture significant portions of America's key industries.

The consumer electronic and automobile industries were the first to feel the bite. The mass output that once justified and drove our robotized manufacturing systems dried up. By the time the 1980s rolled around, 40 percent of our domestic car market and 60 percent of our consumer electronic markets had been captured by foreign competition. Our trade balance was a disaster.

As we proceed through the 1990s, most of the consumer markets will become irreversibly fragmented. Product diversity will become so great that production runs of six months will be considered long runs by today's standards. The big runs that resulted in economies of scale in the "old days" are hard to find today. Mass production, as we use to know it, is dead.

Unfortunately, many of America's corporate leaders have been slow to pick up on the importance of these changes. The lag of corporations to adjust to this paradigm shift has already cost this country billions of dollars in lost markets and American jobs.

Where's the Beef?

So much for the historical tour. What does all this have to do with how you use information to run business today? Everything! Innovation is built on information. Production-controlled automation was great at controlling relatively stable long-term mass-production operations. Very little innovation was required to make it work so we dropped the word from our corporate vocabulary.

That's all changed. Innovation is the hot word in today's competitive environment. There was a last-ditch effort on the part of many automated companies to introduce artificial intelligence into their manufacturing processes so that they could uses computers to generate innovation.

The only ones who were innovative and gained from the experience were the shrewd salespeople who sold artificial intelligence systems. Management failed to realize what Darwin knew back in the eighteenth century. Only human beings are capable of innovative reasoning. It is only through the firsthand experiences and applied imaginations of people that organizations can devise and implement innovative changes to meet the expectations of today's international markets.

Some managers still believe that information knowledge should reside only at the top of the organization. If they continue down this path, they will become a passing character in *The Last Picture Show*. Look around you. Everywhere you look, there is a proliferation of personal computers, intelligent work stations, and sophisticated user-controlled software capturing what employees perceive is information they need to run "their part of the show."

The problem has to do with perception. If they are working for a management team that believes in "information blackout," employees will collect what they perceive to be the right set of information they need to do their jobs. In an information innovative company, information is openly shared throughout the organization.

Winning the Game

In an economy where the only certainty is uncertainty, the one source that you can draw on to get a competitive advantage is information. Today's markets are volatile. New products become obsolete almost before they are introduced. The successful companies are the ones creating information out of mass amounts of data that they process daily.

They are able to disseminate meaningful information throughout their organization. Their employees know how to use it to create new technologies and products. They are the new breed of information empowered corporations.

All this sounds pretty basic, doesn't it? If you've got more information about the game than the next guy on the block, you stand a better chance of winning. And yet, in spite of all the talk about the power of information, only a few managers grasp the importance of an information innovative company.

We still have corporate managers who don't know how to use information and they certainly don't know how to manage information. They do not know how to use information to develop strategic plans, exploit competition, or meet customer requirements. They view the corporation as an organizational machine.

In their minds, the corporate machine generates its own information out of its information processing subsystems. They rely on this information database to make quantifiable decisions related to increasing productivity, lowering cost, and improving returns on investments. Unfortunately, this paradigm is deeply ingrained into the traditions of corporate management.

Our highly successful competitors living outside the United States have a very different view on how to use information to achieve their corporate goals. Companies like Honda, Canon, and Sharp have become famous for their ability to create markets, respond quickly to customer requirements, and to rapidly develop new products at the same time. They all share one thing in common. They're Japanese!

To western executives, the Japanese approach often seems ridiculous. Honda created an original vision statement: "Honda is the theory of automobile evolution." It was an awkward statement, but it excited the Honda workers. Honda collected massive amounts of consumer data from this country. It told them that Americans were ready for an "automobile evolution." They wanted an economy car to commute to work. Detroit wouldn't give it to them so Honda produced the Honda Civic and the rest of the Honda success story is history.

Canon had built up a rather impressive information database that unfortunately revealed that the company would not be a major competitor in the long-term camera business. To survive, Canon's management team had to come up with an alternative product. Management opened up its database to employees and collectively searched for alternatives. The same camera-related information the company had been collecting for years revealed a huge untapped demand for a low-end copier.

None of the copier manufacturers offered low-end copiers. Millions of small businesses throughout the world needed one. The subsequent introduction of Canon's low-end copiers led to Canon's successful entrance into the more lucrative field of office automation. In each of these examples, information played a major role in opening the doors to new product development. Management shared the information with employees to jointly develop a viable solution to a corporate problem.

The Danger of Ignorance

Without access to any strategic information, average employees won't be sure of what it is that they are supposed to know or do for their company. It's not their fault. You can't expect them use the limited information they have to second guess where the company is supposed to be going. They will run around and collect all kinds of meaningless information in an attempt to find the answers they think management is looking for.

The challenge in today's organization is to communicate information to the employees to deepen their understanding of the corporate visions, missions and goals. Companies are discovering interesting situations when this happens. They are discovering that people really can think. In fact, employees can express a collective imagination that is far greater than the sum of all the computers in the world. This living knowledge emerges as people begin to share their perspectives on solving problems. If the process is allowed to continue, it diffuses "it can't be done" attitudes that were previously based upon unfounded assumptions and bad information.

Knowledge Processing

It used to be called data processing. Next, they called it information processing. Now they're calling it *knowledge processing*. Knowledge processing differs from data and information processing in that it evolves out of reason, rather than hard facts that may or may not be supported by information. Knowledge processing draws filtered data and information from multiple sources to produce strategic decisions. It cannot be automated or controlled by the old mechanisms of organizational management.

Many companies have this information processing cycle backwards. They are drowning in a sea of high technology that is supported with piles of data, offering no insights into what they are doing. They end up producing products and services that are inferior in quality, cost too much, or that nobody wants.

This is precisely why you are hearing so much about employee empowerment, employee involvement, self-directed work teams, participatory management, and concurrent engineering. There are a lot of buzz words to choose from. The bottom line is that organizations need knowledge that is supplied from the bottom up, not from the top down, to function effectively in today's business climate.

The New Information Breed

The concept of relinquishing the power of information from top management down to the employee is a major factor fueling a new breed of conferences. The first Collaboration Conference was held in 1992. The conference theme was "Learning to Team, Teaming to Learn." Nationally recognized corporate leaders addressed the information paradigm shifts taking place all over the country. The airline industry was one of the first to apply team learning.

Ever since deregulation, the airlines have been going through some tough times. Information empowered airlines were looking for ways to overcome their financial problems and increase their market share. The airline reservation system provides a classic example of an approach one airline took.

Early airline reservation systems were built around company needs rather than the needs of the customer. The systems told airlines how many seats were available on a flight. They were not programmed to tell the airlines anything about the passenger. Canadian Airline employees decided to apply some innovative reasoning to the process.

They wanted a reservation system that could tell them if a passenger had previously flown with Canadian Air. This would allow Canadian Air to customize its services for that particular passenger. The passenger's seat preference and frequent flyer points could be automatically assigned. Car rental and hotel preferences could be offered and arranged by the airline. As the customer database grew, it could be used to develop marketing joint ventures with the hotel chains and car rental companies. Canadian Air was the first to implement this very successful program.

This concept could be applied to any customer service business. The approach rests in the belief that any business activity can be improved through the application of bottom-up employee ideas. With a refinement and extension of information, a wave of value-added services can be offered to customers to differentiate one company from a competitor.

The apparel industry is being revolutionized by employee-generated ideas. Five basic steps are used to fabricate a piece of clothing:

1. Making fiber
2. Making cloth from the fiber
3. Cutting and stitching garments
4. Stocking retail shelves
5. Final customer sales

It takes an average of one year to complete the five steps. Even if a retailer spots a lucrative fashion trend, by the time the clothing industry actually makes the garments, the trend is probably out. As a result, store buyers have to make style judgments and place orders a year in advance of a perceived fashion trend. It's a risky business. The apparel industry estimates that forced markdowns, lost sales, and warehouse costs account for 25 percent of a garment's total cost.

Levi Strauss challenged its production workers with the task of reducing the one-year response time. They were given access to all the information that Levi had on the problem. If it could be solved, the company could realize bigger profit margins and narrow the foreign competition cost gap.

A Levi employee team came up with what became know as the Livilink system, which included seven new cost and time reduction innovations. They created electronic purchase orders to reduce order entry time. Bar codes were added to shipping cartons and packing slips to speed unloading.

New systems were added to measure color and inspect fabric as it came off the loom so that it could be shipped directly to the cutting rooms. The application of information to solve the distribution problem paid off. Three months were cut out of the one-year cycle, thanks to the effective application of information by Levi's production workers.

What's Happening?

What has happened at Canadian Air and at Levi Strauss are just two examples of what must happen to all U.S. businesses in the years ahead. They must get information into the hands of their employees so that employees can start generating innovative ideas. If they have access to the right information, employees from all levels can be challenged with exciting assignments. Employees can be used as a powerful force to help resolve corporate problems and implement strategic changes.

Unfortunately, there will be some companies that will not be able to make this transition. They will fail to reconfigure their business operations around employee knowledge processing. Most will continue to run "lights out" operations and will, in turn, have their lights "turned out" when they go out of business.

Old standards of service and production efficiency will simply not make the cut in the new world economy. The proper and perpetual application of information will have to be built into every element of the corporate structure if it is expected to reach the new competitive standards. These information usage trends are becoming more and more apparent. They are not isolated trends.

Intelligence Processing

Decision making is the most important function managers perform for the corporation. Everything else is irrelevant if the management perpetually makes the wrong decisions. The organization will ultimately fail.

Processing knowledge and information intelligently is critical to the survival and well-being of any company. Defining problems and identifying the right information that can be used to solve those problems must occur daily. Information is also an essential ingredient in implementing change. You have got to have it in order to determine if the change is viable. Can a proposed change be accomplished based upon your current level of information? How much information do you need?

The accumulation of information can increase to a point where management becomes flooded with unsolicited and irrelevant information. One of the major dangers of an information flood is that by the time you sift through all the information to find what you're looking for, you run out of time. The small problem you were trying to solve has now become a major problem. It now demands more information before it can be solved. The opportunities that could have been realized if the problem under consideration had been resolved in a timely manner have passed.

The solution to the problem of information overload is to devise a filtering system. In a perfect world, the filter would eliminate irrelevant information and retain only relevant information. Ultimately, you want to end up with just the right mix of information which would allow you to make the right decision every time. Unfortunately, we do not have adequate software systems capable of filtering information. The next best thing is the human mind and its ability to reason.

Decision making is a human process of choice that leads to the selection of one alternative rather than others. It requires the processing of information to identify the best alternate solution. In several of our examples, management initiated decisions were made after employee filtered information and applied reason were used to solve the problem.

The Decision-Making Process

Effective decision making occurs in a logical sequence of steps. First, an event must occur to stimulate someone to make a decision. The event may be positive or negative. Let's go back into *The Corporate Game.* Your marketing vice president has just brought you some good news for a change. One of your major car competitors has just gone out of business.

Now for the bad news. The union has just announced a major strike at all your plants. Worse yet, the strike only affects your company. Both of these events hit you just as you entered your office. You haven't even had time to get a cup of coffee. You should have stayed home and taken Joe up on his offer to play golf this morning.

Individuals vary enormously in their responses to stimulating events. In the "good news-bad news" scenario, you have an opportunity to increase sales from a defunct competitor. You need new sales to pump action into your financial statements. But, with the strike on, you're dead in the water. You can't sell more cars if you don't have any way to produce them.

Because you're the CEO, you decide to "rise to the challenge." You've just read a book called *The Corporate Game,* which has given you new ideas on how to use information to make the right decisions. You have got to make some tough decisions today and you need to get all the information that you can, before you make the final decision. If you make the right decision, you get to keep your job. Our story continues.

Information Search

You start your search for information by calling your director of personnel (Kathy) into your office. You like Kathy because she knows how to move in on problems like "smart bombs" did in the Desert Storm War. You start the conversation off in a low and controlled tone. "Kathy, what's this strike all about? I didn't even know that we were having union problems."

Kathy answers in a voice that is not quite as controlled as yours. "To be honest with you, it caught me by surprise too. I knew there were rumblings out there about low salaries and no promotions. We both know we haven't been able to keep up with the cost of living because of our dismal financial performance."

You know she's right on the financial account but you're not going to acknowledge it until you get more information. You make your first decision of the morning. "Kathy, get out there and find out what it will take to end this strike within the next 24 hours. I have an opportunity to sell more cars, but I can't do that if nobody will build them for me."

That was an easy decision to make. You made the decision to get more information so that you can make the "big" decision, whatever that is. Right now, you don't have to worry about it until Kathy gets back with the information you have requested.

As Kathy leaves your office, your vice presidents of marketing and finance (Jim and Dan) walk in for their scheduled 9 a.m. meeting. Jim starts by saying, "We have got a real opportunity to capture some new car sales. The Demon Automobile Company has just announced bankruptcy. All their production facilities will be closed by the end of the week."

Dan quickly adds some financial insights. "This may be just what we need to get our books in order. Our profits have been sagging and, as a result, we may not be far behind Demon." Your circuit boards are becoming overloaded. You think to yourself, "What does he mean by not far behind Demon?" You decide not to think about that prospect for now. You'll think about it tomorrow. You make another one of those easy decisions. "Let's meet again at 3 p.m. this afternoon and ask Kathy to join us. Be prepared to tell me what Demon's bankruptcy means to our current sales forecast. What impact will it have on our bottom line?"

It's now 3 p.m. and your scheduled meeting with Kathy, Jim, and Dan begins. Kathy is the first to speak. "I was right. Everybody out there is frustrated about their wages. I can't blame them. Let me show you what has happened to their wages over the last three years." Kathy uses the overhead projector to display the graph in Exhibit 11-1.

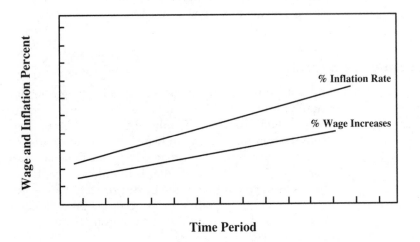

Exhibit 11-1. Wages versus inflation rate.

"As you can see, the exhibit shows a rather dismal picture. The average salary percent increase fell below the average rate of inflation. The net take home pay of our average worker has actually decreased over the past three years. Now, look at the number of voluntary terminations that we have experienced over the same period of time." (See Exhibit 11-2).

"With our net loss in take home pay, we have been losing an increasing number of our people to other better-paying jobs. The people we're losing are, for the most part, our best people. That's because it's relatively easy for them to find a job. The problem compounds itself when you look at what's happening with new hires in Exhibit 11-3.

"Our recruiting and new hire training costs are going out of sight. There are two basic reasons for this. First, it is taking us longer to find replacement workers at our less than competitive pay rates. Second, when we find new people, they don't have enough experience. We have to train them to bring them up to the level of the persons they're replacing. The training program is costing us a lot of money."

"As soon as they gain experience, they quit for a better-paying job, and we start the whole vicious cycle all over again. If we want to settle this strike, we have got to increase our wages by 15 percent across the board to become competitive and meet the union's demands." You have that sinking feeling in your stomach. You thank Kathy for the information she has given and turn to Jim for his part of the presentation.

"As you know, before Demon went bankrupt, we were one of four automobile companies selling cars. With Demon out, there are only three of us left. Simple math says that we can divide the market up three ways instead of four. Here's what it looks like if you assume that we capture one third of the total market" (See Exhibit 11-4).

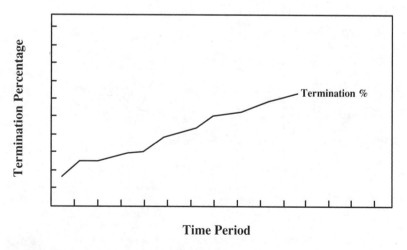

Exhibit 11-2. Percent of voluntary terminations.

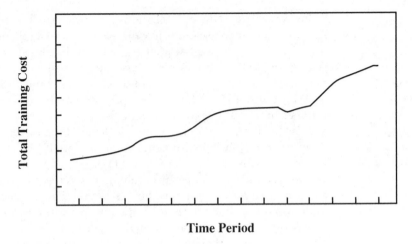

Exhibit 11-3. Cost of training program.

Dan's financial wheels are really beginning to turn. He is so excited that he barely waits for Jim to finish. "Look at what this would do to our financial statements. The increase in sales from Jim's chart would lower our fixed costs." (See Exhibit 11-5).

"This would drive our profit margins and rate of return on assets up (Exhibit 11-6). I need not remind you about how pleased that would make our stockholders and the board of directors."

"We would finally have a positive cashflow (see Exhibit 11-7) to pay off

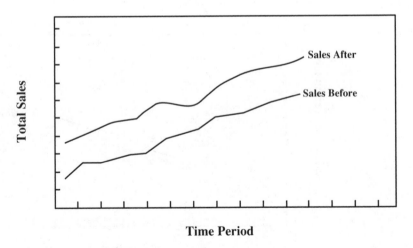

Exhibit 11-4. Projected sales after Demon bankruptcy.

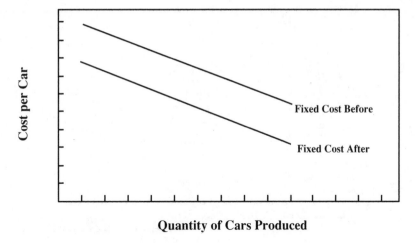

Exhibit 11-5. Average fixed cost per car.

our suppliers, which are key to our just-in-time manufacturing program." When you study Dan's charts, you too begin to get excited. If you work this thing right, you might be able to keep this damn job.

Your team has done a good job and you thank them for their help. They have given you a lot of information to decipher and it is exactly what you'll need to make knowledgeable decisions. You decide to dismiss everybody so you can study, in detail, the information they have given you.

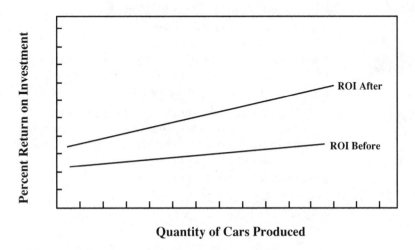

Exhibit 11-6. Return on investment before and after bankruptcy.

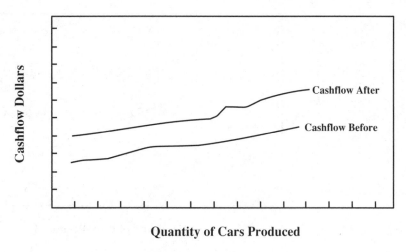

Exhibit 11-7. Cashflow before and after bankruptcy.

Problem Formulation

In the privacy of your office, you finally have a chance to analyze the problems in front of you. This has been one heck of a day. You pull a scratch pad out and start compiling a list of all the problems, based upon the information you have.

1. Your production workers are upset about their wages. The small salary increases you have given them have been eaten up by inflation. They are right to be upset, but what can you do about it?

2. You know your sales have been down. Your profit percent is below what the stockholders could make if they deposited their money into a savings account. If you don't turn the corner pretty soon, that is exactly what they will do. When the stock price heads for rock bottom, you know who the board of directors will come after as their "sacrificial lamb."

3. You need to make sure you capture your share of Demon's car market. But can you move quickly enough to make that happen? You know your two remaining competitors are thinking along these exact same lines. With the strike on, you can't produce any cars and they are likely to take all of Demon's market. You would be left with nothing.

4. You were counting on the new just-in-time manufacturing system to help bail you out of this mess. Once it gets fully implemented, you expect to see some real savings in your total production cost. But, as Dan pointed out, you haven't been able to pay your key suppliers on time. Their deliveries are beginning to lag, which is putting the whole JIT system at risk.

5. The return on asset issue is also causing problems. Your bank has been after you to get your returns up. They are concerned about it and charging you a higher interest on your credit line to cover their concerns.

As you see it, these are the top five problems. You know the problems are all interrelated. The strike is preventing you from capturing your share of Demon's market. Without the increased sales, you can't pay your suppliers on time. As a result, the corporation's stock prices are depressed.

That will delay the implementation of the JIT system, which will put more pressure on costs. As your costs go up, profits go down, and you're in a vicious cycle. You wonder if that is what happened to Demon. What alternatives do you have?

Evaluating Alternatives

You know you must make rational decisions to get out of this mess. What alternatives do you have, based upon the available information? Again, out comes the scratch pad, and you start to list each alternative.

1. If I increase wages by 15 percent across the board, everybody will be happy. The strike will be over and I can begin to produce the extra cars needed to meet the new sales forecast.

2. The total monthly cost of a 15 percent wage hike will be $90,000.

3. It's currently costing the company $18,000 a month in excess recruiting costs. If the wage hike cuts the company's voluntary terminations by 50 percent, recruiting costs should drop by 33 percent to $12,000 per month.

4. New hire training costs are costing the company another $10,000 a month. If voluntary terminations are reduced by 50 percent, training cost, which is costed on a per person basis, could be cut by 50 percent or $5000 per month.

5. The new sales numbers will add an additional $100,000 net profit to the company's monthly bottom line.

Does it all make sense? Will you be able to afford the salary increase when all the numbers are brought together? There is only one way to find out. You construct a "mini" breakeven analysis exhibit (see Exhibit 11-8).

Things are finally looking up. If you can pull all this off, you'll be able to pay everybody a reasonable salary, end the strike, grab at least a third of Demon's car market, and get some profits back into the financial statements. But wait a minute! You forgot one thing.

The anticipated profit of $100,000 a month from the new sales assumes

Profit from new sales forecast	$100,000
Plus: Savings from recruiting	$ 6,000
Savings from training	$ 5,000
Total gross profit	$111,000
LESS: Cost of salary increase	$ 90,000
Total net profit	$ 21,000

Exhibit 11-8. Effect of increases in sales on profit.

that you could produce the additional car units using the current work shifts. How can you do that when you are currently running at 100 percent of capacity? To meet the higher production requirements, you'll have to work everybody on overtime. At the higher rate, that will add an additional $50,000 of labor expenses to the profit and loss statement. Your $21,000 profit just turned into a $29,000 loss (see Exhibit 11-9).

That sinking feeling sets back in. You're running out of answers. You read an article somewhere, about how to get employees involved in helping to solve corporate problems. You have to give them access to the right information. You call Kathy and explain the dilemma you are in. She gives you a ray of hope. "Let me talk to a couple of our production people and see what we can work out. Can we meet with you first thing in the morning?" You

Profit from new sales forecast	$100,000
Plus: Savings from recruiting	$ 6,000
Savings from training	$ 5,000
Total gross profit	$111,000
LESS: Cost of salary increase	$ 90,000
Overtime pay	$ 50,000
Total loss	($ 29,000)

Exhibit 11-9. Effect of increase in labor costs on profit.

agree to the morning meeting, hang up the phone, and head out the door to find the nearest bar.

Kathy shows up the next morning with Hank, your lead production foreman. Kathy starts the conversation. "I told Hank about our $29,000 loss problem yesterday. He immediately formed an empowered employee team to see what they could do to help. They needed access to our production records, which I gave them. Here is what they came up with."

Hank displays a graph on the screen in your office (Exhibit 11-10) and starts his part of the presentation. "Although it may not look like much, my team worked all night to come up with this simple chart. Here is what we have concluded after reviewing our past production information."

"As you know, our prime-time work shift starts at 8 a.m. and ends at 5 p.m. During the course of the day, we can produce a certain number of cars, which is represented by the line marked before on Exhibit 11-10. Look at what happens to our productivity between the hours of 8 to 9 a.m. and 4 to 5 p.m. It takes us an hour in the morning before we start producing any cars. Our productivity drops dramatically between 4 and 5 p.m. as well.

"Here is what the team discovered. For years, we have been religiously shutting down the entire production facility at the end of the shift to conserve energy. When everybody comes in at 8 a.m., all the switches are turned back on, but it takes a hour to power up some of our large machines. A lot of that stuff is computer controlled and it takes time for the computers to go through their own check-out cycles.

"Basically, the same thing happens to us in the afternoon. We have to start shutting everything down at 4 p.m. That's why our productivity drops between 4 and 5 p.m. It doesn't take an entire crew to power the facility up

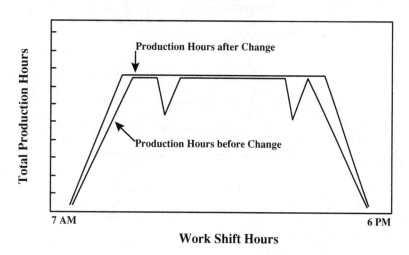

Exhibit 11-10. Effect of shift change on production hours.

or down. In fact, the team concluded that it could be done with a crew of three people. Here is our recommendation. Have three people come into the facility at 7 a.m. to power everything up. When the main crew starts at 8 a.m., they will be immediately productive.

"Do the same thing in the afternoon. The main crew would continue to produce cars right up to the 5 p.m. cutoff point. Another three-person crew would stay until 6 p.m. to shut the equipment down. If we make this simple change, we can increase our car output by at least 15 percent with only a minimum increase in cost (Exhibit 11-11). That's enough to cover the additional car units we need to meet the increased sales forecast."

Everything is suddenly very quiet in your office and you realize that both Kathy and Hank are staring at you. Your mouth is wide open so you decide to shut it. You now have all the information you need to make intelligent decisions. You ask your secretary to come into the office to transcribe your decisions in the presence of Hank and Kathy. You start by saying, "Effective immediately . . . "

1. Initiate a 15 percent across-the-board salary increase to end the strike.

2. Assign a three-person crew to power our facility up in the morning and down in the evening.

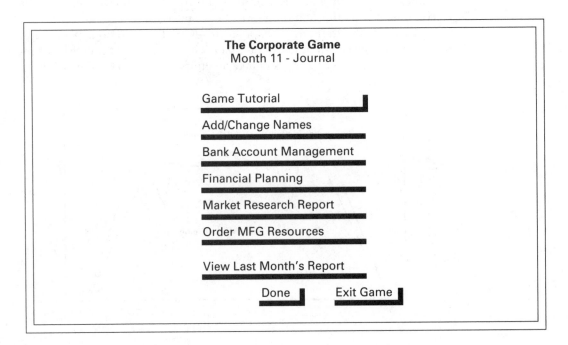

Exhibit 11-11. Month 11—Journal menu.

3. Advise sales and marketing to aggressively pursue capturing a portion of Demon's market-share.

4. Make reservations at the most expensive restaurant in town and invite Kathy, Hank, and his entire team to join me for dinner tonight. Ask Jim and Dan if they want to join us.

Now, Hank's and Kathy's mouths are wide open. There is a roar of applause as they exit your office. This has been "one heck of a day." The sun is out and shining on everything. You wonder if your buddy Joe is still interested in playing golf. You pick up the phone to find out.

Summary and Conclusions

Information technology is moving at a record pace. Using information to make the right decision is absolutely critical in today's highly competitive market. Several examples of companies who have been successful at using information to their competitive advantage were given.

How do you get information to your employees so that they can use it to help you? We showed you how and provided several examples to illustrate the benefits of employee-empowered information processing.

You were confronted with an opportunity and a crisis at the same time. Your major competitor went bankrupt and your employees voted to strike. With help from your staff, you were able to use information to solve the strike problem and increase sales at the same time. This has been one heck of a day. You called Joe and told him you'll meet him at the golf course in five minutes.

PC Game Instructions and Recommendations

When you load the game, you should see the Main Menu for Month 11 (Exhibit 11-11). Make sure you read and study *The Fast Street Journal* before you complete and close out the month. You've got one more month to complete the final round of *The Corporate Game*.

12

Changing Corporate America

Learning to Love Change

You've finally made it to Chapter 12, the last formal chapter in *The Corporate Game*. You have been subjected to "every change in the book." Right after you were appointed as the company's CEO, we encouraged you to develop a strategic plan.

Next, you had to develop a sales and marketing plan that was dynamic and could change to accommodate consumer wants and needs. Everything was going great with one exception. Your manufacturing costs were too high. We convinced you to change your old manufacturing system into a new JIT system. But that wasn't good enough.

You forgot about your employees and had to come up with a scheme to get them to go along with all the changes you made. You capped it all off with a total quality management (TQM) program that was fed data by an information system you developed later.

Your employees were 100 percent behind you as you implemented all these changes. Well, almost! Somewhere in the change process, you forgot about your bottom line and wages. You had to fight off a strike! Thanks to your last-ditch effort to implement an employee-empowered team, you were able to solve the problem.

In retrospect, you have put your company through one heck of a lot of changes over the past 11 months. With the exception of yourself, everybody has adjusted, and settled in nicely. All these changes have overloaded your circuit boards. You wonder if it has all been worth it. Is your company better or worse for having made these changes?

You pick up today's issue of *The Fast Street Journal*. Your eyes focus on the feature article, "Changing Corporate America." You read on to see if you can find some answers to your dilemma.

Changing Corporate America

There are a few excellent American companies. What Tom Peters found when he wrote *In Search of Excellence* was that there were a lot of companies out there trying to flog their way into excellence. In the old days, the parameters for corporate success were relatively simple. If you made money manufacturing the same old product year after year, you were considered "excellent." What was good for General Motors was good for the country. That was before the Japanese entered the car market.

Today, companies are confronted with a chaotic new world where "lean and mean" competitors are springing up overnight. Technological and marketing baselines keep changing. Just when you thought you had the perfect solution, someone comes up with a better one. What's a corporate manager to do?

In today's world, companies that are merely aspiring to change will, at best, survive for a few more years. They will either die or be merged in with the bigger fish. The winners will be companies that are constantly adapting and can instantly implement changes that make sense. They're market driven and are continually creating new market niches. They add value to their products and services daily. Their employees are focused on the corporation's clearly defined visions, missions, and goals.

Learning to Love Change

How do you learn to love and implement change? Be outrageous! You can start by tearing up worthless memos that appear on your desk. Send the pieces back to the idiots who wrote them. Don't attend meetings that last longer than 15 minutes.

The reality of the situation is this: How you play change and effect its implementation in part depend upon your current level and position. Your response may be that if you start being outrageous, you may be out of a job. However, if you sit back and don't do anything, you'll be out of a job anyway when your company goes out of business.

Where do you start? There are a number of proven change strategy programs that have been successfully implemented. You should know what they are, how they work, and what they can do for you. If your corporation is going to survive, you need to make crucial changes that will affect every employee. You must be prepared to implement strategic changes that will significantly alter the way in which you have done business in the past.

The Realities of the Nineties

Over the past 30 years, U.S. productivity has grown slowly. This can be demonstrated by the dismally slow growth of our gross national product. At the same time, the productivity of the nations with whom we compete has significantly increased (see Exhibit 12-1).

Unfortunately, the long-term productivity trends we've experienced have set us up for a productivity crisis of historic proportions. Since 1965, we have managed to increase our average productivity by a mere 1.4 percent a year. In the 20 years prior to 1965, our productivity increased at about 3.4 percent a year. A 1.4 percent increase in annual productivity doesn't translate into much of a pay raise.

Average weekly wages adjusted for inflation have been declining for the past 15 years. If this trend continues, and it probably will until we get serious about correcting it, public sector purchases will decline, unemployment will be a nagging problem, and our educational and government programs will be forced into a spiraling austerity program.

As a result, the economic pressure that this productivity crisis has placed on the average American household has been significant. The number of jobs per household has increased by over 50 percent since 1965. Two working-parent households are common practice today, just to make ends meet.

At the same time, the productivity rate of countries such as Germany, Japan, Britain, and France and the emerging Third World nations like Korea has more than doubled. Nobody, not even the U.S. consumer, can afford to

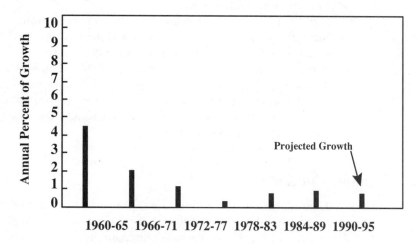

Exhibit 12-1. Percent growth of U.S. GNP.

pay the price for many American products. As a result, our trade deficit has grown to record proportions.

This lack of productivity growth has slowly stripped away the industrial advantage the United States once enjoyed. The playing field of the 1990s will be, at best, level. In fact, the game has already started. We are at the top of the second inning. The score is; World 3, America 0. It's time to play "catch-up ball."

As the U.S. economy moves into the mid-1990s, there is one basic element that will have to change. It should be clear to you by now that we must, at a minimum, double our annual rate of productivity. Our products and services must be competitively priced if they are going to sell both at home and abroad. If we do not achieve this goal, the average standard of living will continue to decline and corporate profits will be hard to come by. This single theme or reality of the 1990s should be the cornerstone of any corporate plan.

Without change, more Americans than ever will be forced by economic necessity to find a job in a shrinking job market. If a job does exist, employers will be looking for highly qualified people with proven productive skills. The burden of finding a job will severely affect the handicapped, new, and untrained workers. The elderly will also feel the pinch.

Light at the End of the Tunnel

There is one ray of light that may help us negotiate the changes that must take place. This country still leads the way in information technology. The information technology industry has been quietly investing billions of dollars in the development of computers and information systems. We may not know how to use them yet, but we already have easy-to-use, powerful, and practical information systems.

Information technology will be common throughout the workplace and our daily lives. If used correctly, it will help us move up the productivity scale and manage the changes that we must make.

Information access must be made available to all employees at all levels. Management must empower them to use this information to make productive decisions on a day-by-day basis. If we are not willing to make this change, our huge investment in information technology and human resources will have been wasted.

The Minimum Changes

If our corporate institutions are to thrive and prosper in the coming years, we will first have to identify what changes we must make to adapt to the realities of the 1990s. We won't be alone in this endeavor. Other countries will be going through this same transition with one big difference. Many of the countries in western Europe and the Pacific Rim have a common focus with economic guidance mechanisms in place. We don't have that.

There is no collaboration between our various levels of government, educational institutions, and industries on a common national focus. Everybody is marching to the tune of his or her own drummer. Individuals are on their own to determine what the long-term international economic forces will be.

The problem will be compounded by the fact that our mighty federal government, the nation's largest corporation, has no strategic economic planning programs in place. Our political leaders refuse to establish an economic program that the country can get behind.

We are beginning to see evidence of government debates over the need for a target industry policy, funding of worker retraining, and the need for a balanced federal budget. Given the political leadership that we have in Washington today, don't expect this to happen in the near future. You are going to be on your own for the next five years in implementing changes to improve productivity.

A Look at Excellence

We're now at the bottom of the third inning of the ball game and it's time to get serious if we want to win this game. Before we change our game strategy, let's take a look at what some winning teams have done.

NCR Cash Register put together one of the most successful JIT manufacturing and production-control programs ever recorded. Their task-driven teams squeezed 85 percent fewer parts out of the company's state-of-the-art cash registers. Suppliers were cut by 65 percent to foster their new materials requirements plan (MRP). Once JIT was fully implemented, it took 75 percent less time to assemble the new cash registers. All this was done under the umbrella of NCR's TQM program.

IBM decided to develop what became known as the Proprinter. It was a dot-matrix printer designed to replace competitive dot-matrix printers. The Proprinter was designed to contain 65 percent fewer parts than conventional dot-matrix printers for reliability. Reliability was a top priority in IBM's total quality management program. Their customers had told them that they wanted a highly reliable, low-cost dot-matrix printer. IBM gave it to them and reduced their printer production time and cost by 90 percent. In the process, they made billions in new sales from the program.

Citibank came up with a unique vision. "Why not use the money we were planning to use for bank expansions for customer loans? We make money off loans and nothing off bank expansion programs." As an alternative to bank expansion, they developed a way to use sophisticated automated teller machines (ATMs), which virtually eliminated the need to expand bank facilities.

How did these companies accomplish such impressive feats? Did they use strategic planning, JIT, and TQM to reach their productivity goals? The answer is "yes," but they also applied the knowledge and expertise of their workers to put each program together. Teams were formed and challenged with the task of "changing the way we do things." They all had access to the information they needed to analyze the problems that had to be solved before major changes could be implemented.

The increased use of information to implement change is catching on. Sales representatives are using mobile computers to capture and transfer customer orders from the field to corporate headquarters. The orders bypass what used to be the order-entry function and now go directly into the production process. Auto repair people rely on computer-generated information to quickly diagnose car problems. Farmers and ranchers use linear programs to routinely determine the best changes to make in livestock feed mix.

A few years ago, the general public thought that the computer revolution at the corporate level meant the use of robotics and the generation of end-of-month accounting reports. We are now beginning to understand how to increase the information flow from the front lines to the back lines to implement change at all levels.

The adage "Let's work smarter rather than harder" is beginning to take hold. The use of more and better information throughout the organization is one of the best ways to analyze and implement change.

The effective use of information technology is only one component in the change formula. In order for the power of information to work, corporations must be prepared to change their management systems and decision-making processes. Individual authorities and responsibilities must be redefined. The information-handling skills of the entire organization must be upgraded.

Productivity Is Not Free

There are social costs associated with our movement up the productivity ladder. The facsimile boom that occurred in the early 1990s is a good example of what's going to happen as changes are made. In the late 1980s, there were less than 300,000 fax machines installed in the United States.

Significant technological improvements were made to the old machines. The new machines were cheaper and faster. When they were introduced in the early 1990s, millions were sold overnight. Electronically transmitted printed information crippled the growth of overnight delivery services, costing thousands of jobs.

Electronic conferences will substantially reduce corporate air travel. Cheap electronic storage media will move us into a paperless society. Electronic speech recognition will dramatically change the way in which we process information. The use of home computers to shop for retail goods will increase in popularity as our streets become more crowded.

Telelearning will become a new word in our vocabulary. Educational lectures will be transmitted by satellite to a student's television. Interactive educational material will be available on computer disks (CDs) that will replace textbooks. All this will help to bring the cost of education under control.

Over time, the benefits of improved productivity through change will be shared by most Americans. Our standard of living will once again begin to rise. Corporate profits will return to their normal levels. How much time we are talking about is anybody's guess. We are just starting the process and are beginning to see signs of improvement. We won't begin to see any real improvements until we are midway through the decade.

The consequences of the continued reduction in our standard of living, the rising cost of health care, and an out of control federal budget are just some of the major obstacles standing in our way.

A Strategy for Change

In a changing world, there are no constants, just variables. The variables are the changes. How can you work the changes to your best advantage? Will you be able to manage the changes and create a more effective organization? Can you do all this in the corporate setting and make money at the same time? The answer is "yes" if you understand why certain approaches to change management work and why others don't.

To get started, you've got to learn how to effectively implement change. Effectiveness includes the ability to do the right thing at the right time, and be right most of the time. What do we mean when we say "right most of the time"? Does that imply that you could be wrong "some of the time"? You bet it does, and you had better be able to stand up to this fact of life. If you are going to be involved in the change process, then you have got to be prepared to make mistakes.

Back to the Game

Let's go back to *The Corporate Game* and set the stage for what is about to happen to your company. You have already given your management team the authorization to implement JIT manufacturing and TQM throughout the company. It will involve major changes, but you're convinced that your management team can rise to the challenge. You've just learned that your hourly employees are "up in arms."

Under the current production-control system, they are paid a production bonus, which can amount to as much as 25 percent of their pay. They don't know what the new JIT or TQM system is going to do to their production bonus, and furthermore, they don't care.

They want to keep the old production system. You're irritated by their reluctance to change. Besides, if you're paying all these production bonuses, why are production costs going out of sight? The link between productivity and bonus payments is "a little foggy" at best.

You meet with Kathy, your personnel director, and tell her in no uncertain terms, "We have got to do something now to get these people to change their attitude. Let's conduct an employee survey and find out what's going on." You and Kathy agree on a set of survey statements. Employees are to indicate whether or not they agree with the statements.

1. I understand the objectives of the company.

2. Management always listens to my ideas.

3. I am encouraged to develop to my full potential.

4. My immediate supervisor shares ideas helpful to me and my group.

5. I can count on the management team for support.

6. My salary and bonus plan are commensurate with the job I perform.

7. This corporation sets realistic productivity plans and goals that I can believe in.

8. We constantly review our work process and make improvements as necessary.

9. Our management team is helpful and effective in developing new ideas to improve our productivity.

The results from the survey revealed some surprises. Employees indicated that they would prefer a higher base salary supplemented with a lower bonus. They felt that their low productivity was a result of poor management. Does that sound familiar? Well, at least you're getting somewhere and are beginning to understand the problems. You organize a joint working team made up of managers and employees to analyze several key areas including:

1. Working practices to improve productivity and quality

2. A new productivity bonus system that links base pay to company performance

3. An approach to motivate all employees to become involved in the implementation of the JIT and TQM systems

One thing is clear from this scenario. When we move to implement fundamental changes, we need to look at how the entire organization sees the problems. Are the existing systems working? If they are not, can they be modified so that they will work? Do they need to be discarded? If they are discarded, do they need to be replaced?

Changes create challenges for all of us. We have already seen the stress and anxiety among the employees when they heard about the JIT and TQM changes. There are also discoveries and opportunities brought about by change.

You developed and deployed a survey. The survey results divulged interesting information about your employees' attitudes that you did not know before. This discovery presented you with an opportunity to form a team to evaluate better ways to implement change.

Block Busting

A *block,* according to Webster, is "something that gets in the way of progress." If you don't know what the block is, you can't remove it. There are a number of blocks to problem solving you need to know about to effectively implement change.

The first is called a *perpetual block.* This is where a problem-solving team is perpetually looking for the problem. They never find it because their focus is either too broad or too narrow. They are typically saturated with data and "can't see the sky through the trees."

Then there is the *emotional block.* The entire team is paranoid about making a mistake. They have an innate fear of risk. As a result, they will sit on problems forever and generate no unique ideas.

Environmental blocks show up when the team perceives that their environment is not conducive to innovation. "Management won't support us" is a common excuse. Any change is seen as a threat and all new ideas are ignored.

How do you work through the blocks? You first need to know what blocks need to be removed. Then, move in with the right tools to bust the blocks down. Before you remove a block, be objective. Listen to all new ideas, even bad ones. Don't interrupt or criticize a person presenting an idea. When all the ideas are in, select the ones that make sense and politely discard the bad ones.

Eliminate status and rank during idea-generating sessions. Control anybody who attempts to dominate the group. Allow people to disagree but discourage arguments. Focus on the good aspects of ideas and build on those good ideas.

Plum Pudding

Before you can implement change, you must first convince all those who are affected by the change that the change is desirable. When you introduce the JIT changes and your production workers say, "Why change . . . we've always done it this way," you've got to remove the block. People get locked into patterns of behavior, systems, and procedures.

Here is an example of a *pattern block*. Many years ago, a corporation ran a chain of restaurants. One day, the CEO decided to visit a company restaurant he had never seen before. As he was talking to the chef, he was glancing at the menu and noticed that plum pudding was not featured in the dessert section. He said to the chef, "I see that you don't serve plum pudding. It's one of my favorite desserts." He completed his tour of the restaurant and left.

The next morning the chef, who was anxious to please the CEO, made up 25 servings of plum pudding. Nobody ordered the plum pudding because it was not featured on the menu. It spoiled and was thrown out that night. Later that year, the CEO retired. Ten years later, the chef was still making plum pudding and throwing it out at the end of the day.

All organizations have some plum pudding left over. What we do need is systematic processes in place to constantly evaluate and diagnose problems in the way we operate. Once the right diagnosis has been made, the change can be made, and the evaluation process continues.

Implementing Change

So far, we have examined how to assess change and some of the human factors that turn change on or off. We have not talked about what it takes to manage change effectively. The management process starts by developing a strategy, which is explicit and clear to everybody who will be affected by the change. The strategy allows for the coordination of all activities necessary to implement the change.

Explicit strategy direction also fosters planning. Planning is of paramount importance to the successful implementation of change. It allows employees to plan change rather than to react to the experience.

The strategy should be simple and clear. It should be based on concepts that employees can understand and appreciate. Priorities should be determined so that there is no mistake as to what has to be done first, second, and so on. All people resources and their respective responsibilities should be clearly identified.

Next, strategies must be deployed throughout the company and reinforced by management with words followed by actions. Visit department meetings on a recurring basis to show, by action, your support for employees' roles in the change process. Implement reward systems to formally recognize excellent performers.

Define the problems you are attempting to solve once the change is implemented. Does everyone understand the problems and agree to a common set of solutions? This is vitally important so that the implementation team can focus on a common set of targets.

Once you identify the problems, identify the forces or blocks which must be removed to solve each problem. Remember, the successful implementation of a change may require that all problem areas be removed before the implementation steps can begin. Are the blocks based upon people, resources, time, or external factors?

Prioritize the opposing blocks. Which block or set of blocks represents the greatest hindrance to the change? What forces can be used to eliminate blocks? Like blocks, forces could be made up of people, resources, time, or external factors.

What are the options and actions you could take to eliminate negative blocks? How could you exploit the strengths of your forces to help remove negative blocks?

Suppose your company has not been receptive to any change. Attempts to implement changes are always met with heavy resistance. Most of the employees never understood what the changes were all about in the first place. As a result, they were always very cautious. What do you do?

Start by making sure that the change is realistic. Explain the need for the change in terms employees understand. Keep everybody informed as more information becomes available.

Whenever possible, involve your people in every phase of the implementation cycle. Actively solicit their feedback. Develop meaningful checklists. Discuss the results of completed checklist items with employees. Start off slow and work the changes through your more receptive people. Implement the change in clear phases. Publicize early successes and provide positive feedback along the way.

Summary and Conclusions

Will there be a happy ending to the corporate game? Will corporate America rise to the challenges of the 1990s? The early data suggest that the number of middle- and upper-income jobs is beginning to rise. Our real income level is still flat. The only way that we can increase the real income of Americans is to increase the value added to the goods and services we produce. That will demand changes in the way we are used to doing things.

We talked about all kinds of productivity-oriented concepts, such as integrated strategic planning, just-in-time manufacturing, and total quality management. All this requires change, teamwork, and total management commitment.

Yet, even with today's harsh economic realities, there are managers who continue to discount new and innovative ideas. They believe "they'll go away in time and we can return to the good old days."

Remember management by objectives (MBO) and "I'm OK, you're OK"? Each scheme lasted for about five years and then faded away into the land of forgotten history. A number of recent surveys bear this out. Employees are resisting the new schemes, in part, because they have committed themselves to other management improvement schemes in the past, only to have management abandon the initiative when the next fad came out.

Without serious leadership at both the corporate and federal government levels, the fundamental organizational changes we must make to beat down the productivity blocks will not happen. A recent Lou Harris survey showed that 75 percent of Americans polled blamed two factors for the economic slide in the United States: the short-sighted attitude of corporate management; and the failure of the federal government to implement a national economic plan. If the bulk of the nation's corporate and government leaders continue to resist implementing the changes we desperately need because of their myopic behavior, then this country could experience an economic revolution the likes of which we have never seen before.

If we do not make a national commitment to increase the skills of America's work force, improve educational systems, and redesign our management systems to effectively use our industrial resources, then U.S. productivity will continue to decline. The economic, sociological, and political consequences of this scenario will not be pleasant.

In order to become competitive without improving U.S. productivity, American firms will have to move more of their production operations abroad. They are already doing this on a large scale. For the part of the operation they keep here, companies will force wage and benefit concessions down through the work force. The end result will be a continued deterioration of our standard of living.

If this continues to happen, the spiral will continue. A shrinking revenue base at home will force further cuts in social safety net programs. This will lead to political debates over health-care rationing, protective tariffs, and cuts in the sacred social security program. At the same time, corporations will seek relief from environmental protection regulations so that they can reduce costs.

The continued deterioration of our general economic performance will inevitably lead to greater social distress and political turbulence. Without a coherent sense of shared purpose, direction, and leadership, we will be subjected to a widening array of meaningless vision statements. At a minimum, the level of uncertainty will increase. It could lead to riots and major acts of civil disorder.

If America is to seriously address its productivity problems, it must begin now to implement the changes we need now! If we are to avoid the social cost and political hazards of further economic degeneration, we must begin to improve our productivity. Americans are a resilient people and they are quick learners.

If history is any indicator, we will work it out in no time at all, and get our productivity levels back to where they belong. When that happens, we will all start playing the corporate game to win.

PC Game Assignment and Instructions

When you load the game disk, the Main Menu should show Month 12, the last month in *The Corporate Game* to play (Exhibit 12-2). When you complete and close out the month, a final Main Menu will appear on your display (Exhibit 12-3).

The menu will allow you to select the View Last Month's Report option to see how well your company did in Month 12. You will have completed 12 months, or one year of play. If you are playing the game against your colleagues, compare your year-to-date corporate profit totals from the income statement to see who made the most profit. If you did, you win!

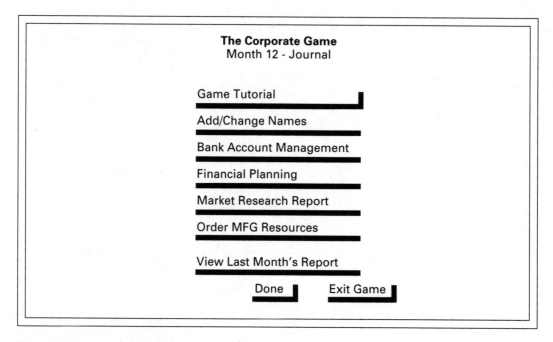

Exhibit 12-2. Month 12—Journal menu.

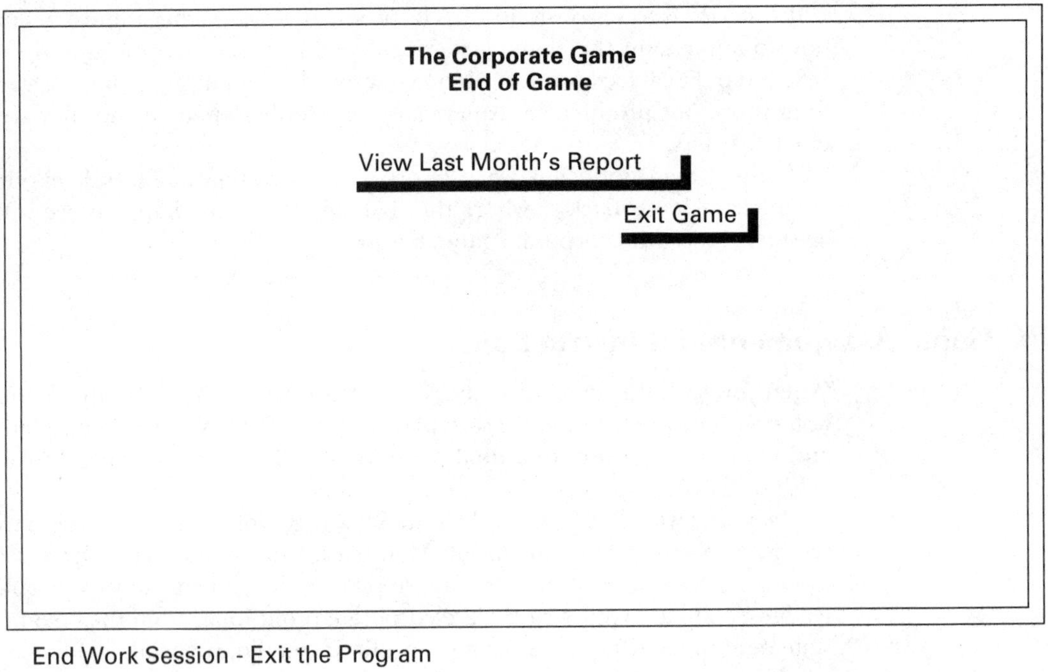

The Corporate Game
End of Game

View Last Month's Report ▉

                              Exit Game ▉

End Work Session - Exit the Program

Exhibit 12-3. End-of-game menu.

13

Playing the Corporate Game

Do You Have What It Takes to Win?

Welcome to the personal computer part of *The Corporate Game*. We'll refer to it as the *game* throughout the balance of Chapter 13. This chapter will show you how to play the game on your personal computer. It's easy and fun. When you complete a chapter in the book, you have the option of testing what you have learned by "playing" the game on your computer. In the process, you will build and run your own company. You have one year of "play time" to get the job done.

There are 12 rounds of play in the game. Each round simulates a one-month period of time, for a total of one year. At the end of each month, the game will ask you to answer various questions and make strategic decisions on behalf of your company. When you complete a month, the game closes out the month and automatically produces end-of-month accounting reports (e.g., income statement and balance sheet).

The reports show you how well your company is doing financially, based upon the decisions you made. As a suggestion, review all reports generated from previous months before you make any decisions affecting the current month. Conflicting decisions can have a devastating effect on your company's profits.

Try to make small progressive changes to your strategic plans as you proceed through the game. Single large changes may prove to be less effective than small progressive improvements. The player who can consistently measure the benefits and adverse consequences resulting from a single change or a combination of changes will generally outperform the "hit-and-miss" corporate player.

If Profit $ Exceed	Then Your Game Ranking Is
$1,750,000	Superb - You would make a great corporate executive
$1,450,000	Outstanding - You substantially beat Demon
$1,150,000	Great - You still beat Demon but not by much
$850,000	Good - You lost to Demon but not by much
$550,000	Fair - You lost to Demon but at least you made a profit
Negative Profits	Terrible - Your company lost money and you went bankrupt

Exhibit 13-1. *The Corporate Game* win table.

How Do You Win?

There are three competitive car companies that live on the game disk. In addition, a very tough economic and business environment has been built into the game. Your challenge is to outsmart your competition and second guess what is about to happen in the game's economic and business world.

The company that achieves the highest profits wins. If you are playing the game against other players, and at the end of Month 12 (December), if your company has earned the highest profits, you win.

If you're playing by yourself, you compete against the game's three competitive car companies. Exhibit 13-1 shows you what profits you must make to beat the Demon Car Company, one of your three major competitors.

Hardware Configuration

The game has been designed to run on an IBM or 100 percent IBM compatible personal computer. You need a minimum of 640KB of random-access memory (RAM) and DOS 3.0 or later version to run the game. If you have a printer, you can print reports on all IBM compatible printers. You have the option of displaying reports on your monitor.

About Your Game Disk

A game disk is included in the back of the book. It contains five files:

TCGAME.EXE

MONTH.DAT

AUTOEXEC.BAT

CONFIG.SYS

MOUSE.COM

Special care should always be taken when handling the game disk.

1. Do not touch or contaminate the magnetic surface of the disk.

2. Do not expose the disk to magnetized objects such as televisions, radios, or metal detectors.

3. Do not expose the disk to excessive heat or sunlight.

Backing Up the Game Disk

Before you get started, you should make a backup copy of the game disk. Consult your DOS manual for instructions on how to copy files from a disk. An example of how files are copied is shown as follows:

PC with floppy drive (e.g., A drive) and a fixed drive:

1. Insert the game disk into drive A

2. At the DOS prompt, ENTER - COPY A:*.* C:\

3. Press the ENTER key

4. All *Corporate Game* files are copied from drive A to drive C

PC with two floppy drives (e.g., drives A and B):

1. Insert the Corporate Game disk into drive A

2. Insert a formatted disk into drive B

3. ENTER - COPY A:*.* B:\ at the DOS prompt

4. Press the ENTER key

5. All *Corporate Game* files are copied from the disk in drive A to the disk in drive B.

You should now have a backup copy of the game disk. As an added precaution, we recommend that you use a write-protect tab on your backup disk. This will prevent you from accidentally copying over or erasing any of the programs on the disk. Write-protect tab instructions are included with boxes of new disks.

Starting the Game

1. Power up your PC system per your normal procedure

2. Insert the game disk into a disk drive (A or B)

3. At the DOS prompt, ENTER - A:TCGAME or the name of the drive that the game disk is in (A: or B:)

4. The game will start

Game Panels

The Main Menu is the first menu you will see on your display (see Exhibit 13-2). It is used to select game options. Initially, there are only two options on the Main Menu. The number of options increases as you proceed through the game.

There are three methods you can use to move around and select options off the Main Menu: (1) tab and arrow keys, (2) hot keys, and (3) a mouse. Depending upon your preference, each method is used to highlight Main Menu options. When a menu option is highlighted, it can then be selected by pressing the ENTER key.

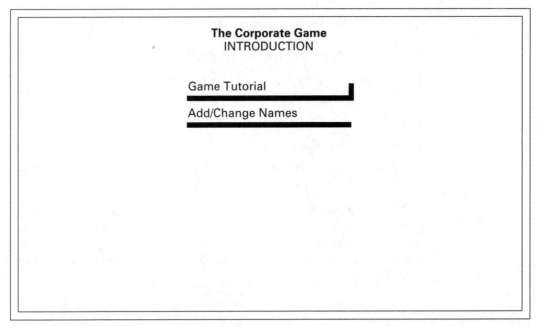

Exhibit 13-2. Introduction menu.

Using Tab and Arrow Keys

To select an option from the Main Menu, press the TAB key until you highlight the option you want. Use the up/down arrow key to move up and down through the options. When you highlight the option you want, press the ENTER key to select that option. Let's try it. Press the TAB key until the Tutorial option is highlighted. Press the ENTER key to select the tutorial. The tutorial appears on your display (Exhibit 13-3) and contains helpful information about how to play each month. You can use the page up (PgUp) and page down (PgDn) keys to scroll through the tutorial or any other displayed report.

There are two options displayed in the bottom left corner of all displayed reports (i.e, tutorial): F2 Print and F3 Return. These are called *function keys*. A set of function keys should be located on the top of your keyboard. If you press the F2 key, the report you are viewing on the display (e.g., Chapter Tutorial) will be printed. If you press the F3 key, you will return to the Main Menu.

The Corporate Game
Welcome to the Corporate Game

Introduction

There are twelve months of play (one year) in the Corporate Game's computer model. Read the test material, and then apply what you have learned by playing the corresponding months in the game. Don't be too concerned if the early rounds of play seem to be "too simple." It gets more complicated when you get into the later months.

When you start Month 1 (January), you'll be given one million dollars, and challenged with building a manufacturing company that makes cars. The creators of The Corporate Game realize that in the "real world," it would be next to impossible to build a car manufacturing company for a million dollars. It would probably take billions of dollars. However, we did not want to clutter up your screen with huge numbers. Therefore, in the interest of simplicity, everything is priced relative to a million dollars.

As you proceed through each month of play, enter your business plans and strategies into the game. You will have the option to purchase raw materials, equipment, services, and a labor force along the way as you build your company. They may be paid for with cash from the corporate checking account, charged to your accounts payable account or from money you borrow from a bank.

F2 Print   F3 Return

Exhibit 13-3. Introduction menu instructions.

Printing Reports

If you want to print a report, your printer must be ON and in the READY mode before you press F2. If your printer is not ready, a Printer Not Ready message is displayed. Press the ESC key to cancel the request or turn your printer on to start printing.

Message panels will pop up as needed to show error messages or warning messages. An example of the Printer Not Ready message menu is shown in Exhibit 13-4. To proceed to the next topic, return to the Main Menu by pressing the F3 key.

Using Hot Keys

You should now be back to the Main Menu. Notice that a single letter is highlighted in the descriptive text of both menu options. For example, the "A" is highlighted in the Add/Change Names option. If you press the "A" character key, the Add/Change Names option becomes highlighted. Next, press the ENTER key. This procedure can be used to select menu options as an alternative to the TAB key. Try it by pressing the "A" and ENTER keys.

The Corporate Game
Welcome to the Corporate Game

Introduction
There are twelve months of play (one year) in the Corporate Game's
computer model. Read the ERROR – ERROR – ERROR ly what you have learned
by playing t   ned if the
early round| If your Printer is ON but not Ready |d when
 you get int| You'll be HUNG UP for 60 seconds |
When you s | OK |
and challen| |rs. The
creators of the Corporate Game realize that in the "real world," it would be
next to impossible to build a car manufacturing company for a million dollars.
It would probably take billions of dollars. However, we did not want to
clutter up your screen with huge numbers. Therefore, in the interest of
simplicity, everything is priced relative to a million dollars.
As you proceed through each month of play, enter your business plans and
strategies into the game. You will have the option to purchase raw materials,
equipment, services, and a labor force along the way as you build your
company. They may be paid for with cash from the corporate checking account,
charged to your accounts payable account or from money you borrow from a bank.

F2 Print   F3 Return

Exhibit 13-4. Printer not ON error message.

Add/Change Names Menu

The Add/Change Names menu now appears on your display. It is an example of the game's ENTRY menu (see Exhibit 13-5). Press the TAB key to select the Title 1 option and then press the up or down arrow key to select the title you want. Repeat these steps for the Title 2 option.

Next, press the TAB key until the Officer's Name input field is selected. ENTER the name you want printed on your corporate reports. Use the same procedure to ENTER your company's name. All the data entry panels work this way. When you're ready to return to the Main Menu, select the Done option. Your name and the name of your company gets updated on the game disk.

Using a Mouse

If you have a mouse, you have probably noticed the mouse cursor that appears on your display. You can use your mouse to point to and select options by moving the mouse cursor to a menu option and pressing the mouse ENTER button. You can also use your mouse to scroll through any of the displayed text reports such as the Chapter Tutorial.

Use your mouse to select the Chapter Tutorial. There is a scroll bar on

```
                         The Corporate Game
                            INTRODUCTION
                           Add/Change Names

          Title 1                        Title 2
          ( ) Dr.                        ( ) President
          ( ) Mr.                        ( ) VP
          ( ) Mrs.                       ( ) CEO
          ( ) Miss                       ( ) CFO
          ( ) Prof.                      ( ) Ph.D.
          ( ) NONE                       ( ) NONE

             Officer's Name
             John D. Doe

             Company Name
             Demon Car Company

                     Done  ▮      Enter  ▮
```

Exhibit 13-5. Company name and title menu.

the right side of the report (Exhibit 13-3). If you place the mouse cursor on top of the scroll bar and hold the mouse ENTER button down, you scroll up or down through the report by moving the cursor up or down.

Completing the Introduction

At this point, we have shown you everything you need to know to manipulate your way through the rest of the game. You know how to select options from the Main Menu, enter data, scroll through reports, and print reports. Let's continue to the first month of actual play to cover a few more points. Select the Done option at the bottom right corner of your display. The Main Menu for Month 1 will appear on your display (Exhibit 13-6).

Playing Month 1

Notice that the "new" Main Menu looks very similar to the previous Main Menu with one exception. We have added a new option called Bank Account Management. New options are also added to the Main Menu in

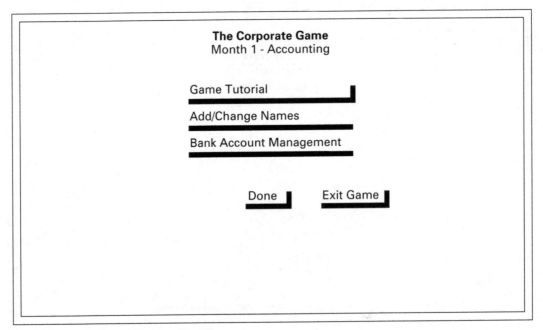

End Work Session - Exit the Program

Exhibit 13-6. Month 1—Accounting menu.

Months 2, 4, 5, and 6. We'll tell you more about these options later. For now, select the Bank Account Management option. The Banking Transactions menu will appear on your display (Exhibit 13-7).

Your display should look like a bank teller machine. You are looking at the bank account balances for your corporation. Look at the balance in your checking account. We promised to give you a million dollars for start-up money and there it is. Your checking account shows an account balance of $1 million. Now that you are a millionaire, what's your next step?

As a prudent corporate executive, you know that most checking accounts do not pay interest. You have decided to transfer $500,000 from your checking account into your interest-bearing corporate savings account. Current interest and loan rates are shown in the Month Tutorial menu. In the Transfer from column, select Checking. In the Transfer to column, select Savings. Next, select Transaction Amount and enter 500000 just as we have done in Exhibit 13-8.

Notice that we did not put any dollar signs, decimal, commas, or any other character in the amount field. The game wants you to enter "whole" numbers in all numeric fields (i.e., no decimal points or cents). If you had entered a number like $500,000 and selected the Enter option, the game would have displayed "????" in the field where it found a signed field. Try it.

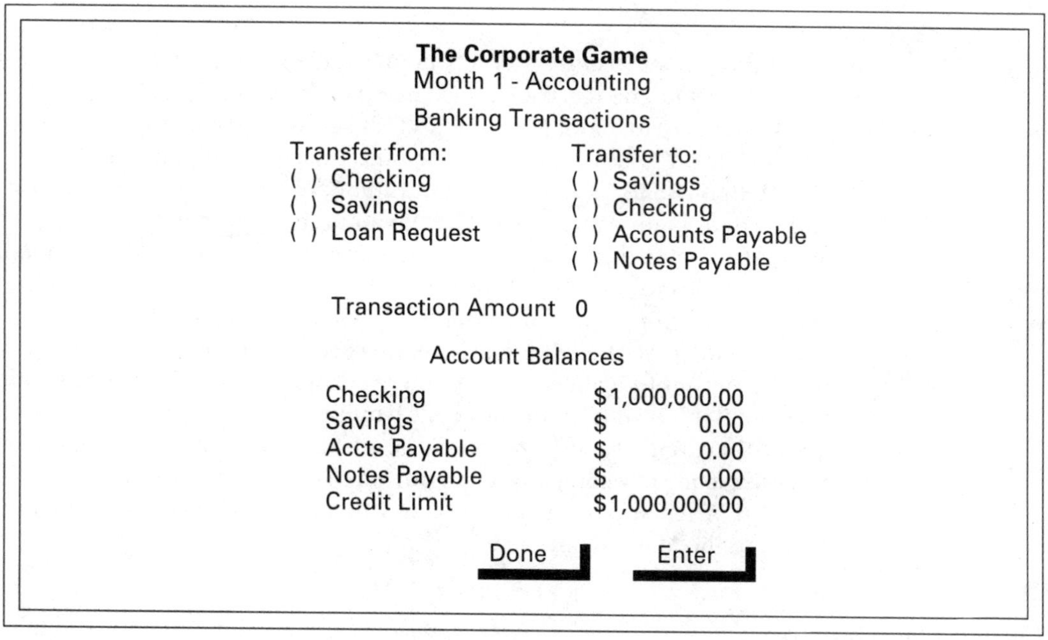

The Corporate Game
Month 1 - Accounting

Banking Transactions

Transfer from: Transfer to:
( ) Checking   ( ) Savings
( ) Savings   ( ) Checking
( ) Loan Request   ( ) Accounts Payable
                                ( ) Notes Payable

Transaction Amount   0

Account Balances

Checking $1,000,000.00
Savings $ 0.00
Accts Payable $ 0.00
Notes Payable $ 0.00
Credit Limit $1,000,000.00

Done ▮   Enter ▮

Exhibit 13-7. Banking Transactions menu.

```
The Corporate Game
Month 1 - Accounting
Banking Transactions

Transfer from:              Transfer to:
( ) Checking               ( ) Savings
( ) Savings                ( ) Checking
( ) Loan Request           ( ) Accounts Payable
                           ( ) Notes Payable

Transaction Amount  500000

Account Balances

Checking              $ 1,000,000.00
Savings               $         0.00
Accts Payable         $         0.00
Notes Payable         $         0.00
Credit Limit          $ 1,000,000.00

        Done  ▮         Enter  ▮
```

Exhibit 13-8. Banking Transactions menu with entry example.

To correct the problem, Enter a "whole" number (e.g., 500000) and select ENTER. If you change your mind after you have made an entry, simply blank out your entry and press the ENTER key to terminate the transaction.

Now select ENTER and you will see the transfer take place on your display (Exhibit 13-9). If you change your mind, you can transfer money back and forth as many times as you like. If you were showing a balance in your accounts payable or notes payable accounts and wanted to apply a payment to these accounts, you would use this same technique (e.g., transfer money from checking or savings to accounts payable or notes payable).

Before we leave the teller machine, there is one other item to cover. Under the Account Balances column, there is a line item called Credit Limit. In Exhibit 13-9, your credit limit is $1 million. If you initiate a Loan Request, the Credit Limit represents the maximum amount of money the bank will loan your company. Loans are charged against your notes payable account. When you are ready to leave the teller machine, select Done to return to the Main Menu.

Closing Out a Month

There are two ways to close out or end a month. The two options at the bottom of the Main Menu are Done and Exit. If you select the Done option,

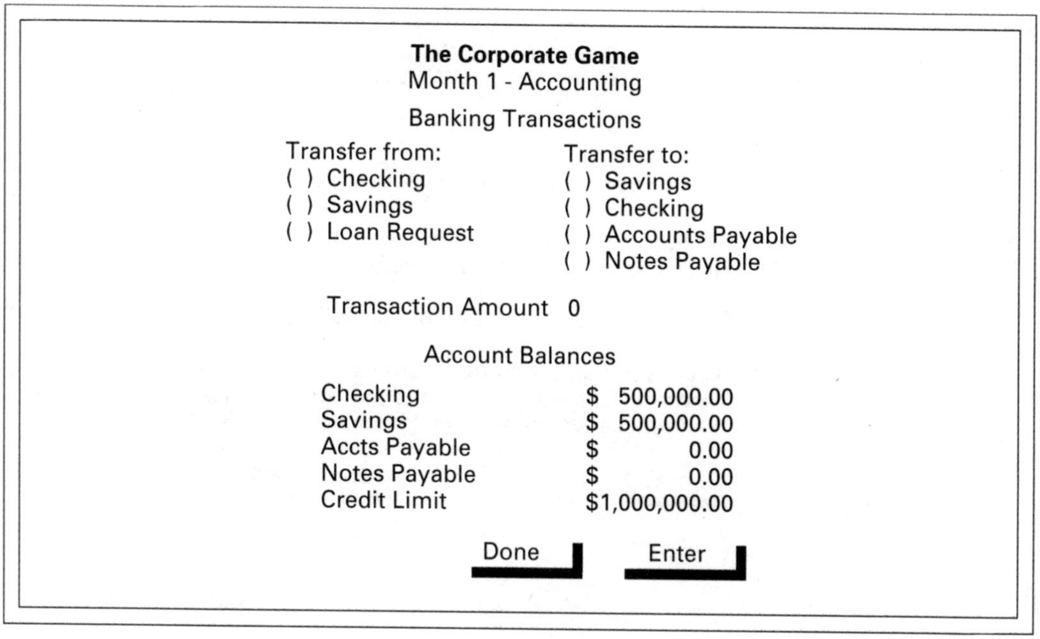

The Corporate Game
Month 1 - Accounting

Banking Transactions

Transfer from: Transfer to:
( ) Checking   ( ) Savings
( ) Savings   ( ) Checking
( ) Loan Request   ( ) Accounts Payable
                                  ( ) Notes Payable

Transaction Amount   0

Account Balances

Checking $ 500,000.00
Savings $ 500,000.00
Accts Payable $ 0.00
Notes Payable $ 0.00
Credit Limit $1,000,000.00

Done ▮   Enter ▮

Exhibit 13-9. Banking Transactions menu with transfer example.

a submenu will appear on your display with two additional options (see Exhibit 13-10).

The message on the menu is self-explanatory. It is a final warning telling you that once you elect to close out a month, you cannot go back and change your answers. This makes sense if you are playing the game in a competitive environment with other players. If you select Done, the game will close out Month 1 and automatically "roll you forward" into the next month (i.e., Month 2).

For now, select the Cancel option so that we can show you the alternative options. You will return to the Main Menu. If you select the Exit option, a submenu will appear on your display with six additional options (Exhibit 13-11).

Exit–Update: You exit from the game and the current month. The game saves (updates) all entries that you have made. You can go back into the game and start where you left off at a later time.

Exit–No Update: Closes out the game without saving (updating) the data or changes you may have made. You are in effect telling the game that you want to start over at a later time.

Run Current Month: Returns you to the Main Menu of the current month to continue the game play.

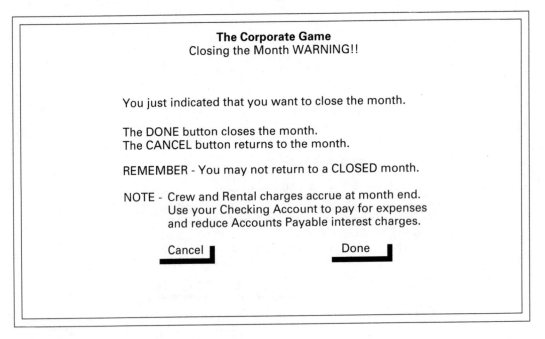

Exhibit 13-10. Closing the Month menu.

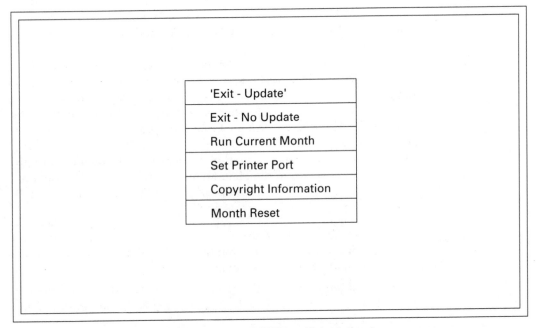

Exit - Saving All Changes Since the Last 'DONE' or 'Exit Update'

Exhibit 13-11. Exit the Game menu.

Set Printer Port: Allows you to direct printed game reports to one of three printer ports (see Exhibit 13-12). Select OK to return to the submenu.

Copyright Information: Provides you with copyright information about *The Corporate Game.* Select OK to return to the submenu.

Month Reset: Allows you to replay any month and includes a submenu as shown in Exhibit 13-13.

Here is how it works. You can use the Month Reset submenu to go back into the game and start over from whatever month you want. For example, if you were in Month 6 and wanted to start over at the beginning of Month 2, simply select Month 2 and the OK option from the submenu. The game automatically moves you back to the beginning of Month 2. All the data that you may have entered including your bank account balances, remain unchanged when you start Month 2. If you want to start the game over and erase (delete) any data that you may have entered, follow these simple steps:

1. Select the Month 0 and OK option from the Month Reset submenu.
2. The Game Introduction menu will appear on your display. Select the DONE option.
3. The Month I menu will appear on your display. Select the EXIT option.

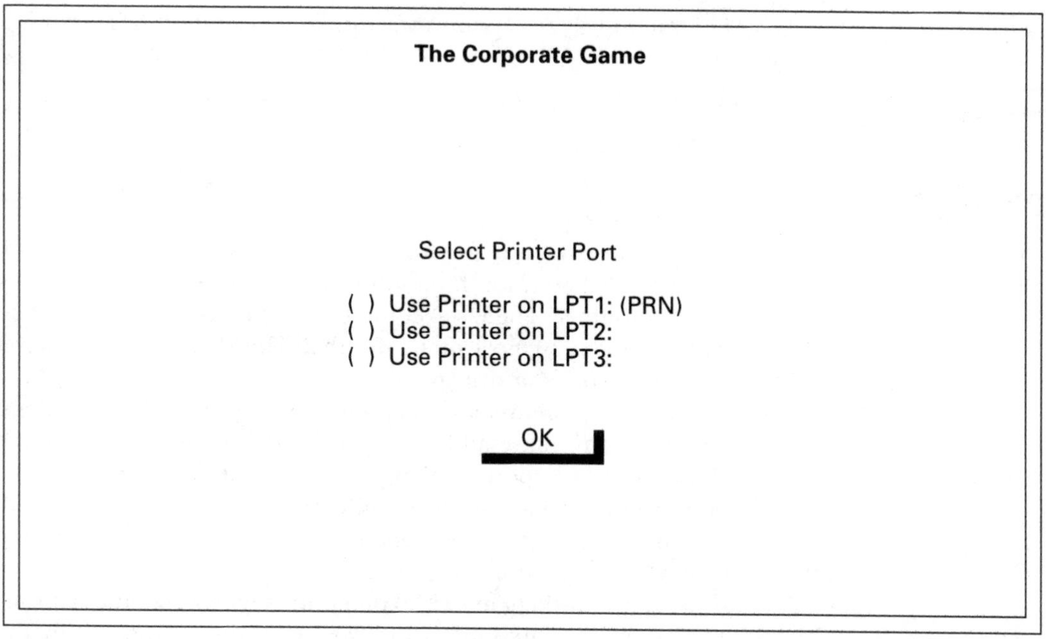

The Corporate Game

Select Printer Port

( ) Use Printer on LPT1: (PRN)
( ) Use Printer on LPT2:
( ) Use Printer on LPT3:

OK

Exhibit 13-12. Select Printer Port menu.

```
┌─────────────────────────────────────────────────────────────┐
│ ┌─────────────────────────────────────────────────────────┐ │
│ │                    The Corporate Game                   │ │
│ │                    Maintenance Utility                  │ │
│ │                                                         │ │
│ │                                                         │ │
│ │                      Reset to:                          │ │
│ │                                                         │ │
│ │             ( )  Month 0  ( )                           │ │
│ │             ( )  Month 1  ( )                           │ │
│ │             ( )  Month 2  ( )                           │ │
│ │             ( )  Month 3  ( )                           │ │
│ │             ( )  Month 4  ( )                           │ │
│ │             ( )  Month 5  ( )                           │ │
│ │             ( )  Month 6  ( )                           │ │
│ │                                                         │ │
│ │                Cancel▌          OK ▌                    │ │
│ │                                                         │ │
│ │                                                         │ │
│ │                                                         │ │
│ │                                                         │ │
│ └─────────────────────────────────────────────────────────┘ │
└─────────────────────────────────────────────────────────────┘
```

Exhibit 13-13. Maintenance Utility menu.

4. The Main Menu will appear on your display. Select the EXIT—No Update option.

5. When you restart the game, you are in effect, starting over.

Playing Month 2

Let's go back to where we were in Month 1, close it, and move on to Month 2. Select the Run Current Month option in Exhibit 13-11 to return to the Main Menu for Month 1. Then, select the Done options on both the Main Menu and the submenu to move on to Month 2. The Main Menu in Exhibit 13-14 should appear on your display.

Again, the new Main Menu looks very similar to the previous Main Menu with one exception. We have added two new options, Financial Planning and View Last Month's Reports. When you closed out Month 1, it was the same as closing out the month for a real corporation. In the real world, end-of-month financial reports are prepared to show the financial results of all the activities for the month.

This also happens in the game. End-of-month reports are automatically generated based upon whatever decisions you made during the month, the

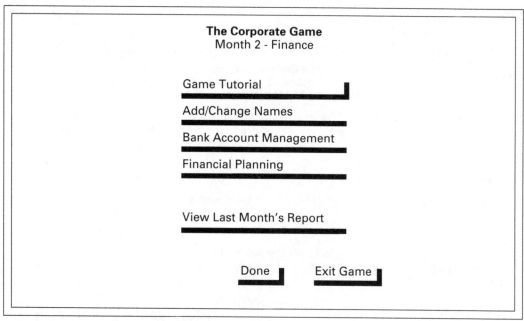

Game Tutorial

Add/Change Names

Bank Account Management

Financial Planning

View Last Month's Report

Done   Exit Game

End Work Session - Exit the Program

Exhibit 13-14. Month 2—Finance menu.

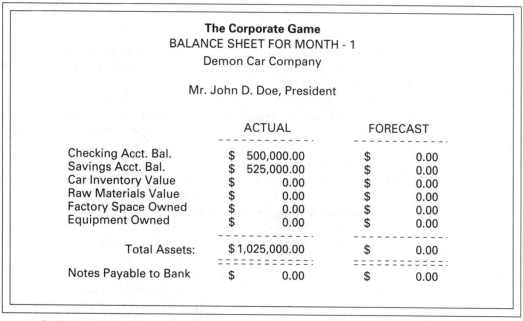

The Corporate Game
BALANCE SHEET FOR MONTH - 1
Demon Car Company

Mr. John D. Doe, President

	ACTUAL	FORECAST
Checking Acct. Bal.	$ 500,000.00	$ 0.00
Savings Acct. Bal.	$ 525,000.00	$ 0.00
Car Inventory Value	$ 0.00	$ 0.00
Raw Materials Value	$ 0.00	$ 0.00
Factory Space Owned	$ 0.00	$ 0.00
Equipment Owned	$ 0.00	$ 0.00
Total Assets:	$ 1,025,000.00	$ 0.00
Notes Payable to Bank	$ 0.00	$ 0.00

F2 Print   F3 Return

Exhibit 13-15. Month 1 balance sheet.

255

The Corporate Game
Month 2 - Finance
FINANCIAL PLAN & MASTER BUDGET

Type of Car	# Cars to Make	Cost to Produce	# Cars to Sell	Minimum Sell. Price
Economy	0	$ 0	0	$ 0
Midsize	0	$ 0	0	$ 0
Luxury	0	$ 0	0	$ 0

Estimates of Month End Account Balances

CHECKING	SAVINGS	ACCTs PAYABLE	NOTEs PAYABLE
$ 0	$ 0	$ 0	$ 0

Estimate the value of your:

FLOOR SPACE	PLANT EQUIPMENT	RAW MATERIALs	INTEREST INCOME
$ 0	$ 0	$ 0	$ 0

NEW--------INVENTORY

'OTHER' INCOME	COST	SIZE	DONE	ENTER
$ 0	$ 0	0		

Exhibit 13-16. Financial planning menu.

state of the game's economy, and business environment. You can review or print last month's reports by selecting the View Last Month's Report option (Exhibit 13-15).

Try it and you will see the top part of your balance sheet followed by the remaining parts of the report and the income statement as you page through (i.e., PgDn) the report. Press the F3 key to return to the Main Menu.

Let's check out the other new option. Select the Financial Planning option to see what its submenu looks like (Exhibit 13-16). Use this option to prepare the corporation's budgets and financial forecasts.

The Financial Planning menu is another example of a game entry menu. Although we have already shown you how to enter data, we'll cover a couple of examples. We have entered several numbers into the Financial Planning menu as shown in Exhibit 13-17.

All the entry fields require the entry of numeric data. For example, in Exhibit 13-17, we said we wanted to produce 10 economy cars at an estimated cost of $120,000. We also said that we wanted to sell five economy cars at a minimum price of $13,000 each. Remember to enter whole numbers. The game will automatically align the fields after you select ENTER (Exhibit 13-18).

The Corporate Game
Month 2 - Finance
FINANCIAL PLAN & MASTER BUDGET

Type of Car	# Cars to Make	Cost to Produce	# Cars to Sell	Minimum Sell. Price
Economy	10	120000	5	13000
Midsize	0	$ 0	0	$ 0
Luxury	0	$ 0	0	$ 0

Estimates of Month End Account Balances

CHECKING	SAVINGS	ACCTs PAYABLE	NOTEs PAYABLE
$ 0	$ 0	$ 0	$ 0

Estimate the value of your:

FLOOR SPACE	PLANT EQUIPMENT	RAW MATERIALs	INTEREST INCOME
$ 0	$ 0	$ 0	$ 0

NEW--------INVENTORY

'OTHER' INCOME	COST	SIZE	DONE	ENTER
$ 0	$ 0	0		

Exhibit 13-17. Financial planning menu with data entries.

The Corporate Game
Month 2 - Finance
FINANCIAL PLAN & MASTER BUDGET

Type of Car	# Cars to Make	Cost to Produce	# Cars to Sell	Minimum Sell. Price
Economy	10	$120,000	5	$ 13,000
Midsize	0	$ 0	0	$ 0
Luxury	0	$ 0	0	$ 0

Estimates of Month End Account Balances

CHECKING	SAVINGS	ACCTs PAYABLE	NOTEs PAYABLE
$ 0	$ 0	$ 0	$ 0

Estimate the value of your:

FLOOR SPACE	PLANT EQUIPMENT	RAW MATERIALs	INTEREST INCOME
$ 0	$ 0	$ 0	$ 0

NEW--------INVENTORY

'OTHER' INCOME	COST	SIZE	DONE	ENTER
$ 0	$ 0	0		

Exhibit 13-18. Financial planning menu after data has been entered.

The number you enter into the Financial Planning submenu will appear in the forecast column in next month's income statement. Let's exit the Financial Planning submenu by selecting the Done option. You can return to it any time you want to review and change your forecasts. Select Done from the Main Menu to start Month 3. We recommend that you read Chapter 3 before you play Month 3.

Playing Month 3

The Main Menu for Month 3 (see Exhibit 13-19) will now appear on your display. No new selection options have been added to Month 3.

If you entered the financial forecast in Month 2, the numbers will appear on your financial statements. Select View Last Month's Report to become familiar with the forecast column in the report. When you are finished with Month 3, select Done from the Main Menu to start Month 4. We recommend that you read Chapter 4 before you play Month 4.

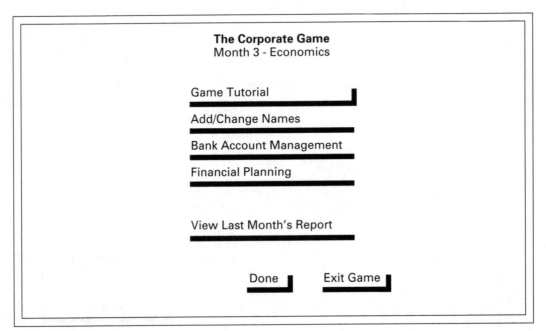

The Corporate Game
Month 3 - Economics

Game Tutorial

Add/Change Names

Bank Account Management

Financial Planning

View Last Month's Report

Done   Exit Game

End Work Session - Exit the Program

Exhibit 13-19. Month 3—Economics menu.

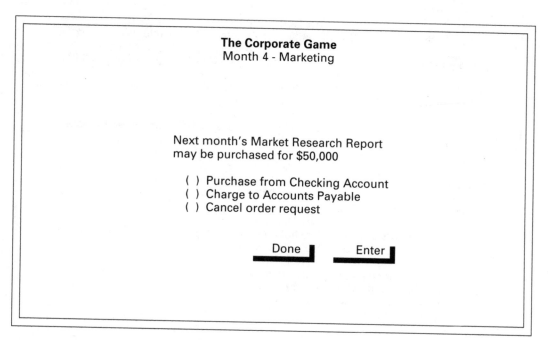

Exhibit 13-20. Month 4—Marketing menu.

Exhibit 13-21. Market-research report order menu.

Playing Month 4

The Main Menu for Month 4 includes a new selection option called Market-Research Report (Exhibit 13-20). This option allows you to order market-research reports from a research firm that has been built into the game.

When you select the Market-Research Report option, the submenu in Exhibit 13-21 will appear on your display. If you order the report, the market-research firm in the game performs a marketing analysis for your company in the current month (e.g., Month 4). The information will not be available for you to review until you start the next month of play (e.g., Month 5).

Here is how you order the report. First, the report is not free. The price of the report is posted in the middle of the menu. To order the report, simply select the option you want to use to pay for it. An example of what the report looks like is shown in Exhibit 13-22.

If you attempt to order the market report a second time in the same month, the game will display an error message (Exhibit 13-4) indicating "you already ordered one." It would be a waste of money to order the same report twice in the same month. If you order the report, it will be delivered to you at the start of next month. We will show how to view the market-

---

The Corporate Game
Car Buyer Survey Questionaire - 1,000 Potential Car Buyers Surveyed

1. Do you intend to buy a car next month? Yes: 30%   No: 50%   Maybe: 20%

2. If your answer was "yes," what type of car do you plan to buy?
   Economy: 32% Midsize: 44% Luxury: 24%

3. If your answer was "no," please check the reason that caused you to make this decision. Already own a car: 26%   Interest rates too high: 52%
   New car prices too high: 22%

4. If your answer was "maybe," please indicate the reason why you are undecided. Interest rates too high: 31%   New car prices too high: 30%
   Economy concerns: 39%

5. If your answer was "maybe," what type of car might you buy?
   Economy: 34% Midsize: 41% Luxury: 25%

Car average sell price and units sold this month by three auto companies:
Economy: 95/$15,500 Midsize: 88/$23,800 Luxury: 59/$28,994

F2 Print   F3 Return

Exhibit 13-22. Example of the market-research report.

research reports you order in Month 5. Return to the Main Menu and select Done to start Month 5. We recommend that you read Chapter 4 before you play Month 4.

Playing Month 5

Month 5 includes a new selection option called Order MFG Resources (Exhibit 13-23). This option allows you to order manufacturing materials, and rent or buy capital equipment and factory space. The option also allows you to hire labor crews.

Select the Order MFG Resources option and we will show you how it works. Exhibit 13-24 will now appear on your display. The left side of the menu shows the current inventory of assets owned by your company. In this example, your inventory is zero since you have not yet placed any orders.

The left side of the menu is where you purchase or rent additional resources as required. The right side of the menu shows current rent and purchase prices. For example, you can select one of four types of machines to buy or rent (e.g., Types A, B, C, or D). Unit rent and purchase prices are

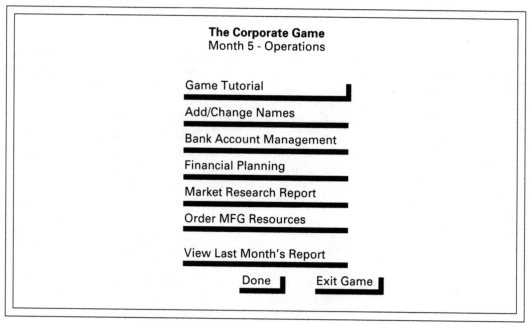

The Corporate Game
Month 5 - Operations

Game Tutorial

Add/Change Names

Bank Account Management

Financial Planning

Market Research Report

Order MFG Resources

View Last Month's Report

Done   Exit Game

End Work Session - Exit the Program

Exhibit 13-23. Month 5—Operations menu.

The Corporate Game
Month 5 - Operations
Acquire Manufacturing Resources

	- - - - - Current Inventory - - - - -		- - - - - Purchase Resources - - - - -		
	# OWNED	# RENTED	# to BUY	BUY PRICE	# to RENT	RENTAL PER MONTH
Type-A Machine	0	0	0	$ 275,000	0	$ 28,645
Type-B Machine	0	0	0	$ 325,000	0	$ 32,500
Type-C Machine	0	0	0	$ 375,000	0	$ 43,750
Type-D Machine	0	0	0	$ 975,000	0	$ 121,875
Floor Space (1000s sq ft)	0	0	0	$ 12,500	0	$ 1,500
Work Crews	Hired 0		Add 0	Per Month $ 2,500	Cancel	
Tons of Steel	Owned 0		Buy 0	Per Ton $ 1,200	Done	
Parts	Owned 0		Buy 0	Per Part $ 10	Enter	

Exhibit 13-24. Manufacturing resources order menu.

shown for each machine type. Each machine has different capacity outputs and requires different levels of resources (i.e., labor and factory space) to operate. Machine capacity and operational information is covered in the Tutorial menu in Month 5.

You can also buy or rent factory space in minimum-order quantities of 1000 square feet. Labor is purchased in work crew units at the purchase price shown on the menu. There are 100 hours of labor in a work crew. Steel and parts are also ordered through this menu. Make sure you read the tutorial before you determine what manufacturing resources you want to order. For purposes of this exercise, select CANCEL to return to the Main Menu.

If you ordered the market-research report last month, this will be your first opportunity to review the report. Select the Market-Research Report option from the Main Menu to bring up the submenu in Exhibit 13-25.

Although we showed you this submenu before, notice that a new option has been added: Review Current Report. This option will appear on the menu if you ordered the report last month (i.e., Month 4). The report is now available for you to review when you select this option.

When you select this option, the report will appear on your display. It can be printed by using the printing procedures we discussed earlier. The re-

```
┌─────────────────────────────────────────────────────────────────┐
│ ┌───────────────────────────────────────────────────────────────┐ │
│ │                                                               │ │
│ │                    **The Corporate Game**                     │ │
│ │                    Month 5 - Operations                       │ │
│ │                                                               │ │
│ │                                                               │ │
│ │                  Review Current Report █                      │ │
│ │                  ─────────────────────                        │ │
│ │          Next month's Market Research Report                  │ │
│ │          may be purchased for $50,000                         │ │
│ │                                                               │ │
│ │              ( )  Purchase from Checking Account              │ │
│ │              ( )  Charge to Accounts Payable                  │ │
│ │              ( )  Cancel order request                        │ │
│ │                                                               │ │
│ │                                                               │ │
│ │                    Done █        Enter █                      │ │
│ │                    ──────        ───────                      │ │
│ │                                                               │ │
│ └───────────────────────────────────────────────────────────────┘ │
└─────────────────────────────────────────────────────────────────┘
```

Exhibit 13-25. Market-research report menu.

port covers what happened to the market last month (Month 4). Use the information in the report to help develop your marketing strategies and financial forecasts. If you want another marketing report for Month 6, make sure you order it before you close out Month 5.

Game Tutorial

We talked briefly about the game tutorials when we showed you how to use the options in the main menu's introduction menu. The tutorial in Month 5 covers important manufacturing resource information needed to make knowledgeable decisions before ordering manufacturing resources. We highly recommend that you print the tutorial so that you can refer to it when you play the remaining months in the game.

When you scroll through the game tutorial, you will come across a new tutorial feature (Exhibit 13-26) called *The Fast Street Journal*. It includes all kinds of economic and business news about what the journal's editors think will happen to the game's economy and business environment in the current month (e.g., Month 5). The journal is free. It's included in the tutorials of all the remaining months.

The Corporate Game
The Fast Street Journal
– – – – – – – – – –

May 1st Edition

Steel Makers Trim Loses

For the steelmakers, the prospect of continued price discounting dims
hope for a third or fourth quarter return to profitability. "There has never
been a price like there is today", complained one marketing executive.

Major Bank Lifts the Prime Rate 1% to 11%

The Great American Bank move comes amid forecasts that interest rates will
continue to increase. The nation's other major banks are likely to follow.

Detroit

Automakers plan to boost output 3% this month. the Demon Auto Company
announced that it will close its Atlanta assembly plant for the next two weeks
to adjust inventories. The plant assembles economy sedans.

F2 Print   F3 Return

Exhibit 13-26. *The Fast Street Journal* example for May.

Producing Product

By now, it should be clear to you that Month 5 is the first month your company can acquire all the resources necessary to produce cars. You can build
a factory, install equipment, hire labor, and acquire the manufacturing materials you need to produce product. At this point, we have shown you every
option you need to know to complete the game with two important exceptions.

First, you must tell the game how many cars you want to produce in any
one month. You do this by selecting the Financial Planning option from the
Main Menu. We showed you how to enter production units into the Financial Plan in Exhibit 13-17.

In Exhibit 13-17, we told the game that we want to produce ten economy
cars. The game takes you at your word and assumes that is the maximum
number of cars you want to build in the current month (e.g., Month 5),
even though you may have resources to produce more. If you do not
change production units when you roll forward to play the next month
(e.g., Month 6), the game will assume you want to produce the same number of cars next month. For this reason, make sure your production units

forecast accurately reflects the number of units you want to produce each month.

If you do not have enough manufacturing resources to produce what you want, the game will allocate your desired production units to match your available production capacity. For example, if you told the game that you want to produce ten cars, but you only have enough steel to produce five, then that will be all the cars you can build.

Selling Cars

In Exhibit 13-18, we entered the number of cars we want to sell in Month 5. We also entered the sales price for each car. Again, the game takes you at your word and assumes that is the maximum number of cars you are willing to sell in the current month (e.g., Month 5), even though you may have been able to sell more. If you do not change these numbers when you roll forward to next month, the game will assume you want to sell the same number of cars next month. Make sure your sales forecast accurately reflects the number of cars you want to sell.

The price you set for each car represents the lowest price you will accept from the game's competitive market for each car. If you tell the game you want to sell ten economy cars and forget to enter a selling price, the game will assume that the ten economy cars are free. Your cars will be donated to the game's charitable organization. Again, as a final warning, make sure your production and sales forecasts accurately reflect the number of cars you want to produce and sell. We recommend that you read Chapter 5 before you play Month 5.

Playing Months 6 through 12

All the remaining months feature the same Main Menu options that are displayed in Month 5. The tutorials include an expanded version of *The Fast Street Journal*. As we stated earlier, the journal is your "window" into the game's economic and business environment. Use it to help develop and fine tune your corporate business strategies.

When you get to the last month of play (e.g., Month 12 or December) and select the Done option, the menu in Exhibit 13-27 will appear on your display. Select the View Last Month's Report option to get your final year-end financial reports. How well did your company do? Did you beat the competition? Good luck at playing *The Corporate Game!*

**The Corporate Game
End of Game**

View Last Month's Report

Exit Game

End Work Session - Exit the Program

Exhibit 13-27. End-of-game report menu.

Index

About the Author

David E. Rye is a senior manager at IBM. He has taught *The Corporate Game* in IBM's professional education program, where it was a huge success. Mr. Rye has an MBA from Seattle University and teaches at the University of Colorado. The author of *Two for the Money* and three other books, he is a frequent speaker at professional conferences on business management issues. He is based in Boulder, Colorado.

DISK WARRANTY

This software is protected by both United States copyright law and international copyright treaty provision. You must treat this software just like a book, except that you may copy it into a computer to be used and you may make archival copies of the software for the sole purpose of backing up our software and protecting your investment from loss.

By saying, "just like a book," McGraw-Hill means, for example, that this software may be used by any number of people and may be freely moved from one computer location to another, so long as there is no possibility of its being used at one location or on one computer while it is being used at another. just as a book cannot be read by two different people in two different places at the same time, neither can the software be used by two different people in two different places at the same time (unless, of course, McGraw-Hill's copyright is being violated).

LIMITED WARRANTY

McGraw-Hill warrants the physical diskette(s) enclosed herein to be free of defects in materials and workmanship for a period of sixty days from the purchase date. If McGraw-Hill receives written notification within the warranty period of defects in materials or workmanship, and such notification is determined by McGraw-Hill to be correct, McGraw-Hill will replace the defective diskette(s). Send request to:

Customer Service
TAB/McGraw-Hill
13311 Monterey Avenue
Blue Ridge Summit, PA 17294-0850

The entire and exclusive liability and remedy for breach of this Limited Warranty shall be limited to replacement of defective diskette(s) and shall not include or extend to any claim for or right to cover any other damages, including but not limited to, loss of profit, data, or use of the software, or special, incidental, or consequential damages or other similar claims, even if McGraw-Hill has been specifically advised to the possibility of such damages. In no event will McGraw-Hill's liability for any damages to you or any other person ever exceed the lower of suggested list price or actual price paid for the license to use the software, regardless of any form of the claim.

McGRAW-HILL, INC. SPECIFICALLY DISCLAIMS ALL OTHER WARRANTY, EXPRESS OR IMPLIED, INCLUDING BUT NOT LIMITED TO, ANY IMPLIED WARRANTY OF MERCHANTABILITY OR FITNESS FOR A PARTICULAR PURPOSE. Specifically, McGraw-Hill makes no representation or warranty that the software is fit for any particular purpose and any implied warranty of merchantability is limited to the sixty-day duration of the Limited Warranty covering the physical diskette(s) only (and not the software) and is otherwise expressly and specifically disclaimed.

This Limited Warranty gives you specific legal rights; you may have others which may vary from state to state. Some states do not allow the exclusion of incidental or consequential damages, or the limitation on how long an implied warranty lasts, so some of the above may not apply to you.